How to Write a BA Thesis

Chicago Guides
to *Writing*, Editing,
and Publishing

How to Write a BA Thesis

A PRACTICAL GUIDE FROM

YOUR FIRST IDEAS TO YOUR

FINISHED PAPER

Charles Lipson

The University of Chicago Press CHICAGO & LONDON

Charles Lipson

is professor and

director of

undergraduate

studies in political

science at the

University of

Chicago.

The University of Chicago Press, Chicago 60637
The University of Chicago Press, Ltd., London
© 2005 by Charles Lipson
All rights reserved. Published 2005
Printed in the United States of America

14 13 12 11 10 09 08 07 06 05   1 2 3 4 5

ISBN: 0-226-48125-5 (cloth)
ISBN: 0-226-48126-3 (paper)

Library of Congress
Cataloging-in-Publication Data
Lipson, Charles.
  How to write a BA thesis : a practical guide from
your first ideas to your finished paper / Charles
Lipson.
     p. cm. — (Chicago guides to writing, editing,
  and publishing)
  Includes bibliographic references and index.
  ISBN 0-226-48125-5 (cloth : alk. paper) —
  ISBN 0-226-48126-3 (pbk. : alk. paper)
  1. Dissertations, Academic—Authorship.
  2. Academic writing. I. Title. II. Series.
  LB2639.L54 2005
  808′.042—dc22

                                    2004026816

To my sons, Michael and Jonathan

CONTENTS

Getting Started

HOW TO READ THIS BOOK

This is a practical guidebook, designed to help you through every stage of your thesis project, beginning with your earliest ideas about writing one. It helps you turn those tentative ideas into a workable project, then a draft paper, and ultimately a polished final version.

Completing a thesis is a substantial project, one that most students find both challenging and rewarding. The most rewarding part, students say, is picking your own subject and reaching your own conclusions. You reach them by doing independent research, writing about it, and discussing your ideas with your adviser.

As you begin, though, the thought of actually finishing this project might seem like a distant goal, perhaps even an unreachable one. In fact, you *can* reach it, and you can teach yourself a great deal in the process. I'll offer suggestions and support at every stage.

The early chapters of this book will help you launch this project on solid footing. They focus on

- Collecting ideas for a thesis
- Picking an adviser
- Writing a proposal
- Starting background reading on your topic
- Taking useful notes on your readings
- Turning broad ideas into a sharply defined thesis topic

They are covered in chapters 1–4.

You'll be doing all these during the first couple of months of your senior year; that's when you should read chapters 1–4, too. This schedule assumes that your thesis will take two semesters. If it's a one-semester project, you need to do the same tasks on a swifter schedule. Chapter 20 offers some ideas about how to do that and provides an abbreviated work schedule.

The middle chapters of this book accompany the middle months of your thesis project, approximately months 3–5, or possibly 3–6, depending on your school's schedule. These chapters concentrate on

- Devising a research strategy
- Conducting focused research
- Planning your thesis in more detail
- Dividing your overall topic into major sections for your paper
- Sorting your research into these sections
- Adding your own ideas to your book notes (a process I describe as "prewriting")
- Shaping this prewriting into a draft of your middle sections (that is, everything but the introduction and conclusion)
- Starting to write your introduction and conclusion (since they give an overview of the entire project, it's best to begin them after you have drafted the middle sections)

For help with all these aspects of your thesis, read chapters 5 and 7–11.

Two other chapters (6 and 12) cover related issues, but ones that aren't relevant to every thesis. Chapter 6 explains how to study individual cases in depth, a common method in the social sciences. Chapter 12 explains how to use maps, graphs, and other visual materials. If you are not using case studies or visual materials, you can skip these chapters.

Chapter 13 discusses everyday issues of working efficiently on your project, everything from study habits to writing. If you have any special problems along the way, such as procrastination, sleep difficulties, or personal issues, you will find chapter 14 helpful and supportive.

As you turn the final corner on your thesis, you will be

- Filling in gaps in your research
- Refining your introduction and conclusion
- Editing and polishing the whole thesis

These tasks should take about three or four weeks. Set aside the time. Doing a good job on them will make your thesis much stronger.

There are no new chapters to read at this stage. You've already covered them. Still, you may find it helpful to revisit some chapters as you complete your work. After you've finished most of your research, for instance, you'll probably discover a few gaps you need to fill. That's covered in earlier chapters on doing research. You'll probably be working on your opening and closing sections, which are covered in chapter 10. You'll need to edit and polish your text. That, too, has been covered—in chapter 11, on editing. Just review these earlier chapters as you move into the final stages of your thesis.

Every chapter has useful tips, all of them specially marked, to assist your research and writing. The most important ones are pulled together in chapter 16, which serves as a summary of the book's main ideas. A related chapter (17) answers some frequently asked questions (FAQs). To help you stay on top of the various tasks, I've included a checklist at the end of most chapters.

Several chapters also have time schedules. They give you a sense of how you should be moving through the various tasks and approximately how long each one should take. Chapter 15 reviews the time schedule for the whole project. Using this schedule as a guide, you can draft a customized schedule of your own, one that suits your pace and your project.

Tip: To get a quick overview of the book and its main recommendations, read chapters 15 and 16.
- Chapter 15 gives a general schedule for completing a thesis and explains the main tasks at each stage.
- Chapter 16 brings together the most important tips for working on the project.
By reading them early, you'll have a clear sense of how to move forward through successive stages of planning, research, and writing.

After you've handed in your thesis, you still have a few small tasks left to do:

- Thanking your adviser
- Getting a good recommendation for future jobs or graduate school

Those are covered in chapter 18.

Some schools add special requirements to the thesis project. One is a thesis defense, where you explain your findings to several faculty members and answer their questions. Other schools require that your thesis be approved by a second faculty member, in addition to your adviser. Chapter 19 explains how to prepare for a thesis defense and pick a second reader.

Some students need to write a thesis in only one semester, either because of their own schedules or the school's requirements. Chapter 20 provides an accelerated timeline for doing that. It offers some concrete suggestions for speeding up your work, and some ideas about what *not* to speed up.

I've also added some useful items in three appendices. The first lists the best places to turn for additional help. If you want to read another book about writing or editing, for example, you can find it there.

The second appendix explains how to prepare footnotes, endnotes, and citations, using the three main styles: Chicago (from *The Chicago Manual of Style*), MLA, and APA. It covers each in detail and shows exactly how to cite books, articles, chapters, Web sites, and much more. With this appendix, you should be able to handle all your thesis references.

A third appendix is intended for new faculty members who are supervising their first thesis projects. Most of it mirrors the advice given to students, but seen this time from the professor's side of the desk.

Taken together, these chapters and appendices provide a full road map for your thesis project and specific guidance for moving successfully from your earliest ideas to a polished final paper. They are not a substitute for working closely with your thesis adviser. Quite the contrary. It is important for you to work well together. I offer suggestions about how to do that, sprinkled across several chapters. The goal, in every case, is to help you work more productively—with your adviser and on your own.

Most of all, I hope this guide will help you write your own best thesis.

TIMELINE FOR READING THIS BOOK

1 INTRODUCTION

Most students write a thesis for a very simple reason: it's required to graduate with honors. In some schools, it's required for all graduates. Even so, the thesis is different from other requirements—more demanding and much more rewarding. Most requirements focus on specific courses, perhaps an introductory course on statistics, social structure, or American fiction. There is not much you can do if the class is at 9 A.M., the subject is boring, or the professor drones on, oblivious to your snoring.[1]

Your thesis, happily, is different. It is in your hands. You will work with an adviser, of course, but you will ultimately select your own topic and do most of the work yourself, independently. You can start at 9 A.M. or 9 P.M., skip work entirely some days, or study straight through the weekend. You own it.

That's the good news and the bad news. To select a topic, you have to think about what truly interests you, and probably meander a bit before you settle on the right path. Once you have decided on a general subject—say, marriage and divorce in nineteenth-century fiction—you need to hone it down to a manageable size. That might be "The Scar of Divorce in the Fiction of Henry James and Edith Wharton." In international studies, your broad interest in America's wars might lead to a thesis on "The Evolution of American Air Power in Kosovo, Afghanistan, and Iraq." These

---

1. One student recalls just such an experience: "Dr. Duncan's lectures [on medical matters] at 8 o'clock on a winter's morning are something fearful to remember. Dr. Munro made his lectures on human anatomy as dull as he was himself. . . . I attended Jameson's lectures on Geology and Zoology, but they were incredibly dull. The sole effect they produced on me was the determination never as long as I lived to read a book on Geology or in any way to study the science." The student was Charles Darwin. Despite the dreadful lectures, he grew more interested in these subjects and, apparently, even conducted some independent research and writing. Charles Darwin, *The Autobiography of Charles Darwin and Selected Letters,* ed. Francis Darwin (New York: Dover, 1958), 12, 15.

topics capture your general interests and encourage you to grapple with them, but they are not too large and unwieldy. They are feasible thesis topics because they allow you to do the necessary research and then enter the conversation with your own ideas.

This reading, research, and writing builds on your previous work: your courses and seminar papers. Together, they lay the foundations for a longer, more challenging project: your thesis. If doing a thesis seems harder than your earlier work, it is also more satisfying. As you select your topic, you can explore issues that interest you deeply. As you move gradually from reading and research to writing and revising, you can develop a real sense of mastery. As you work out your perspective and begin writing, you can develop your own distinctive voice. In all these ways, your thesis is the capstone of your undergraduate education. And it is something more: a vital step toward lifelong learning, where you will *always* pick your own subjects to explore.

Because your thesis requires independent work, it is useful to have a guide, a mentor by your side. That's what this book is. It is designed to help you and your adviser as you proceed along the trail, from selecting a good topic to turning in your final draft, with a sigh of relief. My goal is to offer suggestions you can use at every stage of your work.

One of the challenges of writing a thesis is that you need to combine a lot of tasks: selecting a topic, reading the best books and articles, conducting sustained research, arriving at your own viewpoint, planning your paper, writing a first draft, and then revising and polishing it, all while managing your own time. This is not a 100-meter dash. It is a hike through the woods, requiring a variety of skills and some persistence.

This book will guide you past the mileposts, flag the main issues, warn you about the stumps along the trail, and give you some brief, practical advice about each aspect of the project. If you want more details on some, I will point you to the best sources. But I will keep this book focused on the main issues so you can focus on your primary goal: completing your own best thesis, one you find satisfying to work on and pleased to turn in.

For now, let me begin with some reassurance, based on years of working with thesis students. You've made it this far, and you can complete your thesis. In fact, you can complete a thesis you'll be proud of. You just need to approach it thoughtfully and stick with it. If you are committed to that, you'll do just fine.

Tip: Be persistent. If you work steadily on your thesis, you'll complete a rewarding project and learn a lot in the process.

That leads me to the most important advice of all: *Pick a topic that truly interests you.* If you care about the subject, you will pursue interesting questions because you want to know the answers. That, more than anything else, will draw you into the subject, enrich your work, and sustain you for the long haul.

Tip: Pick a thesis topic you really care about.

Good luck!

2 USEFUL NUTS AND BOLTS

Every thesis student has to handle a number of nuts-and-bolts issues, from departmental requirements to picking an adviser. A little advice can ease the way.

WHAT ARE YOU INTERESTED IN?

Well before you start looking for a thesis adviser, you should begin to highlight areas that interest you and start taking courses in them. At this stage, probably in your junior year, you don't need to narrow your focus much. Just pick a field or two to emphasize within your major. In art history, that might be modern or classical art. In political science, it might be international relations or political philosophy. These are broad topics, and you may already have some more detailed interests within them. In modern art, you might be most interested in German expressionists or, alternatively, in American abstract artists like Jackson Pollock. In international relations, you might be concerned with relations between rich and poor countries, but beyond that you aren't sure. That's fine. You will zero in on a specific research topic later, and I'll help. For now, what matters is getting the best preparation, as you fulfill the requirements in your major. In the process, you'll discover some areas that interest you and others that don't.

Two kinds of preparation matter most for your thesis: learning more about your field and learning more about writing research papers.

PREPARING FOR YOUR THESIS BY CHOOSING THE RIGHT COURSES

In choosing courses, the key is to move beyond the basics into more advanced, specialized fields since your thesis will come from these specialized fields. In economics, for instance, you will build on basic micro and macro courses to take classes in labor economics, international trade, or capital markets—whatever interests you. In sociology, you might take advanced courses in immigration, crime, or changing gender roles. You'll be learning what really matters to you (and what doesn't) as you lay the foundation for your thesis research. You will also be doing essential background reading, familiarizing yourself with the debates, and discovering the hot issues. You'll be looking for puzzles and questions that interest you.

> *Tip:* Take advanced courses in your field. You'll explore important issues, learn the best methods to study them, identify research topics, and develop skills for writing a thesis.

As you advance within your major, ask faculty and advisers if you need to take some essential courses in other fields. In economics, for instance, calculus and statistics are extremely valuable—the more, the better. For European history, you might want to take a course in French literature or Enlightenment philosophy. These "extra" courses are important in every field. But you need to ask. The faculty aren't going to search for you. If you want their help, you should approach them with clear questions.

> *Tip:* Ask about courses outside your major that complement your interests.

To get the best advice, you also need to say something about your own interests. If you are concerned with the sociology of religion, for instance, you might take related courses in theology or anthropology. These same courses would be less useful for sociology students concerned with racial segregation. Those students would benefit more from classes on urban education, labor markets, or African American literature. The point is simple. Before embarking on your thesis project, take some advanced courses to deepen—and widen—your knowledge of your specialty. You should continue taking such courses as you conduct thesis research.

SEMINAR PAPERS PREPARE YOU TO WRITE A THESIS

You also want to gain some experience in writing research papers. It is a lot easier to plan and write your thesis after you have written a few seminar papers. You'll know much more about how to conduct research and how to present it effectively. You also learn how to manage your time as you organize an independent project. These skills will prove useful in your thesis.

You may also discover that you want to learn more about a particular topic. An interesting class paper might be the basis for an interesting thesis.

> *Tip:* Before beginning your thesis, take some courses that require research papers. They might be the seeds of a thesis project. Even if they're not, they'll give you valuable experience in researching and writing.

Fortunately, most advanced courses require papers rather than exams. Still, some large schools rely on exams, even in upper-level courses, to cope with heavy enrollments. Check out the requirements for specific classes with an eye to doing some research and writing. A few longer papers will prepare you for the thesis project.

By the same token, don't load up with three courses requiring papers the same semester. If they all come due on Tuesday of exam week, believe me, it will be an ugly train wreck. Balance your load.

GENERATING IDEAS FOR YOUR THESIS

As you take these advanced courses, start thinking tentatively about your thesis. By junior year, you will probably be settled into your major, taking some specialized classes and learning which topics you enjoy and do well in. You need not spend a lot of time thinking about your thesis, and none at all worrying about it. Just mull over what interests you and what might be worth exploring further.

Now is the time to start collecting ideas for possible thesis topics. Do it in writing, even if the ideas themselves are tentative and exploratory. Make a special computer file where you can jot down ideas and have a manila folder where you can put handwritten notes and photocopies, marked up with your observations. Lots of professors do this, collecting ideas for their next book or article. You should do exactly the same thing for your thesis.

If you don't have such files set up already, go ahead and do that now, even if you don't have anything to put in them. You will have some ideas soon, and having the files ready to go encourages them. As you add new items to your files, remember that your goal is not to find a single topic but to collect multiple ideas. You'll narrow them down later, and I'll explain how.

> *Tip:* To collect potential ideas for a thesis, set up a computer file (and perhaps a manila folder, as well).

A happy by-product of collecting these ideas is that you'll begin to write. At least you'll begin to write some brief notes to yourself. They don't need to be anything fancy, just notes for your files, done without any pressure or deadlines. But do make a regular practice of writing down your ideas.

Thinking on paper is very helpful—at least, I've always found it is—and it's important to make it a regular part of your thesis project from the very beginning. The more you write, the easier it becomes. These notes will jog your memory, prompt your imagination, and help you puzzle out the issues.

Try not to censor yourself. Nobody is judging you. Nobody is grading you. Don't worry if your ideas seem vague, a little dumb, or too ambitious. You can always drop them later or combine them with others. At this stage, you are planting a garden, not weeding it. Just write down your ideas as they pop up, before they wilt away. When you think of something, write down a few casual sentences so that next month you'll remember what you were thinking. Don't fret about grammar or style. The goal is simply to generate ideas and begin writing, at least informally.

To begin this file, think over the various classes you have taken. Which issues fascinated you? Which ones did you want to learn more about? Which paper topics were most rewarding to work on? Scribble down your answers. See if you can expand on any of them. *Why* did these topics intrigue you? *Which aspects* were most interesting? The more you can write about these questions, the better.

> *Tip:* Remind yourself to keep adding material to your thesis ideas file. Fill it with
> * Brief notes and comments on articles you've read
> * Questions that interest you
> * Any ideas that suggest possible paper topics

From now on, jot down any ideas you might want to delve into. Do it as you take notes in class, read assignments, or write seminar papers. Just add them to your thesis ideas file. That's exactly what professional writers do. They keep a file of ideas for their next project. It's easy, and it works. The only trick is to make it a habit.

> *Tip:* Make it a habit to put notes in your thesis ideas file. A little informal writing is good practice and will develop your ideas. Review these notes occasionally and see if they prompt still more thoughts. Cull the ones that no longer interest you.

Every so often, review your file, see what still intrigues you, and toss out what no longer does. See if your ideas fall into two or three groups, and if they do, organize them that way, under a few major topic headings. If a few ideas keep cropping up—the same basic themes in different dress—make a special note of that. Bounce ideas around with professors and friends. Don't hoard them; share them. Debate them. As you do, you will understand your own ideas better and come up with still more. Write them down, too. It can become a virtuous circle, as your thoughts build on each other. Equally important, it will become easy and natural to write about them.

Behind this playfulness is a serious purpose. One of the most meaningful—and difficult—elements of your thesis project is formulating your own topic. Professors could easily assign topics to students, but they are reluctant to do so for a very good reason. Handing out assignments would cast aside one of the main educational aspects of writing a thesis: picking your own topic.

Choosing your own topic makes the thesis different from any course you have ever taken. All of them define the subject matter for you. Take seminar papers, for example. If the course is about Jane Austen, you can't write about Emily Dickinson. Your thesis is different because you have so much freedom. This freedom is challenging, as freedom often is, but it also makes your thesis the most personal part of your education. You can define the range of subjects that interest you, and then, working with a faculty adviser, select your own topic. Later, we'll talk about how to choose a topic and refine it. For now, what matters is to figure out your interests and generate some ideas worth pursuing.

PICKING AN ADVISER

With your thesis file set up, a few ideas percolating, and some advanced courses under your belt, you are ready to look for a thesis adviser, probably toward the end of your junior year or, at the latest, the beginning of senior year.

> *Tip:* Start looking for a thesis adviser during the latter part of your junior year or, at the latest, early senior year.

So, what makes a good thesis adviser? Better yet, what makes a good thesis adviser *for you?* Two criteria stand out above all others. Your adviser should know your thesis subfield. And you should feel comfortable, intellectually and personally, with your adviser. Everything else is secondary.

> *Tip:* Pick an adviser who is
> - Comfortable for you to work with
> - An expert in your area of interest

Your adviser will work with you as a one-on-one teacher: a tutor and mentor. He or she will help you shape your topic, select the best background readings, find the most useful data, and use the right research methods. You, in turn, will come to the faculty member's office every week or two to discuss your progress. Most times, you'll hand in some writing and get some feedback. You'll hash out your latest ideas and leave with directions for the next steps to take. These meetings are often brief, but they are vital.

Just listing all the adviser's responsibilities makes it clear why you want someone who is a good teacher, someone you feel comfortable with and eager to learn from.

Fortunately, it's easy to find out if your prospective adviser is a good teacher. Just read student evaluations and ask other students in your department. What you hope to find is a professor who excels in small groups and one-on-one. That's more important than being a great lecturer, at least for thesis advising. Does she make time for students, read papers promptly, and give helpful advice? Are her interests narrow and her approach rigid? Or does she have an open-minded interest in lots of issues?

The best evaluations come from students who have written seminar papers in your major and from seniors who are completing theses. Seek them out during your junior year. It's worth the extra effort. They will know this more personal dimension of advisers' abilities. Ask them which advisers are good, and which ones are good riddance.

In addition to these teaching skills, there is one more critical dimension to your choice: your adviser's professional expertise. What is the professor's specialty?

PICK AN ADVISER WHO SPECIALIZES IN YOUR TOPIC

Let's say you want to write a thesis on marketing plans for a small business. You suspect, rightly, that all business professors know a little something about marketing and small businesses. That's part of their broad professional training, just as all professors of Spanish literature know something about *Don Quixote*. But you should seek something more: an adviser who knows your specific subject well. Otherwise, you're tilting at windmills. In this case, you want a professor who specializes in entrepreneurship or marketing, or, if you are lucky, both.

To find the right expertise for your thesis, you need to know how your major is organized. Every subject has its own specialties and faculty members who are experts in them. What are the usual academic specialties in *your* major? Which professors concentrate on which topics? Learn the lay of the land before you pick an adviser.

> *Tip:* Learn how your major is organized into specialties and who are the best thesis advisers in your area of interest.

Some fields are divided into a few clear-cut categories. Political science, for instance, has four or five major subfields, such as American politics. Within that, however, some faculty know more about U.S. voting behavior, others about Congress, and still others about courts and law enforcement. If several professors specialize in your general area, ask around to find out which ones are the best teachers and the most attentive mentors. It helps to know this terrain when you choose a thesis adviser.

Some departments have many more specialties than political science. Historians usually concentrate on a specific time period within a specific country. This intersection of times and locations forms a kind of grid: Italy during the Renaissance, colonial India in the nineteenth century, Mexico in the twentieth, and so on. In still other fields, the pattern is more like a maze. English literature marks out its subfields by time periods (Tudor, Victorian), by location (colonial, American), by ethnicity (African American, Latino), by methods of analysis (rhetoric, discourse theory), by creative medium (film studies, poetry), and by other academic practices (gay and lesbian studies).

You can see how this gives you some interesting choices. If you are drawn to recent American poetry, for instance, you might seek a specialist in poetry or perhaps in contemporary American writing. If the poetry happens to deal with feminist themes or racial issues, you have still more potential advisers.

Of course, if you attend a small college, you have fewer specialists to choose from but other advantages that compensate fully. You know the faculty well, and you probably have written seminar papers for several of them. Most important of all, you know they care deeply about teaching.

Learn a little about these pathways before looking for an adviser. The course catalog will tell you most of what you need to know. Supplement that with a quick Internet search to see what books and articles your prospective advisers have written and which courses they have taught recently. And, of course, ask around.

MEETING WITH YOUR (PROSPECTIVE) ADVISER AND SELECTING A TOPIC

Once you have learned who specializes in your area and who teaches effectively (especially one-on-one), you should set up meetings with one or two faculty. The agenda is simple. You want to discuss your budding thesis ideas and find out if a prospective adviser is a good match for you.

In your first meeting, you want to establish a rapport, determine if your interests fit well with the faculty member's, and ultimately decide if you want to work together. The best way to do that is to discuss possible thesis topics and get some concrete advice about how to approach the project. (In chapter 4, I'll discuss the actual thesis proposal.)

If your interests overlap with several faculty, schedule meetings with all of them. Don't think of this as "interviewing faculty." It is really just trying to find a good fit. You want an adviser who knows your subject well and is comfortable to work with. Normally, it's best to schedule this initial meeting during regular faculty office hours, although most professors will find another time if you have work or classes. This meeting will probably take fifteen or twenty minutes, but it could run longer if you discuss thesis topics in depth.

> *Tip:* Schedule brief meetings with potential thesis advisers late in your junior year or early in your senior year. Hold them during the faculty member's office hours if possible.

Come prepared. That way you can relax (or at least try to!), talk about your interests and course background, ask some questions, and get a good sense of how well you might work together.

What does it mean to "come prepared"? Think, for just a minute, about what any prospective adviser wants to know:

- What is your area of interest?
- What kind of questions do you have about it?
- Are you well equipped to undertake a research paper in this general area?
- Am I the best faculty member to advise you?
- What's your name again?

Even if your prospective adviser doesn't ask all those questions, she'll be thinking about them. So it's a good idea for you to think about them, too. As usual, the best way to answer them is with a little writing in advance.

Assemble a small packet of items for this meeting, beginning with your name and e-mail address on a contact sheet. Next, write a list of pertinent courses you have taken, with professors and course names (not just course numbers). Leave out courses that are far removed from your thesis, but include everything in your major plus those "extra" courses that I mentioned earlier. You can include grades if you wish. Add any courses you plan to take, along with the notation that they are upcoming.

Feel free to write some brief comments next to any of these courses. Next to one on French literature, for example, you might add that you wrote a seven-page paper on Victor Hugo and a fifteen-page paper on *Madame*

Bovary. It's a good idea to bring extra copies of any relevant papers to this meeting, just in case the professor wants to look at them. Of course, what's relevant depends on your thesis topic.

If you have any other skills that bear on the thesis project, list them on your course sheet, just as you would on a résumé. If you are thinking about a thesis on U.S. immigration, for instance, it helps an adviser to know if you have worked with survey data or speak Spanish.

Sometimes, nonacademic information shapes your topic or approach. Add that to the packet, too, if you feel comfortable. For a thesis on immigration, for instance, you might note that your grandparents emigrated from Poland and you have always been interested in their experience.

Finally, if your department requires faculty advisers to sign a thesis form, bring that along.

Tip: Prepare a small packet of written materials for an introductory meeting with any prospective adviser. List the

- Relevant courses you've taken
- Seminar papers you've written
- Special skills you have, such as languages or advanced statistics

Print your name and e-mail address on the first page. (Do it on all future papers, too.)

Bring along any thesis forms your new adviser needs to sign.

This packet not only answers essential questions; it shows the professor you care about the subject and are organized and ready to move forward. The professor can review the materials quickly, and you can begin a useful conversation immediately. That's exactly what you want to do.

How can you make this conversation more productive? By moving directly into a discussion of your thesis interests. Here's my suggestion. Before the meeting, write down the thesis topic or question you are considering. This is *not* part of your packet, so do it on a separate sheet. You are not going to share it with faculty, at least not right away and not in this form. Later, you will share plenty of writing with your adviser, but not this time.

This brief sketch is just for you, and you should linger over it. Go to your thesis ideas file, review your clippings and notes, and try to organize them into a few categories to guide your thinking. Feel free to write down more than one potential thesis topic.

Then do one more thing. Try to write at least a couple of sentences about each possible topic you've listed, saying *why* each one interests you and *which aspects* most intrigue you. The more you can write, the better. If you return to it the next day, you can probably add still more thoughts, stimulated by what you've already written. Your writing might consist of intellectual puzzles, or it might list some very personal reasons why you are interested in the topic, such as future career goals. In either case, probe your interests as you embark on the project. It will sharpen your focus. The better you understand your own interests, the better you can convey them to your prospective adviser.

> *Tip:* For yourself alone, write a paragraph or two summarizing your main ideas for a thesis topic. That might be a single idea or it might be several. It might be a question or puzzle that interests you. Do this after you've reviewed your file of thesis ideas.

To illustrate the process, let's stick with the general topic of immigration. With a little exploration, it may become clear that you are interested mainly in what kinds of jobs immigrants get and how those differ for legal and illegal immigrants. Or you might be interested in a different facet of immigration: how local communities respond to new arrivals from abroad. Does it matter if the immigrants come from Mexico or Russia? Does it matter if they arrive in Southern California, East Texas, or North Dakota? Or perhaps you are more interested in bilingualism and cultural interactions. You may be interested in why the second generation fares so much better in some groups than others. The more you coax out your own interests and hunches, the better start you will make.

Most of all, you should aim for good questions. The answers will come later, as you conduct the actual thesis research. Right now, focus on the questions. *Good theses begin with good questions or intriguing puzzles.* So sniff around for an interesting question or puzzle.

> *Tip:* One of the best ways to find a thesis topic is to search for a good question or puzzle. But what *is* a good thesis question?
> - It should genuinely interest you.
> - It should concern something you want to understand better . . . but cannot answer yet. (It's fine to have a hunch or tentative answer, but if you really know the answer, move on.)
> - It should be something you can study well—in the time available, with your skills. (Your adviser can help here, saying whether a topic is manageable.)
>
> Good questions form the basis for an interesting thesis. The answers will come later.

Review your private notes and draw on them when you meet your prospective adviser. Even if your ideas are unformed, they can launch a useful conversation about your interests and what you hope to study. In return, the professor might suggest some pertinent readings or ways to refine the topic. As you talk about these issues, ask how your subject fits her interests and whether your approach seems sensible. If things go well, you might be able to line up an adviser then and there and begin clarifying your topic.

WHAT IF YOU ARE STILL UNSURE ABOUT A TOPIC?

What if you don't yet know the specific topic you want to pursue? By now, you know the general area, but you may still be searching for the exact topic. Here's a technique I have found helpful.

I ask students to propose three topics or questions—briefly, in writing, and in order of priority. You may be thinking: "Well, that's not exactly a Nobel Prize–winning suggestion. If I can't settle on one topic, how can I possibly propose three?" Because, believe it or not, it is often easier to jot down three ideas than to pick just one. When you try to generate the "single best idea," there is a lot of pressure to pick exactly the right one. After all, you will have to work on it for some time. Knowing that, you hesitate. You delay not because you lack ideas but because you are reluctant to choose the single best one.

Writing down two, three, or even four ideas lessens the pressure dramatically. You are not committed to any one of them. Equally important, this little list makes it easy to talk with faculty about what matters most to you. Your prospective adviser will learn about your chief interests, and as you talk, you may discover that seemingly different ideas have a common theme. (If you hold these talks during your junior year, you will have a head start on your thesis and can get some useful advice on which classes to take as preparation.)

> *Tip:* If you are unsure about what thesis topic to pursue, try generating a tentative list of three topics or questions. You can narrow them later in discussions with faculty.

To illustrate, let's look at a student list of three thesis topics in American politics. The first item mentions the riots that followed Martin Luther King's 1968 assassination. The second is on welfare reform during the Clinton administration. And the third is about affirmative action.

What does the student himself think about this list? For him, the items might suggest one underlying interest or several different projects. Talking with an adviser will explore that. The underlying interest could be racial politics, which is a dominant feature of both the riots and affirmative action and a major component of welfare policy. Perhaps the focus is really political resistance by the poor, whether black, white, or Latino. Perhaps it's the federal government's role in responding to large-scale social problems. Or it could be something else entirely. The list itself will prompt a constructive discussion. Writing it down will help you think about it—beforehand and during your meetings with potential advisers.

Even if you have not settled on a topic, it is easy enough to generate a list like this. And it's surprisingly useful. In discussions with faculty, you may be able to identify some core interests and move beyond them to find a specific research topic. That topic might be one already on the list, or it might emerge from your discussions. Even if you don't nail down your topic in this first meeting, you should move much closer to defining it.

GOALS FOR MEETING WITH A POTENTIAL ADVISER

Beyond learning more about possible topics, your meeting with a potential adviser should accomplish two or three concrete goals.

First, if you are comfortable with the professor, personally and professionally, go ahead and seal the deal. Ask her to sign the school's paperwork and formally become your adviser. If you prefer to talk with other faculty before choosing, go ahead. That may seem a little awkward, but it's a small matter compared to picking the wrong adviser. Just thank the faculty member you spoke with—courtesy counts—and say you hope to decide on an adviser soon. Then make appointments with other professors you are considering. Do it fairly soon, make your choice, and then complete the departmental paperwork. Don't hesitate to return to the first or second teacher you spoke with, if that turns out to be the best adviser for you.

Second, once you have chosen an adviser, work together to set specific tasks for your next meeting. Don't settle on a vague goal. Don't promise more than you can deliver. Pick one or two clear-cut tasks you can accomplish in the time available. Do that at every meeting, beginning with the first. Simply ask what you should do for next time, or make a suggestion yourself. It will keep you and your adviser on the same page and keep you moving forward. Do that every time, be concrete, and don't overpromise.

Third, set a date for your next meeting. Again, do that every time. Don't leave any regular meeting with your adviser without setting a specific day and time for your next meeting. That will reduce confusion and eliminate needless calls and e-mails to schedule. Most important of all, it will give you a firm deadline for the tasks you have just settled on. If you are unsure how soon your next meeting should be, just ask your adviser, "Should we meet again next Thursday afternoon or in a couple of weeks?"

> *Tip:* At the end of *each* meeting with your adviser, set a date for your next meeting and specific tasks to accomplish for it.

DIVIDE YOUR PROJECT INTO
SMALLER TASKS AND SCHEDULE THEM

These meetings and tasks are crucial because nobody can complete a thesis all at once. It is simply too big. You may be great at cramming for exams, but you cannot crank out a whole thesis that way. It would be a miserable task with uncertain results. To do good work (and certainly to do your best work) you need time—time to think through the topic and discuss it with your adviser, time to conduct research carefully and revise your writing.

Fortunately, there is a straightforward solution: *Slice your large thesis project into a series of smaller tasks, each with its own deadline.* Rather than focusing on a distant target date for the whole thesis—many months away—focus on completing a series of smaller tasks, due every week or two. Out of these small components, you will build a large successful project.

> *Tip:* To make the thesis project manageable, divide it into small doable projects. You can set deadlines for each as you move along.

This step-by-step approach will help you organize the project and keep it on schedule. The same approach works just as well for a master's thesis, a PhD dissertation, or a book—indeed, for all large tasks. In each case, you subdivide the big project into a series of specific manageable tasks (such as chapters of a book or sections of a paper) and then complete each one in turn. Later, I'll show you how to carve up your thesis project into its major components, and I'll suggest a schedule for these various tasks.

Working from this general schedule, you should write a customized one for your own project. You should probably do that in the second or third month, after you've completed and revised your thesis proposal. (More on that later.) This schedule provides a rough guide, not fixed marching orders. You'll update it periodically as you complete your work and share it with your adviser so you can both monitor your progress.

Working steadily on these smaller tasks has many advantages. It is certainly more comfortable than weeklong binges of research and writing. Occasionally, you may need to do a sprint of intensive work. That's fine. But don't let your normal work schedule resemble a roller coaster, with weeks of slow uphill movement followed by a heart-pounding weekend of frenetic activity. Save that for parties.

For your thesis, *do some work every day.* It is much calmer and more sustainable. You can learn more from your research and writing since you'll have time to think things over and get regular feedback. As your adviser reads your work and discusses it with you, you can make useful midcourse corrections.

Tip: Work steadily, with interim deadlines.
- Set due dates for smaller projects as you go along. Set them yourself; your adviser won't.
- Incorporate these due dates into your own customized thesis schedule.
  - Write this schedule yourself, probably in the second or third month.
  - Use the schedules in this book as guidelines (summarized in chapter 15).
  - Revise your schedule as you move deeper into the project.
- Try to do at least a little reading, writing, or research on the thesis every day.

In the end, this approach is simply more pleasant and more productive. You know that already; I'm just reminding you. It's the ancient fable of the tortoise and the hare: Slow but steady wins the race. The longer the race, the more important a steady pace.

HOW LONG SHOULD YOUR THESIS BE?

Just how long is this race? Think of it as an intensive seminar paper, one that requires more planning, research, and polishing than any you've written before. It should take at least one semester to complete; most schools consider it a two-semester (or two-quarter) project.

How long should the paper be? That varies from school to school and from department to department, but the best model is a good article in your field. In some fields, such as economics and psychology, published articles generally run fifteen or twenty pages. They often state hypotheses as mathematical formulas and present extensive data in compact graphs and tables. A great deal of intellectual work and data analysis is compressed into a few pages. Supplementary data might be included in an appendix or Web site. In other fields, journal articles are longer because data is presented in descriptive paragraphs and the relevant context is conveyed in richer detail. As a result, articles in the *American Historical Review* are two or three times longer than those in the *American Economic Review*. Articles in comparative literature or English are as long as those in history, mainly because they quote extensively from primary texts and major critics. BA theses in these fields differ in the same ways, matching the subject matter and research methods.

> *Tip:* Your thesis should be modeled on a good article, *not* on a book. It should be roughly the same length as major articles in your field.

It helps to know what's expected from the beginning. Start by looking at the top journals in your field. Check out the length of articles and the breadth of material they cover. Then talk it over with your adviser. (When you discuss the paper's length, be sure to say whether you mean double-spaced or single-spaced. Big difference!) Finally, see if your department has specific requirements. Some do. They specify the minimum and maximum word length, single- or double-spaced lines, proper margins, appropriate citation styles, standardized cover pages, and so on.

All of these requirements are easy to handle, and most of them don't matter until you are deep into your research and writing. I'll remind you then. Only two of them matter now. First, as you think about the scale of your project, it helps to know the target length of the paper. Second, as you start assembling your reading list and turning in draft papers, it helps to know what kind of citations to use. You might as well use the right style consistently from the beginning. See if your department requires a particular style or if your adviser recommends one. (Appendix 2 shows how to handle different citation styles.)

> *Tip:* See if your department has requirements for the length and format of your thesis. Even if it doesn't, you should discuss these issues briefly with your adviser. Use a consistent citation style from the beginning.

START ASSEMBLING A READING LIST

For your first thesis task, I recommend putting together a reading list. I've talked with lots of advisers, and almost all of them recommend it as a first task. The reasons are simple. It is essential for every thesis, and you can begin right away. Ask your adviser to suggest a few books and articles to get you started. Pursue them and follow their footnotes to other readings.

Don't just compile a list. Begin exploring it. Read some important works carefully and skim others to familiarize yourself with the topic. Don't read everything at the same pace. That's like talking in a monotone.

Tip: As one of your first tasks, start assembling a reading list.

You can start constructing the reading list as soon as you've settled on your basic topic, even before you have completed your thesis proposal. If you know your general topic by the end of junior year, start then. That way, you can do some background reading over the summer and hit the ground running when senior year arrives.

FIVE FAST WAYS TO BUILD A READING LIST

There are several shortcuts to building a good reading list, little tricks that insiders know and you can take advantage of. First, identify the leading scholarly journals in your field and thumb through the past few years, looking for articles on your topic. Each field has its own top journals. Ask your adviser which ones you should examine. Supplement that by searching your library's database. You will probably want to do a general Web search, too, but be wary of the quality of what you find. Check to see if the work has been published in a reputable place.

Second, see if your library has a specialist in your area. Reference librarians are an excellent source of advice about readings. They know about new books and journals, specialized bibliographies, and primary documents. After all, they are the ones who order them. Later, as your research develops, they can show you how to request research materials from other libraries.

Third, check for recently published guides to the literature. Again, a reference librarian can help. Some fields publish regular surveys, such as the *Annual Review of Anthropology* or the *Annual Review of Psychology,* in which specialists evaluate recent developments.[1] For historians, there is *The*

---

1. *Annual Review of Anthropology* (Palo Alto, CA: Annual Reviews, 1972–present); *Annual Review of Psychology* (Stanford, CA: Annual Reviews, 1950–present). There are similar volumes (from the same publisher) in other social sciences.

American Historical Association's Guide to Historical Literature, now in its third edition.[2] It is filled with useful essays on various topics and periods, followed by annotated bibliographies. (The annotation explains what each book covers and offers some assessment of its quality and reliability.) There are similar works in other fields, such as *The Humanities: A Selective Guide to Information Sources.*[3] These guides are valuable in every field; they are essential if you are looking for archival items such as personal letters. Volumes like Steven Fisher's *Archival Information: How to Find It, How to Use It* explain where the originals are and whether microfilms or electronic versions are available.[4] For American archives, the most comprehensive guide is the National Union Catalog of Manuscript Collections, available online from the Library of Congress at http://lcweb.loc.gov/coll/nucmc/ nucmc.html.

Fourth, look closely at the footnotes and bibliographies in everything you read. Some are very thorough, listing all the relevant literature. You can share the fruits of this hard work—but only if you look for it.

Fifth, and most important of all, search for top-notch book reviews. There are two basic kinds:

- Brief evaluations of individual books
- Longer "literature reviews," surveying major trends and comparing recent books in a field

It's not hard to find reviews of individual books. Many journals include them as a professional service. Skim these reviews, looking for new publications on your topic. Your main goal is to decide whether to read the book itself.

Even more valuable are full-scale literature reviews. Search hard for

---

2. Mary Beth Norton, ed., *The American Historical Association's Guide to Historical Literature,* assoc. ed. Pamela Gerardi, 3rd ed., 2 vols. (New York: Oxford University Press, 1995). Also see Francis Paul Prucha, *Handbook for Research in American History: A Guide to Bibliographies and Other Reference Works,* 2nd ed., rev. (Lincoln: University of Nebraska Press, 1994).

3. Ron Blazek and Elizabeth Aversa, *The Humanities: A Selective Guide to Information Sources,* 5th ed. (Englewood, CO: Libraries Unlimited, 2000).

4. Steven Fisher, ed., *Archival Information: How to Find It, How to Use It* (Westport, CT: Greenwood Press, 2004).

them and read them carefully. In most fields, one or two journals are known for their in-depth surveys, usually written by leading scholars. Every issue of *Diplomatic History,* for instance, has a major review article.[5] So does the prominent journal of medieval studies, *Medium Aevum.*[6] In English literature, several journals do the same for their different specialties, such as Victorian studies.[7] Some, such as *Studies in English Literature, 1500–1900,* go even further and provide annual surveys of new work in various areas.[8] Still others publish occasional surveys. The Spring 2004 issue of *International Security,* for example, includes an essay examining five recent books on American foreign policy.[9]

A few journals concentrate exclusively on review articles. *Reviews in American History, Reviews in Anthropology,* and *Reviews in Religion and Theology* examine individual books and survey entire topics. One recent

---

5. For example, Mark J. White's feature review "New Scholarship on the Cuban Missile Crisis," *Diplomatic History* 26 (Winter 2002): 147–53, covers books by Jutta Weldes, Philip Nash, and Aleksandr Fursenko and Timothy Naftali, plus a number of scholarly articles, and compares them to earlier works on the Cuban Missile Crisis.

6. For example, H. L. Spencer's review article "The Study of Medieval English Preaching: What Next?" *Medium Aevum* 69 (2000): 104–9.

7. Roger Cooter, for example, reviews four books and cites many more in "The Traffic in Victorian Bodies: Medicine, Literature, and History," *Victorian Literature* 45 (Summer 2003): 513–27, http://search.epnet.com/direct.asp?an=11685101&db=aph.

8. To give you a flavor of these surveys, consider Dympna Callaghan's "Recent Studies in Tudor and Stuart Drama," *Studies in English Literature, 1500–1900* 44 (Spring 2004): 405–44. She begins by noting that she "can discern no seismic break with criticism from last year," but that recent work "has taken a decisively philosophical turn. . . . [And it has] thoroughly absorbed and integrated theory and new historicism" (405). After reviewing dozens of books and articles, she concludes by emphasizing their theoretical and methodological diversity: "What drives the books considered above is, I believe, a very clear sense of specifically historical, and very often archival, work that remains to be done on the texts of our period combined with a sense of the priority of the literary and dramatic text over the tools used to interpret it" (444).

9. Colin Dueck, "New Perspectives on American Grand Strategy: A Review Essay," *International Security* 28 (Spring 2004): 197–216, compares books by Robert Art, John Ikenberry, Charles Kupchan, Henry Nau, and Joseph Nye. The article is also filled with references to recent articles on the topic.

article in *Reviews in Anthropology,* for instance, compares several books on emotion.[10] Another evaluates recent work on nomads. Other articles deal with "gender, the state, and globalization in Latin America" and "the Roma of Central and Eastern Europe."[11] Reviews like these provide a quick overview of the best new works, compare their approaches, and highlight the most prominent issues.

If you are fortunate enough to find a major review article on your thesis topic, you have a tremendous jump start on your reading and research. To see if you're the lucky winner, check the journals in your library and online, ask a reference librarian, and talk with your adviser.

After you've finished the reviews and found the best books and articles, buckle down and start reading them. No matter how useful the review, the original work is far richer—and far more valuable for your thesis research. There is simply no shortcut here. You have to read the best scholarship on your topic. Immersing yourself in this literature will give you a much deeper understanding of the subject as you begin research.

> *Tip:* To jump-start your reading list, look for major review articles in your subject. Also, go through the top journals in your field, looking for articles on your topic. Pay special attention to footnotes and bibliographies in these articles.

You'll be searching for the right books and articles throughout your project. Fortunately, your adviser can play a vital role here. She knows the literature and can usually point you to prominent works on your topic. Even

---

10. James M. Wilce Jr., "Passionate Scholarship: Recent Anthropologies of Emotion," *Reviews in Anthropology* 33 (January–March 2004): 1–17. Wilce reviews books by Jean Harkins and Anna Wierzbicka, Zoltán Kövecses, and Sally Planalp.

11. Bahram Tavakolian, "Multiplicities of Nomadism and Varieties of Anthropological Theory," *Reviews in Anthropology* 32 (January–March 2003): 297–314; Richard Giulianotti, "Forging Identities: Reviewing Key Studies in the Relations between Gender, the State, and Globalization in Latin America," *Reviews in Anthropology* 33 (October–December 2003): 345–58; David Z. Scheffel, "The Roma of Central and Eastern Europe," *Reviews in Anthropology* 33 (April–June 2004): 143–61.

if she doesn't know which articles to read on a specific issue, she will certainly know where to look. She does this all the time for her own work. Just remember, it's your job, not hers, to assemble a reading list.

As you collect these titles, include all the information you will need to cite them later. Why waste your time chasing down the articles a second time? Write it down the first time and put it in your computer file.

When I make my own reading lists (something I do for each writing project), I take an extra moment to include the call numbers, too. That way, I don't have to return to the library catalog every time I need a particular book. Incidentally, if I find several similar call numbers, I usually wander into the library stacks and see what other books are nearby. I've made some great discoveries that way.

Tip: Your reading list should
- Grow as your project develops
- Be used as a working document, filled with your notes about books and articles
- Include citation information and call numbers so you can cite the work or find it again

As you hunt for these books, remember that you are putting together some initial readings, not a definitive bibliography. You'll keep adding to the list as your thesis progresses. Your goal right now is simply to initiate the bibliography, dip into the literature, and learn how others are approaching your topic. You want to discover the main questions, the shared understandings, and the big debates that roil the field.

YOUR SECOND MEETING

In a couple of weeks, after you've made some headway on these readings, return for a second meeting with your adviser. By then, you'll know more about your topic and have more to talk about. To reach this stage, you need to explore some of the books and articles you've found, take good notes, and think about how these readings bear on your thesis topic. These, too, are nuts-and-bolts features of thesis research. They are the subject of the next chapter.

CHECKLIST: TIMELINE TO BEGIN YOUR THESIS

Junior year	• Collect ideas for thesis topics.
	• Take advanced courses relevant to your thesis.
Late junior year/ early senior year	• Develop a thesis topic (or, if you are unsure, a list of three).
	• Meet with potential faculty advisers.
	• Start assembling a reading list on your general topic.
Early senior year	• Select your thesis adviser.
	• Pick a general thesis topic and begin to focus within it.
	• Develop your reading list and begin to explore it.
	• Schedule regular meetings with your thesis adviser.

Framing
Your Topic

3 TAKING EFFECTIVE NOTES AND AVOIDING PLAGIARISM

Good notes will make the most of your reading. That doesn't mean slowing to a crawl to write down everything. You're not a human photocopier. Rather, it means focusing on important books and articles—the ones that really matter to your research—and then summarizing their chief points, crucial data, and major ideas so you can draw on them later.

To take effective notes, you should think about what you'll be using them for. One is to learn more about your subject. Another is to find specific sources dealing with specific points in your thesis. A third is to help you categorize and synthesize the work of others so you can situate your work within the wider field. The fourth and most important goal is to spur your own well-informed ideas.

Taking notes is mental work, not menial work. And that work will find its way into your thesis: the broad learning, the specific sources, the synthesis of materials, and your original ideas. To meet these goals, your notes should

- Capture the main points of each article
- Focus on parts of the work most closely related to your topic
- Use clear markings to distinguish your comments from the author's language, preventing any accidental plagiarism
- Record the bibliographic information you need for citation
- Develop your own insights, as prompted by the readings, so you can draw on them later

I should add that these notes should be written or typed, not simply marked on photocopies. It's fine to copy articles and underline some sentences, though you should *never* mark a library volume. The real problem is that underlined sentences and a few marginal comments are not effective notes. To make your notes worthwhile, you need to extract the main points from each reading and express them in your words. You might add some critical comments or ideas of your own, connecting the reading to your topic.

Then, once you have taken such valuable notes, don't file them away. Out of sight, out of mind. Take them out occasionally and review them as you develop your thesis project. Going over them will jog your memory and prompt new ideas.

> *Tip:* Don't file away your notes. Review them regularly. That may seem like a waste of time since you've "already finished them." Actually, it's quite valuable since it will remind you of important points and suggest new ones.

CAPTURE THE MAIN POINTS OF EACH ARTICLE

First, make sure your notes capture the heart of what you are reading, phrased in your own words. For example:

My summary: Milton Friedman argues that the Great Depression was caused by a contraction in the money supply. The problem got worse, he says, as banks failed in the early 1930s and the Federal Reserve refused to print more money. He rejects Keynesian explanations that there was a "liquidity trap," or that the Depression could have been solved by higher government spending. For Friedman, the real problem was America's plummeting money supply, not inadequate government demand.

To produce summaries like this, you not only need to read the article; you need to review the introduction, conclusion, and abstract. Then you need to ask yourself, "What is the author's main point?" To figure that out, look away from the article, try to state the main point to yourself, and then write it down.

What if you can't do that? Then you missed the main point. It's much better to know that now than to discover it later. You need to look at the work again, at least briefly, and take another stab at summarizing the main point.

Tip: Your notes on each book, article, or Web site should include a brief summary in your own words. To do that, you should look away from the article, think about its main point (probably only one; rarely more than two or three), and write it down.

Naturally, you also want to include more detailed notes along with your summary. If some ideas are presented on specific pages, rather than throughout the article, your notes should reflect that. For example:

U.S. money supply contracted more in 1932 and 1933 than in 1929 (pp. 55–59).

This pagination will be important later when you start writing. Detailed citations help your readers, who may want to look up a point or check some data you present.

Before completing your notes, pause and reflect on the article as a whole. You might want to add something to your summary or include some additional comments and criticism of your own. If the article prompts some questions, jot them down, too, so you can talk them over with your adviser. To make these queries stand out, I put two question marks at the beginning. For example:

?? Why did the government allow the money supply to contract?

Tip: If you don't understand something you've read, flag it with a question mark. Keep a list of these questions and raise them with your adviser or other teachers.

In my experience, *most of us spend far too little time thinking about what we've just read compared to the time spent reading it.* That's as true for faculty as it is for students. After ninety minutes poring over an article, we close the journal with relief and go directly to the next task or, more likely, stroll out for a well-deserved pizza. Far better to spend eighty-six or eighty-seven minutes reading and three or four minutes simply thinking about what the article says. Same time, better results. You'll understand the material more thoroughly. You'll see more connections to your thesis project.

You may even come up with some ideas of your own (which you should jot down right away).

> *Tip:* After you finish a book or article, spend a couple of minutes just thinking about it. Try to restate the main points to yourself. Ask yourself what you learned from it. As you mull over this reading, be sure to jot down any additional ideas it prompts about your own work.

FOCUS ON ARTICLES AND BOOK CHAPTERS CLOSELY RELATED TO YOUR TOPIC

As you read, it's important to concentrate on works closely tied to your thesis topic. Early in the project, as you immerse yourself in the subject, you need to do some general background reading. A little meandering is par for the course, and it's fine. But as your topic takes shape, your focus should become clearer, sharper.

Maintaining this focus is particularly important when you read longer books. Some parts may bear on your thesis, but others do not. Read shrewdly. Use the table of contents and the index. Feel free to skip some chapters and skim others. You have my permission! Zero in on the key material in your reading and in your notes. Your goal is to extract what you need without getting bogged down in the rest. Remember: *You are reading to write.*

> *Tip:* Read selectively.
> - Don't read everything; focus on works directly related to your topic.
> - Don't read everything at the same speed; read the most important works more carefully.
> - Remember that you are reading to write.

TAKING NOTES WITH Q-QUOTES

Some honest writers find themselves in hot water, accused of plagiarism, because their notes are so bad they cannot tell what they copied and what they wrote themselves. You can avoid that by clearly distinguishing your words from others".[1]

All you need is a simple way to identify quotes and keep them separate from your own words and ideas.

The common solution—using ordinary quotation marks in your notes—doesn't actually work so well in practice. For one thing, quotation marks are small, so it's easy to overlook them later when you return to your notes to write a paper. Second, they don't tell you which page the quote comes from, something you need to know for proper citations. Third, if there's a quote within a quote, it's hard to keep your markings straight.

There's a better way. To avoid all this confusion, simply use the letter Q and the page number to begin all quotations in your notes. To end the quote, write Q again. It's painless, and it's easy to spot the Q's when you read your notes and write your papers.

Example of Q-quotes used to identify exact words:
Q236 Goya's paintings of the civil war in Spain, now two centuries old, are still vivid, immediate, and chilling.Q

Begin your notes for each new book, article, and Web site by writing down the author, title, and other essential data. (The exact information you need is described later in this chapter and in appendix 2: "Footnotes 101.") You'll need this information for each book, article, and Web site you use. With this publication data plus Q-quotes, you'll be able to cite effectively from your own notes, without having to return to the original publication.

---

1. The next several pages are drawn from my book *Doing Honest Work in College: How to Prepare Citations, Avoid Plagiarism, and Achieve Real Academic Success* (Chicago: University of Chicago Press, 2004), chapter 3. I have made some changes to the original text.

Tip (and example) on how to begin notes:
- Top of page 1: bibliographic information and call number
- After that: your notes about the text, including Q-quotes

For example:

Michael Ryan, *Literary Theory: A Practical Introduction* (Malden, MA: Blackwell, 1999). PN45 .R93 1999

Q26 Structuralists applied the insights of linguistics to literature and culture.Q

Some of the earliest structuralists were Russian formalists in 1920s (pp. 26–27).

This system is simple, clear, and effective. It works equally well for typed and handwritten notes. It easily handles quotes within quotes. Looking at your notes, you'll know exactly which words are the author's and which page they are on. You'll know if he is quoting anyone else. And you'll know that anything *outside* the Q-quotes is your own paraphrase. In this example, you know that the observation about linguistics is a direct quote, the one about Russian formalists is your paraphrase.

Tip on paraphrasing: Make sure your paraphrase does not closely resemble the author's words. When in doubt, double-check your wording against the original.

EXAMPLE OF A MORE COMPLICATED QUOTE

Because quotes can be complicated, let's see how these Q-quotes work in more detail. First, some quotes begin on one page and end on another. To show where the page break falls, insert a double slash (//) inside the quote. (A double slash stands out, just as Q does.) That way, if you use only part of the quote, you can cite the correct page without having to chase down the original again. To illustrate:

Q132–33 Samuel Eliot Morison was not only a great historian, he was an experienced sailor. His life-long love of the sea // is apparent in his work.

It gives special depth to his treatment of the European voyages of discovery.Q

The first sentence is on page 132; the next one is on both pages; the third is only on page 133. Using Q-quotes with a double slash gives you all this information quickly and easily.

> *Tip:* After writing down a quotation, compare your notes to the original to ensure you have transcribed it correctly.

Quotes can be complicated in other ways, too. You may wish to cut out some needless words or add a few to make the quote understandable. Fortunately, there are straightforward rules to handle both changes.

SHORTENING QUOTATIONS WITH ELLIPSES . . .

Although quotes need to be exact, you are allowed to shorten them if you follow two rules. First, your cuts cannot change the quote's meaning. Second, you must show the reader exactly where you omitted any words. That's done with an ellipsis, which is simply three dots . . . with spaces before and after each one.

If the omitted words come in the middle of a sentence, an ellipsis is all you need. Take this original sentence:

Original   I jogged around the park, which took at least an hour, and returned home exhausted. Naturally, I took a shower. Then I had dinner and watched a movie before falling asleep.

Here's a shortened version of the first sentence, with an ellipsis to show the omission:

Shortened,   I jogged around the park . . . and returned home exhausted.
ellipsis only

If the two parts of your quote come from two separate sentences, use an ellipsis plus a period (that is, three dots plus a period) to separate the two parts. Here's an example, joining the first and last sentences:

Shortened,	I jogged around the park . . . . and watched a movie be-
ellipsis and	fore falling asleep.
period	

Here's another example:

Original	I walked downtown. After walking more than thirty min-
	utes, I rounded the corner and saw her.
Shortened 1	I walked downtown. . . . and saw her.
Shortened 2	I walked . . . . more than thirty minutes.
Explanation	Both shortened sentences use three ellipses plus a period.
	In the first, the period comes immediately after the word
	"downtown," because that's where the period falls in the
	original sentence. In the second, there is a space before
	the period because the original sentence continues.

Omissions like these are perfectly acceptable as long as you signal them (with ellipses) and you don't change the quoted author's meaning.

ADDING WORDS [IN BRACKETS] TO CLARIFY A QUOTE

Occasionally, you need to add a word or two to clarify a quote. Perhaps the original sentence uses a pronoun instead of a person's name. For clarity, you might wish to include the name. Again, you cannot change the quote's meaning, and you need to signal the reader that you are modifying it slightly. You do that by using [brackets] to show exactly what you have inserted. Consider this original text:

Original	Q46 Hamlet is one of Shakespeare's most complex and
	enduring characters. When he appears onstage, the ac-
	tion quickens as the young prince's rage melds with his
	madness.Q

Now, let's say you want to quote only the second sentence. An exact quote wouldn't make much sense since the reader won't know who "he" is. To correct that, you need to add a word in brackets to make it clear that you've added it to the original:

Your quote   "When [Hamlet] appears onstage, the action quickens as
with brackets the young prince's rage melds with his madness."

That's an accurate quote even though you added a bracketed word. If you
added the same word without brackets, however, it would be a misquotation.

Or, to take our earlier quote, you might say, "Naturally, I took a shower
[after jogging]." That's fine. What you cannot say is "Naturally, I took a
shower [after bicycling]." That's a misquotation and a distortion, perhaps
a deliberate one. Big mistake.

Follow the rule: Additions [with brackets] and omissions (with ellipses . . .) should not change the quote's meaning in any way. The quoted
statement belongs to another writer, not to you. You're welcome to praise
it or to damn it, but not to twist it.

QUOTES WITHIN QUOTES

The phrase you are quoting may itself contain a quotation. One advantage of using Q-quotes for your notes is that you can simply put quotation
marks wherever they appear in the text. For example: Q47 He smiled and
asked for "a double latte with skim milk, please" and she walked over to the
machine to make it.Q Since you are using Q's to mark off the entire quote,
there will be no confusion later when you write a paper with these notes.

USING Q-QUOTES TO HANDLE COMPLICATED QUOTATIONS

Now that we've covered the basics of Q-quotes plus ellipses, brackets,
and quotes within quotes, you are equipped to handle even the most complex quotes accurately, first in your notes and then in your thesis writing.
To illustrate that, let's combine all these elements in one example:

Q186–87 Boswell's biography of Samuel // Johnson is a wondrous work.
It not only invented the genre, it remains the finest example. . . . The
writer and [his subject, Dr. Johnson] are perfectly joined, and Johnson
is, as one critic said, "surely one of the great figures of his age, or any
other."Q

This notation makes the following things clear:

- Only the first few words appear on page 186; the rest are on page 187.
- Some words from the original are omitted after the word "example."
- There is a period after "example" and then an ellipsis (three dots), indicating that the omission does not come in the middle of a sentence. Rather, it separates two sentences.
- The bracketed words, "his subject, Dr. Johnson," are not in the original text.
- The final words are actually a quotation from someone else. They are included as a quote by the author you are citing.

With clear notation like this, you will be able to cite portions of this complicated quote later, without returning to the original article and with no chance of accidental plagiarism. It's not difficult. Actually, it takes more time to explain it than to use it!

PLAGIARISM AND ACADEMIC HONESTY

Because the Q-quote system prevents confusion over who wrote what, it eliminates a major source of plagiarism: simple mistakes caused by bad notes. Of course, that's not the only reason for plagiarism. Students rushing to finish a paper may forget to include the necessary citations. Some are sloppy. Others don't understand the citation rules. Sadly, a few cheat deliberately.

Whatever the cause, plagiarism is a serious violation of academic rules—for undergraduates, graduate students, and faculty alike. The rules are the same for everybody. Misrepresenting someone else's words or ideas as your own constitutes fraud. It is a basic principle of academic integrity that when you say you did the work yourself, you actually did it. Likewise, when you rely on someone else's work, you cite it. When you use someone else's words, you quote them openly and accurately. When you present research materials, you present them fairly and truthfully. Quotations, data, experiments, and the ideas of others should never be falsified or distorted. These are basic principles of academic honesty.[2]

---

2. These principles are explained in *Doing Honest Work in College*, chapter 1.

CITE OTHERS' WORK TO AVOID PLAGIARISM

Citation rules follow from these principles of openness and honesty. If the words are someone else's, they must be clearly marked as quotations, either by quotation marks or block indentation (for longer quotes), followed by a citation in a footnote, an endnote, or an in-text note, depending on your paper's citation style. It's not enough merely to mention an author's name. If it's a direct quote, use quotation marks and a full citation in a note. If it's a paraphrase of someone else's words, use your own language, not a close imitation of the work being cited, and include a proper citation.

The same rules apply to visual images, architectural drawings, databases, graphs, statistical tables, spoken words, and information taken from the Internet. If you use someone else's work, cite it. Cite it even if you think the work is wrong and you intend to criticize it. Cite it even if the work is freely available in the public domain. Cite it even if the author gave you permission to use the work. All these rules follow from the same idea: Acknowledge what you take from others. The only exception is when you rely on commonly known information. When you say the world is round, you don't need to cite Christopher Columbus.

The penalties for violating these rules are serious. For students, they can lead to failed courses and even expulsion. For faculty, they can lead to demotion, loss of tenure, or outright dismissal. The penalties are severe because honesty is central to academic life and the pursuit of knowledge.

Tips on avoiding plagiarism: When in doubt, give credit by citing the original source.
- If you use an author's exact words, enclose them in quotation marks and include a citation in a footnote, an endnote, or an in-text note. If the quote is longer, use block indentation (without quotation marks), followed by a citation in a note.
- If you paraphrase another author, use your own language. Don't imitate the original. Be sure to include a citation.
- If you rely on or report someone else's ideas, credit their source, whether you agree with them or not.

USING THE INTERNET WITHOUT PLAGIARIZING

You need to be especially alert to these citation issues when you use the Web. Internet research is very efficient, especially when you don't need to read long stretches of text. You can do extensive targeted searches, quickly check out multiple sources, access sophisticated databases, click on article summaries or key sentences, and then drag-and-drop material into your notes. That's all perfectly fine. In fact, it's often the best way to conduct research. But it's also crucial to be a good bookkeeper. You need to use a simple, consistent method to keep straight what some author said and what you paraphrased. After all, you have to cite Web sources just as you do print sources.

The easiest way is to stick with the method you use for printed books and articles: *Put Q-quotes around everything you drag-and-drop from electronic sources.* You can supplement that, if you wish, by coloring the author's text red or blue, or by using a different font. Just be consistent. That way you won't be confused in three or four weeks, when you are reviewing your notes and writing your paper.

One more thing: Be sure to write down the Web site's address so you can cite it or return to it for more research. Just copy the URL into your notes. It's probably a good idea to include the date you accessed it, too. Some citation styles ask for it. If the item appears in a database and has a document identification number, copy that, too. It's very helpful for finding the document again.

QUOTING AND PARAPHRASING WITHOUT PLAGIARIZING: A TABLE OF EXAMPLES

A simple example can illustrate how to quote and paraphrase properly, and how to avoid some common mistakes. The following table shows the main rules for citation and academic honesty, using a sentence written by "Jay Scrivener" about Joe Blow. I'll use footnote superscript 99 to show when that sentence is cited.

QUOTING WITHOUT PLAGIARIZING

Joe Blow was a happy man, who often walked down the road whistling and singing.

Sentence in the book *Joe Blow: His Life and Times,* by Jay Scrivener.

WHAT'S RIGHT

"Joe Blow was a happy man, who often walked down the road whistling and singing."[44]
According to Scrivener, Blow "often walked down the road whistling and singing."[99]
"Joe Blow was a happy man," writes Scrivener.[99]

Correct: Full quote is inside quotation marks, followed by citation to *Joe Blow: His Life and Times.*
Correct: Each partial quote is inside quote marks, followed by citation. The partial quotes are not misleading.

According to Scrivener, Blow was "a happy man," who often showed it by singing tunes to himself.[99]

Correct: Partial quote is inside quotation marks; nonquoted materials are outside. The paraphrase (about singing tunes to himself) accurately conveys the original author's meaning without mimicking his actual words. Citation properly follows the sentence.

Joe Blow seemed like "a happy man," the kind who enjoyed "whistling and singing."[99]

Correct: Two partial quotes are each inside quotation marks; nonquoted materials are outside. Citation properly follows sentence.

Joe appeared happy and enjoyed whistling and singing to himself. [99]

Correct: This paraphrase is fine. It's not too close to Scrivener's original wording. The citation acknowledges the source.

WHAT'S WRONG

Joe Blow was a happy man, who often walked down the road whistling and singing. (no citation)

Wrong: It is plagiarism to quote an author's exact words or to paraphrase them closely without both quotation marks and proper citation. Acknowledge your sources!

Joe Blow was a happy man, who often walked down the road whistling and singing.[99]	**Wrong:** These are actually Scrivener's exact words. It is plagiarism to use them without indicating explicitly that it is a quote. It is essential to use quotation marks (or block indentation for longer quotes), even if you give accurate citation to the author. This example is wrong, then, because it doesn't use quotation marks, even though it cites the source.
Joe Blow was a happy man and often walked down the road singing and whistling. (no citation)	**Wrong:** Although the words are not exactly the author's, they are very similar. (The words "singing" and "whistling" are simply reversed.) Either use an exact quote or paraphrase in ways that are clearly different from the author's wording.
Joe Blow was a happy man. (no citation)	**Wrong:** There are two problems here. First, it's an exact quote so it should be quoted and cited. Second, even if the quote were modified slightly, Scrivener should still be cited because it is his personal judgment (and not a simple fact) that Joe Blow is happy.
Joe Blow often walked down the road whistling and singing. (no citation)	**Wrong:** Same two problems as the previous example: (1) exact words should be both quoted and cited, and (2) Scrivener's personal judgment needs to be credited to him.
Joe Blow appeared to be "a happy man" and often walked down the road whistling and singing.[99]	**Wrong:** Despite the citation, some of Scrivener's exact words are outside the quotation marks. That creates the misleading impression that the words are original, rather than Scrivener's. This is a small violation, like going a few miles over the speed limit. But if such miscitations occur often or include significant portions of text, then they can become serious cases of plagiarism.

"Joe Blow was an anxious man, who often ran down the road."[99]	**Wrong:** The quote is not accurate. According to Scrivener, Joe Blow was not anxious; he was "happy." And he didn't run, he "walked." Although this misquotation is not plagiarism, it is an error. You should quote properly, and your work should be reliable. If such mistakes are repeated, if they are seriously misleading, or, worst of all, if they appear to be intentional, they may be considered academic fraud. (Plagiarism is fraud, too, but a different kind.)
Joe Blow "walked down the road" quietly.[99]	**Wrong:** The words inside the partial quotation are accurate, but the word following it distorts Scrivener's plain meaning. Again, this is not plagiarism, but it does violate the basic principle of presenting materials fairly and accurately. If such mistakes are repeated or if they show consistent bias (for example, to prove Joe Blow is a quiet person or hates music), they may be considered a type of academic fraud. At the very least, they are misleading.

WHEN YOU RELY HEAVILY ON A SOURCE, SAY SO

The "Joe Blow" table refers to single sentences, but some citation issues involve paragraphs or whole sections of your paper. Let's say you are writing about European rivalries before World War I and one part of your paper relies on Paul Kennedy's analysis of the subject. Whether or not you quote Kennedy, you should include several citations of his work in that section, reflecting its importance for your paper. You could accomplish the same thing by including an explanatory citation early in the section. The footnote or endnote might say, "My analysis in this section draws heavily on Paul M. Kennedy's work, particularly *The Rise of the Anglo-German Antagonism, 1860–1914* (London: George Allen & Unwin, 1980), 410–31." Or you could include a similar comment in the text itself. Whichever you choose, give readers fair notice that you are leaning on Kennedy. Of course, you still need to include citations for any direct quotes.

Tip: Tell readers when you are relying heavily on a particular source. You can explain that
- In the text itself
- In a descriptive footnote or endnote
- By citing the author multiple times

Any of these is fine.

PARAPHRASING

When you paraphrase an author's sentence, don't veer too close to her words. That's plagiarism, *even if it's unintentional and even if you cite the author.*

What's the best technique for rephrasing a quote? Set aside the other author's text and think about the point *you* want to get across. Write it down in your own words (with a citation) and then compare your sentence to the author's original. If they contain several identical words or merely substitute a couple of synonyms, rewrite yours. Try to put aside the other author's distinctive language and rhythm as you write. That's sometimes hard because the original sticks in your mind or seems just right. Still, you have to try. Your sentences and paragraphs should look and sound different from anyone you cite.

If you have trouble rephrasing an idea in your own words, jot down a brief note to yourself stating the point you want to make. Then back away, wait a little while, and try again. When you begin rewriting, look at your brief note but *don't look at the author's original sentence.* Once you have finished, check your new sentence against the author's original. You may have to try several times to get it right. Don't keep using the same words again and again. Approach the sentence from a fresh angle. If you still can't solve the problem, give up and use a direct quote (perhaps a whole sentence, perhaps only a few key words). It should either be a direct quote or your distinctive rephrasing. It cannot be lip-synching.

Why not use direct quotes in the first place? Sometimes that's the best solution—when the author's language is compelling or when it says something important about the writer. When Franklin Roosevelt spoke about the attack on Pearl Harbor, he told America: "Yesterday, December 7, 1941—a date which will live in infamy—the United States of America was suddenly and deliberately attacked . . . ."[3] No one would want to paraphrase that. It's perfect as it is, and it's historically significant. When you analyze novels and poems, you'll want to quote extensively to reveal the author's creative expression. Other phrases speak volumes about the people who utter them. That's why you might quote Islamic fundamentalists calling the United States "the Great Satan" or George W. Bush responding that they are "evil." Direct quotes like these convey the flavor of the conflict.

Because there are so many times when quotations are essential, you should avoid them where they're not. Overuse cheapens their value. Don't trot them out to express ordinary thoughts in ordinary words. Paraphrase. Just remember the basic rules: Cite the source and don't mimic the original language.

> *Tip:* Choose whether to quote or paraphrase. If you paraphrase, it should not resemble the original quote.

These rules apply to the whole academic community, from freshmen to faculty. A senior professor at the U.S. Naval Academy was recently stripped of tenure for violating them. Although Brian VanDeMark had written several well-regarded books, his *Pandora's Keepers: Nine Men and the Atomic Bomb* contains numerous passages that closely resemble other books.[4] Most were footnoted, but, as you now know, that doesn't eliminate the problem.[5]

Here are a few of the questionable passages, compiled by Robert Norris. (Norris compiled an even longer list of similarities between VanDeMark's work and his own book *Racing for the Bomb*.)[6]

---

3. President Franklin D. Roosevelt, Joint Address to Congress Leading to a Declaration of War against Japan, December 8, 1941, http://www.fdrlibrary.marist.edu/oddec7.html (accessed June 1, 2004).

4. Brian VanDeMark, *Pandora's Keepers: Nine Men and the Atomic Bomb* (Boston: Little, Brown, 2003).

5. Jacques Steinberg, "U.S. Naval Academy Demotes Professor over Copied Work," *New York Times* (national edition), October 29, 2003, A23.

6. Robert Norris, *Racing for the Bomb: General Leslie R. Groves, the Manhattan Project's Indispensable Man* (South Royalton, VT: Steerforth Press, 2002).

Brian VanDeMark, *Pandora's Keepers* (2003)	Richard Rhodes, *The Making of the Atomic Bomb* (1986) and *Dark Sun* (1995)
". . . Vannevar Bush. A fit man of fifty-two who looked uncannily like a beardless Uncle Sam, Bush was a shrewd Yankee . . ." (60)	"Vannevar Bush made a similar choice that spring. The sharp-eyed Yankee engineer, who looked like a beardless Uncle Sam, had left his MIT vice presidency . . ." (*Making of the Atomic Bomb,* 336)
"Oppenheimer wondered aloud if the dead at Hiroshima and Nagasaki were not luckier than the survivors, whose exposure to radiation would have painful and lasting effects." (194–195)	"Lawrence found Oppenheimer weary, guilty and depressed, wondering if the dead at Hiroshima and Nagasaki were not luckier than the survivors, whose exposure to the bombs would have lifetime effects." (*Dark Sun,* 203)
"To toughen him up and round him out, Oppenheimer's parents had one of his teachers, Herbert Smith, take him out West during the summer before he entered Harvard College." (82)	"To round off Robert's convalescence and toughen him up, his father arranged for a favorite English teacher at Ethical Culture, a warm, supportive Harvard graduate named Herbert Smith, to take him out West for the summer." (*The Making of the Atomic Bomb,* 120–121)
"For the next three months, both sides marshaled their forces. At Strauss's request, the FBI tapping of Oppenheimer's home and office phones continued. The FBI also followed the physicist whenever he left Princeton." (259)	"For the next three months, both sides marshaled their forces. The FBI tapped Oppenheimer's home and office phones at Strauss's specific request and followed the physicist whenever he left Princeton." (*Dark Sun,* 539)

Source: Robert Norris, "Parallels with Richard Rhodes's Books [referring to Brian VanDeMark's *Pandora's Keepers*]," History News Network Web site, http://hnn.us/articles/1485.html (accessed June 22, 2004). For convenience, I have rearranged the last two rows in the table, without changing the words.

Unfortunately, VanDeMark does not cite Rhodes or quote him directly in any of these passages. Some, like the last one, are virtual quotations and would raise red flags even if they occurred only once. A few others are a little too close for comfort but raise problems mostly because there are so many of them in VanDeMark's book.[7]

This is only one of several tables covering VanDeMark's poor paraphrasing or unquoted sources. Each was prepared by a different author who felt violated. According to the Naval Academy's academic dean, "The whole approach to documenting the sources of the book was flawed."[8] The dean and VanDeMark himself attributed the problem to sloppiness rather than purposeful theft (which is why VanDeMark was demoted rather than fired). Still, the punishment was severe and shows how seriously plagiarism is taken at every level of the university.

PLAGIARIZING IDEAS

Plagiarizing doesn't just mean borrowing someone else's words. It also means borrowing someone else's ideas. Let's say you are impressed by an article comparing *The Catcher in the Rye* and *Hamlet*.[9] The article concludes that these works are variations on a single theme: a young man's profound

---

7. Besides copying words and phrases from Richard Rhodes and Robert Norris, VanDeMark took passages from Greg Herken, William Lanouette, and Mary Palevsky without proper quotations or full attribution. Some passages are *not* obvious cases of plagiarism—deliberate or accidental—but some are nearly identical to other works and still others are too close for comfort. The overall pattern is troubling. These parallels between VanDeMark's work and other books are documented online with similar tables. See History News Network, "Brian VanDeMark: Accused of Plagiarism," May 31, 2003, http://hnn.us/articles/1477.html (accessed June 22, 2004). That page links to several tables comparing VanDeMark's wording to various authors'.

8. Nelson Hernández, "Scholar's Tenure Pulled for Plagiarism: Acts Not Deliberate, Naval Academy Says," *Washington Post,* October 29, 2003, B06, http://www.washingtonpost.com/wp-dyn/articles/A32551-2003Oct28.html (accessed March 5, 2004).

9. Although I thought of this comparison between the characters of Hamlet and Holden Caulfield myself, I suspected others had, too. Just to be on the safe side, I decided to do a Google search. The top item offered to sell me a term paper on the subject!

anguish and mental instability, as shown through his troubled internal monologues. If your paper incorporates this striking idea, credit the author who proposed it, *even if every word you say about it is your own.* Otherwise, your paper will wrongly imply you came up with the idea yourself. Holden Caulfield would call you a phony. The moral of the tale: It's perfectly fine to draw on others' ideas, as long as you give them credit. The only exception is when the ideas are commonplace.

> *Tip:* Cite borrowed ideas as well as borrowed words.

DISTORTING IDEAS

A recurrent theme of this chapter is that you should acknowledge others' words and ideas and represent them faithfully, without distortion. When you paraphrase them, you should keep the author's meaning, even if you disagree with it. When you shorten a quote, you should indicate that you've shortened it and keep the essential idea.

There are really two goals here. The first is to maintain honesty in your own work. The second is to engage others' ideas fully, on a level playing field. That's the best way to confront diverse ideas, whether you agree with them or not. That's fair play, of course, but it's more than that. It's also how you make your own work better. You are proving the mettle of your approach by passing a tough, fair test—one that compares your ideas to others without stacking the deck in your favor.

The danger is setting up straw men, constructing flimsy arguments you can knock down without much effort. That's not only dishonest; it's intellectually lazy. Believe me, your own position will be much stronger and more effective if you confront the best opposing arguments, presented fairly, and show why yours is better.

> *Tip:* When you use others' words or ideas, don't distort them. Confront their real ideas, not a pale imitation.

THE RIGHT WAY TO PARAPHRASE AND CITE: A SUMMARY OF KEY POINTS

To summarize, the rules for citation and paraphrasing are based on a few core ideas:

- You are responsible for your written work, including the ideas, facts, and interpretations you include.
- Unless you say otherwise, every word you write is assumed to be your own.
- When you rely on others' work or ideas, acknowledge it openly.
  - When you use their ideas or data, give them credit.
  - When you use their exact words, use quotation marks plus a citation.
  - When you paraphrase, use your own distinctive voice and cite the original source. Make sure your language doesn't mimic the original. If it still does after rewriting, then use direct quotes.
  - When you rely heavily on an author for part of your paper, say so.
- When you draw on others' work, present it fairly. No distortions. No straw men.
- When you present empirical material, show where you acquired it so others can check the data for themselves. (The exception is commonly known material, which does not need to be cited.)

These principles of fairness and disclosure are more than simple rules for citation, more than just "good housekeeping" in your paper. They are fundamental rules for academic integrity. They promote real learning. They apply to teachers and students alike and encourage free, fair, and open discussion of ideas—the heart and soul of a university.

WRITE DOWN INFORMATION YOU NEED FOR CITATIONS

Since you will eventually want to cite many of the books and articles you read, you need to write down the full titles so you can refer to them later. If you photocopy a few pages from an article, be sure to record all the bibliographic information, including the page numbers for the whole article.

Tip: Include full citation information in your notes, on your photocopies, and in downloaded articles.

Aside from the author and title, what information do you need? That differs slightly for books, journal articles, and chapters in edited books, but the basic idea is the same. Don't be put off by the mechanics, which are not difficult and are fully discussed in appendix 2, "Footnotes 101."

For a book, you only need three pieces of information besides the author and title: the publisher's name, where it was published, and when. For this book: Charles Lipson, *How to Write a BA Thesis: A Practical Guide from Your First Ideas to Your Finished Paper* (Chicago: University of Chicago Press, 2005). Done.

For an article, you need to tell the reader where it appears within a particular journal. That means you need the volume and publication date, plus page numbers for the entire article: Jill Frank, "Citizens, Slaves, and Foreigners: Aristotle on Human Nature," *American Political Science Review* 98 (February 2004): 91–104.

For a chapter in an edited volume, you essentially combine the information needed for a book and an article: Gerald Feldman, "Mobilizing Economies for War," in *The Great War and the Twentieth Century,* ed. Jay Winter, Geoffrey Parker, and Mary R. Habeck (New Haven, CT: Yale University Press, 2000), 166–86.

If a book has been translated or is a second or third edition, include that in the citation (normally, after the title). Finally, if your information comes from the Internet, write down the full URL and the date you accessed it.

And that's it. That's basically all you need to know to cite books, articles, and Web sites. It is not hard or arcane. It's just the information anyone needs to find the material you used, all presented in standard form. In some fields, you cite this information at the bottom of the page (footnotes) or after the body of the paper (endnotes), with a bibliography at the end of the paper. Others prefer what is called "in-text" citing, such as (Frank, 2004), followed by a reference list at the end of the paper, covering only those books and articles that you have cited.

Whether you use footnotes, endnotes, or in-text citations, the information you collect is the same. Just ask your adviser which form she prefers or which one the department requires. You can find more information in appendix 2. It covers the three main citation styles in some detail and provides plenty of examples.

> *Tip:* For details on proper citation, covering all three major citation styles, see appendix 2: "Footnotes 101."

If you need more information or want to use other citation styles, the details are provided in Charles Lipson, *Doing Honest Work in College: How to Prepare Citations, Avoid Plagiarism, and Achieve Real Academic Success* (Chicago: University of Chicago Press, 2004), part 2. It is a work of exquisite beauty, and the chapters on citations are thrill-packed.

My examples in appendix 2, however, should cover most of what you need. If you have any questions about a particular footnote or endnote style, simply write out two or three citations and ask your adviser to correct them for you. It will only take a moment, and you'll be on track. Or turn to the mother lode of information on academic style, *The Chicago Manual of Style.*[10]

Collect citation information as you write your notes. I speak here as a reformed sinner. Many times, I've looked over my notes and found an article that came from volume 49, but I don't know what year. That means another trip to the library, mumbling under my breath. Worse, I've often stared at a single photocopied page, stuck in my files, with no idea which article it came from, which journal, or which planet. Earth, I suppose, but I'm just guessing.

DEVELOP YOUR OWN INSIGHTS AS YOU READ—
AND WRITE THEM DOWN

Your reading may spark genuinely new ideas, which you want to expand and include in your thesis. That is one of the great joys of active reading, where you engage the material and respond to it. My suggestion is to write out these ideas immediately, expand on them as much as you can right away, and mark them clearly as your own. Nothing is more important than developing your own ideas on the topic, particularly when they are solidly grounded in research. So seize the moment.

> *Tip:* Write down your ideas as you take notes. Identify them clearly as your own.

---

10. *The Chicago Manual of Style,* 15th ed. (Chicago: University of Chicago Press, 2003).

You probably won't confuse your ideas with anyone else's work, but you might inadvertently bury them amid the notes you are taking. I avoid that by indenting my comments and putting them in brackets, beginning with my initials. For example, while reading an anthropology article, I might write:

[CL: Anthropologists' descriptions of tribal communities without formal government are remarkably similar to descriptions of the international system, where there is no overarching government, either. But there are important differences. Cultural ties and social norms are much stronger in tribal groups than in international politics.]

You could go further and highlight your comments with color, boldface, or italics. I don't do that, but I do look through my notes and copy all my comments to a special file. What matters is that I arrange these comments so I can find them easily when I want them.

SOME TIPS FOR TAKING NOTES EFFECTIVELY

As a senior, you've already taken a lot of notes in college, and by now you have your own system for doing it. Here are some additional ideas that might make your system more efficient.

- Always write down page numbers in your notes.
    - Because your thesis should attribute specific information to specific sources, you need to write down page numbers when you find key data and ideas.
- Get your information from several sources and check them against each other. Underscore any important conflicts.
- Get an overview of each book or article before reading it in detail.
    - Before reading the material carefully, read the abstract, introduction, and conclusion and skim the rest quickly. That will orient you to important materials, reinforce major points, and allow you to skip some minor chapters or sections entirely.
- When you paraphrase, use language that is truly your own, not a close imitation of the author's. It is your paper, and it should be your distinctive voice.
- Don't use highlighters.
    I know, everybody uses them. But, in fact, they don't help and can actually hurt your work. They create two problems:

- ○ Highlighting too many points
- ○ Remembering too few

Highlighters create the illusion that you have thought about the main points, when all you have done is painted them.

Rather than wasting time highlighting, spend a few minutes after you finish the reading actually *thinking about the article*. What's the author's main point? What kind of evidence or arguments are used to support it?

True story: A few years ago, I ran across an old college history book of mine. One *entire* page was highlighted. Everything was solid yellow, except for one solitary sentence. I stared and stared at the unmarked sentence. As best I could tell, it was no more or less important than the others. Frankly, no sentence on that page was worth a second glance. I still have no idea why I marked them all. That page just sat there, line after line painted bright yellow, reminding me that I was completely clueless about what was really important.

- Use consistent abbreviations in your notes.
  - ○ If your notes deal with nineteenth-century Britain, for example, you might use "CD" to mean Charles Dickens. Just remember that you need a different abbreviation for Charles Darwin.
- Transfer your handwritten notes to the computer. They will be much more usable.
- If you photocopy or download articles, make some marginal notations and underline a few crucial lines of text. (Restrain yourself from underlining much more.)

Here are the main marks I use in the margins of photocopied articles:

Mark	Meaning
NB	The most important points to be noted well, usually only one or two per article. (NB = *nota bene* = note well)
✓	Check mark, used sparingly to note important supporting points or data. Similar to NB but for less important points.
Def	Definition of key term. I sometimes add the term itself in the margin, as in "def-Democracy."
?	A question I have about the material; perhaps I don't understand it.

The main point about photocopies, though, is that you should take good notes so you don't have to return to the article itself to get ideas and information.

SOMETIMES THE MOST IMPORTANT PART OF TAKING NOTES IS WHEN YOU ARE *NOT* WRITING

Good notes are based on your judgment about what is important in the readings and what is relevant to your thesis. You are not a stenographer, trying to write down everything you read. Be selective because, in the end, *you are reading to write your own paper.*

Your reading is part of your thesis research, and your notes should be crafted to help you in the writing process. To do that effectively, your notes should focus on what's important for your thesis topic. Use your editorial judgment to decide which articles and ideas matter for your thesis and concentrate on them. That editorial process—your decision whether to write something down and, if so, how to summarize it in your own words—is the crux of taking good notes. Jot down key ideas, facts, and quotes that bear directly on your thesis; exclude the rest.

> *Tip:* Take notes that focus on ideas and data relevant to your thesis. Omit the rest.

Another major part of taking notes is deciding which articles (and which parts of articles) bear on your thesis topic. Some are essential, others completely irrelevant. That means you should mull over what you are reading, decide what is germane to your thesis, and choose what is most important to include in your notes. You will return to these notes later, as you write, so you want to be sure they include the main ideas and facts you need.

Think as you read, and think as you transform your reading into notes. Ask yourself whether a particular point is significant to your thesis—not to the author's thesis but to yours. Write it down only if it contains important information and bears directly on your topic. Students waste time writing down marginal information that has little impact on their thesis. Their hands get tired because their minds are resting.

You should pause several times as you read and take notes. In the midst of an article, look away and see if you can explain to yourself what the main point is, why it is important, and how the author supports it. Most articles have only one main point, not more. A good test of whether you truly understand the article is to see whether you can restate that point. Beyond that, ask yourself questions about what the article means and see if you can answer them. Ask what kind of evidence or logic it uses. Then make sure your insights are reflected in your notes.

After this summary of your reading, you should do two more things. First, give your own candid assessment of the author's claims and evidence. Second, as you think over the article and your notes, see if it prompts any original ideas of your own. If it does, write them down immediately and put them in brackets to identify them as yours.

> *Tip:* Your notes on books, articles, and other readings should
> - State the main point (or claim) of the article
> - List any significant secondary points
> - Highlight the evidence or logic used to support these points
> - Offer your own (brief) critical assessment of the reading
> - Include any ideas that the article suggests for your thesis

DON'T FILE 'EM AND FORGET 'EM

The notes you have just created are too valuable to be filed away, unseen for weeks. Often, your most valuable ideas about a day's readings come the next day, as you review your notes. (That's true of your draft writing, too, which should also be reviewed first thing the next day.) *Read yesterday's notes before beginning another day's reading and research.* Make it a routine, and do it with all your writing, from notes to drafts. It won't take long—probably ten or fifteen minutes—and it's incredibly productive. It will reinforce major points, suggest ideas, point you toward new readings, and get you back into the flow of your work.

> *Tip:* Reread yesterday's notes and writing before beginning today's work.

If you don't review the materials you have studied, your retention will fall off rapidly. That means some of the time you spent reading was wasted. You can retrieve that time simply by reviewing your notes.

Reviewing your notes and writing should be an active process, not a passive one. Read your work critically and add comments or summary statements. I sometimes add "NB" to the margins of my notes or amplify a point I left undeveloped. If my notes are unclear to me, I go back and fix them or reread part of the article. I flag questions and try to repeat the author's main points. I look for connections between this reading and others I have done. If I find such connections, I mention them in the notes. It is at least a small step toward the synthesis of readings I am aiming for. Most important of all, I look for any new ideas of my own stimulated by this review, and I write them down immediately, usually in the same file as the notes. As you know, I put my own comments in brackets and label them with my initials.

> *Tip:* Reviewing your notes should be an active process. Engage the ideas.

BACKING UP YOUR FILES

Your notes and reading list are too valuable to leave unguarded, where they can be stolen, misplaced, or lost in a computer crash. Copy all your computer files and physical notes at regular intervals and store them in a safe place. Their loss would be devastating, and you can prevent it easily.

You've heard it a million times before: Back up your data. You can now make that a million and one. The horror stories of computer crashes, theft, and fire are not urban legends. They are rare, but they do happen. Fortunately, you can guard against them with little cost or effort. All you have to do is remind yourself.

The most convenient way to back up your data is on the school server. It may even be possible to do that automatically each day, a perfectly painless way to handle the problem. Check with your local geek.

> *Tip:* Back up your data. The best arrangement saves your computer data regularly and automatically stores it at a separate location. Be sure to back up your handwritten materials, too.

Everything else is a little less convenient, but still well worth doing. The most obvious is to back up your files on a disk and store it in a separate location. Or you could e-mail the files to a friend or even to yourself, simply for storage. You can probably figure out several other options. Start by making a simple plan now. Then start backing up your files regularly, before the computer gremlins strike.

Different gremlins could strike your handwritten notes. Nobody wants to steal your spiral notebooks or thesis outline, but they might grab your backpack or you might misplace it. Photocopy your notes occasionally and do exactly what you do with computer files: store them in a separate place, just in case. It's cheap insurance.

We'll talk more about your notes and other useful nuts-and-bolts ideas later—this is a practical guide, after all—but the last two chapters covered the main points that you need to get started. Now that you've done some reading and begun taking good notes, it's time to meet with your adviser again, refine the thesis topic, and hand in a proposal. That's where we'll turn next.

CHECKLIST: READING AND TAKING NOTES

- Assemble a working bibliography and keep adding to it.
- Read important works intensively; skim others.
- Take Q-notes on readings.
- Develop your own ideas as you read and file them in your thesis ideas file.
- Back up your notes and other data.

CHECKLIST: INFORMATION NEEDED FOR CITATIONS

- Author or editor (and translator)
- Title of book, article, or chapter in an edited book
- Book publisher's name, location, and date of publication
  - Edition number of book, such as 3rd ed.
  - Date of original publication for reprinted books, such as 1776
- Journal's name, volume number, and date
- Pages of article, book chapter, or relevant part of a book
- Web page address and the date you accessed it

---

4 REFINING YOUR TOPIC, WRITING A PROPOSAL, AND BEGINNING RESEARCH

By now, you are reading about your topic, taking notes, and preparing to meet with your adviser again. You should get together fairly soon, probably within a couple of weeks of your first meeting. But don't come back until you've had a chance to do some reading and think about it. That will ensure a more substantive, fruitful meeting. It will also show your adviser that you follow through when either of you suggest some work—a very good message to send. Demonstrating you are serious about your thesis project will kick off your working relationship the right way.

This follow-up meeting has three main purposes, beyond learning something more about your topic (which you hope to do at every meeting). First, you should talk with your adviser about what you hope to accomplish in the project, personally and intellectually. If some aspects of the project are particularly interesting to you, be sure to mention that.

If your thesis bears on your goals beyond college, mention that, too. For example, you might talk about how this project fits into your plans for business, law, or teaching. If you are considering graduate studies in your major, be sure to discuss that with your adviser at the outset. Graduate programs in the arts and sciences train students to do research, so their admissions process closely examines each applicant's ability to handle major projects and reach thoughtful conclusions. Your adviser can make an important contribution to your success here.

Different students have different goals for their thesis projects. Now is a good time to think about yours. What do you really want to accomplish? Answer that as honestly as you can. Is your goal simply to meet your department's requirements? If so, you might choose to write a shorter thesis outside the honors program, if your department offers that option. At the other end of the spectrum, you may wish to gain a real sense of mastery and confidence in a subject you relish. An honors thesis is an excellent opportunity to do that. It's also an opportunity to see if you want to go further, perhaps entering an MA or a PhD program. Likewise, it can be a useful step toward a career in law, business, or teaching and an important credit on any résumé.

Second, you should use this meeting to set up a comfortable, efficient program for working with your adviser over the next several months. Ask how often you should meet, when the best times are, and how you should schedule these meetings. Ask about the best way to contact your adviser if you need to change a meeting or ask her a quick question. Finally, ask how she wants to receive your written materials, which you will be dropping off every week or two. Does she want you to hand in a hard copy (where? when?) or send an e-mail attachment? Does she want it double-spaced? Your adviser has done all this before and will have some preferences. She'll appreciate your asking about them.

> *Tip:* Set standard working arrangements with your adviser early. Find out how often you should meet, what are the best times, and how you should prepare written materials.

Let me add one suggestion myself — one that both you and your adviser will appreciate. Each time you visit, bring *two* stapled copies of any written work you plan to discuss. If you both have copies of the material, it is easy to refer to specific items and discuss them in detail, even though you are sitting across the desk from each other.

> *Tip:* Bring two stapled copies of papers to meetings—one for you, one for your adviser.

Put some essential information on each copy:

- Your name
- E-mail address
- Today's date
- Page numbers
- A simple title, even if it's tentative

Because your paper has today's date, your adviser won't confuse it with next week's updated version. Because it has your e-mail address, your adviser can easily pass along more comments after any meeting. Because it has page numbers, your adviser can say, "I notice you say something very interesting on page 3."

Because each paper has a title, you and your adviser can easily refer to specific documents, perhaps comparing today's paper with one you completed a couple of weeks ago. It will also give you a chance to try out different titles. For example, if you plan to study the quality of urban schools and your first paper is a list of readings, you might call it "Student Performance in Inner-City Schools: A Working Bibliography."

I know these seem like niggling points—actually, they *are* niggling points—but they have an important purpose: to aid communication between you and your adviser. That's a major step toward a successful thesis project and a valuable learning experience.

> *Tip:* Each paper should include your name, e-mail address, and date. Pages should be numbered. Give each document a title, however tentative.

For heaven's sake, proofread everything you turn in. Nothing says "I really can't be bothered about this project" like a few dreadful typos. Everybody goofs up; the point is to catch these errors before you inflict them on your adviser. Obviously, you will run spell-check. Do that *each time* you turn in a draft, even if the draft is brief and informal. Informal ≠ sloppy. I've gotten into the habit of hitting spell-check before I print, even if I'm the only one who will read it. By now, I hit that function key by rote. Why bother? Because it's easy and I don't want to be distracted by typos as I review the document for language and content. Or maybe it's just that I'm a teacher and grade myself.

> *Tip:* Proofread *everything* you hand in to your adviser.

Go beyond spell-check. Reread the document carefully, looking for errors the computer missed. Grammar software is still not very good; it won't stop you from using "there" when you meant to say "their." And spell-check won't catch the mistakes if you leave out words or punctuation marks after cutting and pasting. I've learned all this the hard way. I make these mistakes every day and have to catch them myself.

Since you should be editing and changing the text constantly—I'll discuss that later—you need to proofread it each time you hand it in. It only takes a few minutes, and it shows real courtesy to your reader. If you want your adviser to read your work with care and attention, then you must do the same. It builds a relationship of mutual respect.

BUILDING YOUR READING LIST

As you do background reading, you should also be building a reading list. My advice is to show your adviser the list periodically. She ought to know which articles, books, and Web sites you're using, which ones you find most valuable, and which ones you expect to read in the near future. If you are currently focusing on a particular author or facet of your topic, mention that. If you are reading Tolstoy or Proust in translation, explain which edition you are using. Open up all these issues for discussion.

Why should you talk about the readings? For several reasons. First, your adviser probably has some well-informed views about your sources. She might think these readings are the best place to start or, alternatively, that they are better approached after you've done some other reading. She might think your sources are excellent, or she might consider them a bit dated or one-sided. All that is helpful to know before you spend too much time on them. As your adviser looks over the list, she'll probably remember a few more readings you should check out and perhaps a related issue you should think about. If you are having trouble finding useful readings, be sure to mention it. Your adviser might know a resource.

Besides getting new leads, you'll probably end up discussing some of the individual readings. That's often the best way to move into a topic and thrash out your own ideas. In effect, you and your adviser are beginning a tutorial on your thesis topic.

> *Tip:* Discuss your reading list with your adviser. You can talk about how different authors approach your topic and get valuable suggestions for other readings.

In some fields, particularly history, your reading and discussion will cover not only books and articles but also primary documents. Letters, pamphlets, treaties, old newspapers, and county records are the stuff of historical research. You should begin to explore these primary materials as you delve deeper into the topic.

Working with these source materials not only enriches your work; it shows you how research is conducted in many fields. "Often a student will develop an interest in a particular subject after reading a major book or article," one thesis adviser remarked. "However, the 'real' topic emerges only after the student consults the primary source or chases down a footnote. Especially when a student is in the early stages of research, this process of going back and forth between secondary and primary texts can yield unexpected views on well-worn subjects or turn up smaller topics that the professional scholar passed over."

That's excellent advice, and it applies not only to history but to many other disciplines as well. In economics, political science, or sociology, the primary sources are raw data about government expenses, voting records, or migration patterns. Many fields rely on public opinion surveys and census data. There is a unique excitement in beginning to work with source materials like these. They offer a chance to find something new, something no one has ever seen before.

> *Tip:* In many fields, students want to explore primary source materials, ranging from private diaries to elaborate databases. Ask your adviser whether you should use such source materials, which ones are most appropriate, and when you should begin working with them. If you do use primary materials, work back and forth between them and secondary works, which set the documents or data in context and offer interpretations.

REFINING YOUR TOPIC: THE MAIN GOAL
FOR EARLY MEETINGS WITH YOUR ADVISER

One reason these early readings are so important is that they help you frame your principal questions and your approach. That's actually the number one goal for these first weeks. *Your chief aim is to refine your thesis topic, to sharpen and delimit your main question.*

You should start distilling and reshaping your topic now, even though you will continue to do so as you research and write. It's not something you do once at the beginning and then put behind you. Honing your topic is vital to producing a first-rate thesis, and you should keep doing it throughout the thesis project. The question is, how exactly do you refine your topic?

You begin by understanding what makes a thesis topic *manageable*. Some topics, no matter how significant and interesting, are simply too big and amorphous to research well. You can't get your arms around them. You will never really master them, and it's very hard to write a coherent thesis that truly does them justice. That leads to a second point: You need to figure out how to move from a compelling general idea to a *sharply focused topic*, one you can research and analyze within the time available.

> *Tip:* Refining your thesis topic is the top priority for the first months of your project. The goal is to move from a general topic to a sharply focused one that you can manage. This should be a major item in early meetings with your adviser.

WHAT MAKES A THESIS TOPIC SUCCESSFUL AND MANAGEABLE?

A successful thesis poses an interesting question you can actually answer. Just as important, it poses a question you can answer within the time available for the project.

The question should be one that interests you and deserves exploration. It might be an empirical question or a theoretical puzzle. In some fields, it might be a practical problem or policy issue.

Whatever the question is, you need to mark off its boundaries clearly and intelligently so you can complete the research and not get lost in the woods. That means your topic should be manageable as well as interesting and important.

A topic is manageable if you can

- Master the relevant literature
- Collect and analyze the necessary data
- Answer the key questions you have posed
- Do it all within the time available, with the skills you have

A topic is important if it

- Touches directly on major theoretical issues and debates, *or*
- Addresses substantive topics of great interest in your field

> *Tip:* A successful thesis poses an interesting question you can actually answer within the time available for the project.

Ideally, your topic can do both, engaging theoretical and substantive issues. In elementary education, for example, parents, teachers, scholars, and public officials all debate the effectiveness of charter schools, the impact of vouchers, and the value of different reading programs. A thesis on any of these would resonate within the university and well beyond it. Still, as you approach such topics, you need to limit the scope of your investigation so you can finish your research and writing on time. After all, to be a good thesis, it first has to be a completed thesis.

Some problems are simply too grand, too sweeping to master within the time limits. Some are too minor to interest you or anybody else. This is a Goldilocks problem: you need to find a happy medium.

The solution, however, is *not* to find a lukewarm bowl of porridge, a bland compromise. Nor is it to abandon your interest in larger, more profound issues such as the relationship between school organization and educational achievement or between migration and poverty.

Rather, the solution is to select a well-defined topic that is closely linked to some larger issue and then explore that link. Your thesis will succeed if you nail a well-defined topic. It will rise to excellence if you probe that topic deeply and show how it illuminates wider issues.

> *Tip:* The best theses deal with important issues, framed in manageable ways. The goal is to select a well-defined topic that is closely linked to some larger issue and can illuminate it.

You can begin your project with either a large issue or a narrowly defined topic, depending on your interests and the ideas you have generated. Whichever way you start, the goals are the same: to connect the two in meaningful ways and to explore your specific topic in depth.

MOVING FROM A GENERAL IDEA TO A MANAGEABLE TOPIC

Let's begin as most students actually do, by going from a "big issue" to a more manageable thesis topic. Suppose you start with a big question such as, "Why has the United States fought so many wars since 1945?" That's certainly a big, important question. Unfortunately, it's too complex and sprawling to cover well in a thesis. Working with your adviser, you could zero in on a related but feasible research topic, such as "Why did the Johnson administration choose to escalate the U.S. war in Vietnam?" By choosing this topic, your research can focus on a specific war and, within that, on a few crucial years in the mid-1960s.

You can draw on major works covering all aspects of the Vietnam War and the Johnson administration's decision making. You have access to policy memos that were once stamped top secret. These primary documents have now been declassified, published by the State Department, and made available to research libraries. Many are readily available on the Web. You can also take advantage of top-quality secondary sources (that is, books and articles based on primary documents, interviews, and other research data).

Drawing on these primary and secondary sources, you can uncover and critique the reasons behind U.S. military escalation. As you answer this well-defined question about Vietnam, you can (and you should) return to the larger themes that interest you, namely, "What does the escalation in Southeast Asia tell us about the global projection of U.S. military power since 1945?" As one of America's largest military engagements since World War II, the war in Vietnam should tell us a great deal about the more general question.

The goal here is to pick a good case to study, one that is compelling in its own right and speaks to the larger issue. It need not be a typical example, but it does need to illuminate the larger question. Some cases are better than others precisely because they illuminate larger issues. That's why choosing the best cases makes such a difference in your project. I'll say a bit about that now and discuss it further in chapter 6 ("Using Case Studies Effectively").

Since you are interested in why the United States has fought so often since 1945, you probably shouldn't focus on U.S. invasions of Grenada, Haiti, or Panama in the past two decades. Why? Because the United States has launched numerous military actions against small, weak states in the

Caribbean *for more than a century.* That is important in its own right, but it doesn't say much about what has changed so dramatically since 1945. The real change since 1945 is the projection of U.S. power far beyond the Western Hemisphere, to Europe and Asia. You cannot explain this change—or any change, for that matter—by looking at something that remains constant.

In this case, to analyze the larger pattern of U.S. war fighting and the shift it represents, you need to pick examples of distant conflicts, such as Korea, Vietnam, Kosovo, Afghanistan, or Iraq. That's the noteworthy change since 1945: U.S. military intervention outside the Western Hemisphere. The United States has fought frequently in such areas since World War II but rarely before then. Alternatively, you could use statistics covering many cases of U.S. intervention around the world, perhaps supplemented with some telling cases studies.

Students in the humanities want to explore their own big ideas, and they, too, need to focus their research. In English literature, their big issue might be "masculinity" or, to narrow the range a bit, "masculinity in Jewish American literature." Important as these issues are, they are too vast for anyone to read all the major novels plus all the relevant criticism and then frame a comprehensive thesis.

If you don't narrow these sprawling topics and focus your work, you can only skim the surface. Skimming the surface is *not* what you want to do in a thesis. You want to understand your subject in depth and convey that understanding to your readers.

That does not mean you have to abandon your interest in major themes. It means you have to restrict their scope in sensible ways. To do that, you need to think about which aspects of masculinity really interest you and then find works that deal with them.

You may realize your central concern is how masculinity is defined in response to strong women. That focus would still leave you considerable flexibility, depending on your academic background and what you love to read. That might be anything from a reconsideration of *Macbeth* to an analysis of early twentieth-century American novels, where men must cope with women in assertive new roles. Perhaps you are interested in another aspect of masculinity: the different ways it is defined within the same culture at the same moment. That would lead you to novelists who explore these differences in their characters, perhaps contrasting men who come from different backgrounds, work in different jobs, or simply differ emotionally. Again, you would have considerable flexibility in choosing specific writers.

However you refine and narrow your topic, your goals are the same: to make the topic more manageable while still giving yourself the opportunity to explore broad issues that intrigue you.

> *Tip:* The goal is not just to narrow your topic. The goal is to narrow it the right way—so your inquiry still matters, so it still offers real insights into larger issues.

CONNECTING A SPECIFIC TOPIC TO A BIGGER IDEA

Not all students begin their thesis concerned with big issues such as masculinity or American wars over the past half century. Some show up at their first or second meeting with very specific topics in mind. One example might be the decision to create NAFTA, the North American Free Trade Agreement encompassing Canada, the United States, and Mexico. Perhaps you are interested in NAFTA because you discussed it in a course, heard about it in a political campaign, or saw its effects firsthand on local workers, companies, and consumers. It intrigues you, and you would like to study it in a thesis. The challenge is to go from this clear-cut subject to a larger theme that will frame your project.

Why do you even need to figure out a larger theme? Because NAFTA bears on several major topics, and you cannot explore all of them. Your challenge—and your opportunity—is to figure out which one captures your imagination.

One way to think about that is to finish this sentence: "For me, NAFTA is a case of _____." If you are mainly interested in negotiations between big and small countries, then your answer is, "For me, NAFTA is a case of a large country like the United States bargaining with a smaller neighbor." Your answer would be different if you are mainly interested in decision making within the United States, Mexico, or Canada. In that case, you might say, "NAFTA seems to be a case where a strong U.S. president pushed a trade policy through Congress." Perhaps you are more concerned with the role played by business lobbies. "For me, NAFTA is a case of undue corporate influence over foreign economic policy." Or you could be interested in the role of trade unions, environmental groups, or public opinion.

The NAFTA decision is related to all these big issues and more. You cannot cover them all. There is not enough time, and even if there were, the resulting paper would be too diffuse, too scattershot. To make an impact, throw a rock, not a handful of pebbles.

Choosing one of these large issues will shape your research on NAFTA. If you are interested in U.S. decision making, for example, you might study the lobbying process or perhaps the differences between Democrats and Republicans. If you are interested in diplomacy, you would focus on negotiations between the United States, Canada, and Mexico. Either would be an interesting thesis, but they are *different* theses.

Although the subject matter and analysis are decidedly different in the humanities, many of the same considerations still apply to topic selection. In English or comparative literature, for example, you may be attracted to a very specific topic such as several poems by William Wordsworth. You are not trying, as a social scientist would, to test some generalizations that apply across time or space. Rather, you want to analyze these specific poems, uncover their multiple meanings, trace their allusions, and understand their form and beauty.

As part of this project, however, you may wish to say something bigger, something that goes beyond these particular poems. That might be about Wordsworth's larger body of work. Are these poems representative or unusual? Do they break with his previous work or anticipate work yet to come? You may wish to comment on Wordsworth's close ties to his fellow "Lake Poets," Coleridge and Southey, underscoring some similarities in their work. Do they use language in shared ways? Do they use similar metaphors or explore similar themes? You may even wish to show how these particular poems are properly understood as part of the wider Romantic movement in literature and the arts. Any of these would connect the specific poems to larger themes.

In both the Wordsworth and NAFTA examples, you begin with an interest in a quite specific topic and ultimately link it to larger issues. But the process could just as easily be reversed. You might initially come to your adviser with an interest in economic integration and whittle it down to NAFTA. Or you might come with a general interest in Romantic poets and decide to write your thesis on some specific works by Wordsworth or Coleridge.

> *Tip:* If you begin with a well-defined topic, then look for some connections to larger themes. That's not only important for your conclusions; it will direct your whole approach to the topic, highlighting some aspects instead of others.

You can start with either a big issue or a narrow topic. Either way is fine. A first-rate thesis will eventually make some connections between the two, between a well-defined topic and a more encompassing theme.

WRITING A THESIS PROPOSAL

Now that you know what makes an interesting, manageable thesis, you also know the main points to include in a proposal. It should briefly explain *why it is interesting* and *how you are going to manage it.*

Different departments have different rules for proposals, saying when they are due (usually near the end of junior year or the beginning of senior year) and how long they should be (usually a page or two). You can find out the specifics from a departmental administrator or perhaps from the department's Web site. It's essential to know these administrative details, and you should find them out now. But they are separate from the intellectual issues I cover here.

Whatever the department regulations, *all* proposals need to contain a few key points about what you intend to do. In clear, concise language, your proposal should explain

- What your main question or topic is
- Why it matters
- How you plan to approach the analysis

The proposal should briefly state your topic, its importance to your field, and the way you intend to analyze it. The trick is to be brief without being vague.

What you need *not* do is answer the hard questions you pose. That's not the job of the proposal. That's the job of the thesis itself. If you can already answer the main questions you pose, then they are probably the wrong ones. You should pose other, more challenging questions.

> *Tip:* Your thesis proposal should outline your topic, its importance, and your approach to studying it. It should pose one or two major questions, but it does not need to answer them. The thesis itself will do that.

One way to explain your topic's importance is to describe current debates surrounding it and how leading scholars treat it. Are there major disputes among theorists or practitioners? What is at stake in these debates? If your topic is not particularly prominent, then you should say why it deserves more attention. What's wrong with just ignoring it? In some fields, such as medical ethics, environmental regulation, or educational policy, you should also underscore the topic's practical significance. Does it affect many people or perhaps affect a few with great intensity?

Once you have identified an important question and stated it clearly, you need to say how you will examine it. Again, you are not trying to answer the question. You are saying how you intend to find the answer. You need to show that the investigation is a manageable task and is likely to yield answers. You may wish to illustrate your approach with a little preliminary analysis, probably only a paragraph or two.

In the social sciences, you should also mention what data you will use. Do you plan to use case studies, interviews, large databases, original documents, or some combination of these? Will this be more a quantitative study or a qualitative one?

In the humanities and less quantitative social sciences, you should say which primary texts you will study, such as Wordsworth's early poems or Abigail Adams's letters. Will you be studying particular drawings by Leonardo or particular movies by Tarantino? If you plan to rely on (or contend with) some major secondary works, such as several major books about Wordsworth, mention that and explain how they fit into your project.

Normally, a thesis proposal does not mention your academic background or special skills unless they directly affect your planned research. (That is why I suggested you list them separately for your adviser.) For instance, you would not mention that you have taken advanced statistics courses, but you might mention the techniques you plan to use for data analysis. For a thesis on World War II in the Pacific, you might say that you will rely on important documents in the original Japanese. If these documents have never been translated, be sure to mention it. It shows the excitement and originality of your project. In discussing these skills, your goal is never to show off. It is to show *what* you will study and *how* you will study it.

REVISING YOUR PROPOSAL

Getting your adviser to approve your proposal is often seen as just a bureaucratic hurdle, yet another dull requirement among so many you have to meet in college. In fact, it can be much more useful to you. A good proposal would be worth doing even if it were not required, because it will start your thesis research on the right path.

That's also why it is valuable to *revise* your proposal, to make sure it lays out the research questions intelligently and explains how you intend to study them. Few departments require these revisions, but they are still worth doing to make certain the project is well conceived at the outset.

You can learn a great deal from drafting a proposal, discussing it, and revising it in response to faculty comments. Trying to explain your project will help you understand it better. Discussing it with faculty will help, too, because your adviser's suggestions and clarifications come at a critical moment, while you are still framing your focal questions and your basic approach.

That is why, if you have time, you should do more than ask for your adviser's approval and signature. You should meet to discuss a first draft of your proposal and incorporate the comments in a revised version. Then return to discuss it before moving on to more focused research. The draft proposal and its revisions will point you in the right direction.

> *Tip:* Revising your proposal is well worth the time. It will help you clarify your topic, your questions, and your approach. It will point you in the right direction as you begin the project.

This is a perfect time to think about the project as a whole and how you will approach it. Your revised proposal should reflect your reappraisal, putting you in a much stronger position to launch your research. That is why revisions are standard operating procedures for much larger projects such as dissertation proposals. They can aid your thesis for exactly the same reasons. By treating your proposal thoughtfully, you are doing more than simply clearing another bureaucratic hurdle. You are molding and improving your project at its most pliable moment.

REFINING YOUR TOPIC WITH ADVISERS AND WORKSHOPS

As this chapter makes clear, one of your adviser's most valuable contributions is to help you refine your topic. She can help you select the best cases for detailed study or the best data and statistical techniques for quantitative projects. She can help you find cases that shed light on larger questions, have good data available, and are discussed in a rich secondary literature. She may know valuable troves of documents to explore. That's why it is so important to bring these issues up in early meetings. These discussions with your adviser are crucial in moving from a big but ill-defined idea to a smart, feasible topic.

> *Tip:* Begin sharpening your question and refining your topic early in the project. Your adviser can play a vital role in this crucial early stage.

Some colleges supplement this advising process by offering special workshops and tutorial support for thesis students. These are great resources, and you should take full advantage of them. They can improve your project in at least three ways.

First, tutors and workshop leaders are usually quite adept at helping you focus and shape your topic. That's what they do best. Even if they are relatively new teachers, they have been writing papers themselves for many years. They know how to do it well and how to avoid common mistakes. To craft their own papers, they have learned how to narrow their topics, gather data, interpret sources, and evaluate conjectures. They know how to use appropriate methods and how to mine the academic literature. In all these ways, they can assist you with their own hard-won experience. To avoid any confusion, just make sure your main faculty adviser knows what advice you are getting from workshop leaders and tutors. You want everyone to be pulling in the same direction.

Second, you will benefit enormously from batting around your project in workshops. The more you speak about your subject, the better you will understand it yourself. The better you understand it, the clearer your research and writing will be. You will learn about your project as you present your ideas; you will learn more as you listen to others discuss your work; and you will learn still more as you respond to their suggestions. Although you should do that in sessions with your adviser, you will also profit from doing it in workshops and tutorial sessions.

Third, workshops, tutors, and other readers remind you that you are writing for an audience. This is a vital lesson for all writers. Others will read your work, and it should be directed toward them. (By the way, in good thesis workshops, students read each others' work and take it seriously. That's probably what differentiates them from mediocre workshops, where students don't bother to read each others' work, so they cannot provide helpful, informed comments.)

If you want to imagine a good target audience, think about juniors and seniors in your major and intelligent laypeople who are not specialists in your area. Of course, some topics go beyond the technical expertise of ordinary educated readers. If that's true for your topic, then focus on an audience of fellow thesis writers in your major.

> *Tip:* Take full advantage of thesis workshops to get feedback on your project. They offer
> - Evaluations from skilled workshop leaders
> - Opportunities for you to discuss your project
> - Comments from fellow students about your work
> - A constant reminder that you must convey your ideas to others

ZEROING IN ON YOUR READINGS

With your topic better defined, your reading can now become more sharply focused. Remember to add any new articles you read to your bibliography so you can discuss them with your adviser and cite them later.

> *Tip:* As your project develops, your reading should become more tightly focused.

You will inevitably find that a few articles you read are worthless, some are too complex, and still others are unrelated to your topic, despite their promising titles. Jot that down in your working bibliography so you don't forget and waste time next month tracking down the same useless articles. Similarly, when you photocopy an article or check out a book, note that briefly in your bibliography file. Marking up your bibliography with personal comments like this makes it more than a list of works for eventual citation. It becomes your working guide for day-to-day research.

> *Tip:* Your bibliography should be a *working* document, a day-to-day guide for your research.
> * Record full information for later citation.
> * Mark up your list with comments next to various items.
> * Divide your reading list into sections, reflecting the different subtopics you are working on.

Besides annotating your bibliography, you might begin dividing it into sections. For the Vietnam War thesis, for instance, you might have one set of readings on "the Johnson administration's decision making," another on "military advice," and still another on "U.S. opponents of escalation." These divisions may also help you think about how you will eventually organize the paper. The divisions in your bibliography could well become sections in your paper.

> *Examples of a working bibliography (earlier and later versions):*
>
> **Early version of bibliography on U.S. war in Vietnam:**
> David Kaiser, *American Tragedy* FULL TITLE?? (City?? Publisher?? 2000).
> Stanley Karnow, *Vietnam: A History* (New York: Viking, 1983).
> Neil Sheehan, *A Bright, Shining Lie: John Paul Vann and America in Vietnam* (City?? Publisher?? Year??).
>
> **Later, annotated version of bibliography on U.S. war in Vietnam** (includes full citations; organized into subtopics with comments on different readings):
> Earlier accounts:
> Stanley Karnow, *Vietnam: A History* (New York: Viking, 1983).
> DS558.K370 1983 (at main library only)
> Not read yet

Neil Sheehan, *A Bright, Shining Lie: John Paul Vann and America in Vietnam* (New York: Random House, 1988).
DS558.S470 1988
War as seen through the transformation of one soldier; useful and filled with personal detail but superseded by treatments that use recently released documents. (Skimmed; some notes)

Recent histories of U.S. policy, based on newly released documents:
David Kaiser, *American Tragedy: Kennedy, Johnson, and the Origins of the Vietnam War* (Cambridge, MA: Harvard University Press, 2000),
DS558 .K35 2000 (at main library and law school)
Excellent treatment; uses full official documents; supplements Logevall because it also covers the Kennedy administration's role. (Read about half book so far, with good notes)

Fredrik Logevall, *Choosing War: The Lost Chance for Peace and the Escalation of War in Vietnam* (Berkeley: University of California Press, 1999).
DS558.L6 1999 (I purchased)
Probably the best single treatment I've read on the Johnson administration's decision to escalate. Covers only the period 1963–65; analyzes U.S. decision making rather than the war itself. (Read whole book; thorough notes)
Need to read *Foreign Relations of the United States* volumes for Vietnam policy in early to mid-1960s (Reading Room 2 at main library and law library: JX233.A3). Check to see if these are online.

Keep marking up and reorganizing your bibliography as you take notes and work in the library and online.

BE AN ACTIVE READER

As you continue to read and learn, join the dialogue in your field. Think of yourself as a participant in your field's larger discourse. Authors talk back and forth to each other through their written work. Notice how they do it in your area of interest. In what ways do they agree, disagree, emphasize different issues, and build on each other's work? What is their conversation about? How do they conduct it?

Your goal is to be an alert reader, not a passive recipient. Pay special attention to theoretical arguments and analytic perspectives, as well as the evidence that authors marshal to support their ideas. Look for styles to imitate, questions to ask, and research designs to follow. The best articles should serve as silent teachers, models for your own work. But they can teach only if you seek to learn. That's an active process.

Active reading is easier than you might think. I pay closer attention to others' work when I'm busy doing research myself, probably for the same reasons I'm more alert to new cars when I am thinking of buying one. All around me, I suddenly notice sunroofs, taillights, and wheel covers—details I usually ignore—and realize that I want my new car to have some features and not others. Similarly, as I research and write, I notice the meaningful details of others' work and try to learn from them. You will probably notice the same things as you work on your thesis. If you foster this learning process by trying to read actively and critically, you will discover even more.

WRITE A SHORT BIBLIOGRAPHIC ESSAY

As you conclude your background reading, consider writing a brief essay (perhaps three to five pages) on the readings you've done so far. The essay serves several purposes. First, it draws together the readings you've done so far. You'll understand the terrain much better as you then begin more focused research and reading. Second, a brief essay like this is an excellent topic for discussion, either with your adviser or in a thesis workshop. There is a clear agenda: where do the major authors in your area agree and disagree? Third, it invites you to begin thinking about where you stand in this debate. Finally, it prompts you to begin writing as a regular part of your thesis project.

Don't postpone putting your ideas on paper for months, waiting to complete all your research and begin a first draft. Far better to write several short pieces as you go along, each of them covering discrete aspects of your work. I'll make the same suggestion later, after you've divided your paper topic into its major sections. You can write separate informal papers on each section. Parts of these papers, beginning with your bibliographic essay, will find their way into your first draft.

Tip: Write a three- to five-page paper on your background readings, concentrating on major areas of agreement and disagreement among the authors. As you lay out this terrain, begin thinking about where you stand.

THESIS TIME SCHEDULE

To keep your work on track, it helps to have a target time schedule. I've included one here for the first couple of months, based on the assumption that you have a couple of semesters (or quarters) to complete the thesis.

This is not a rigid schedule. It's a rough guide to the progress you should be making through various stages of thesis research and writing. Of course, individual projects differ, and you should discuss your own timing with your adviser and workshop leaders. Don't discuss it once at the beginning and then consider it settled. Bring it up occasionally as your thesis project moves along. The schedule I've included here can serve as a starting point for that continuing discussion and for drafting a schedule suited to your project.

I'll update this schedule as we move further into thesis research and writing. For now, the main point is that you should spend the first couple of months doing general reading about your topic, formulating a draft proposal, and then revising it with feedback from your adviser.

TIME SCHEDULE FOR MONTHS 1, 2:
THESIS PROPOSAL AND BACKGROUND READING

Reading: Background reading

Writing: Proposal and revised proposal
            Bibliographic essay

CHECKLIST: REFINING YOUR TOPIC AND BEGINNING RESEARCH

- Meet regularly with your adviser.
  - Establish standard times and other arrangements for these meetings.
  - Think of your own agenda for each meeting.
  - Try to bring some written work to most meetings.

- ○ Bring two copies of all written materials (with name, e-mail address, and date).
- Take advantage of thesis workshops.
- Narrow your general ideas to make the thesis manageable.
- Write a first draft of your thesis proposal.
- Revise your thesis proposal, based on feedback from your adviser.
- Search for connections between your manageable idea and larger issues in your field.
- Zero in on readings directly related to your thesis project.
- Create a working bibliography and keep it up-to-date.
- Conclude your background readings by writing a three- to five-page paper.
  - ○ It should outline the main debates in your field and associate specific authors with different positions.
  - ○ If you have a perspective on these debates, include it.

Conducting
Your Research

5 WHAT IS GOOD THESIS RESEARCH?

Doing research will occupy most of your time on the thesis. Actually, you will be performing three overlapping tasks: reading, research, and writing. As your reading becomes increasingly focused, it becomes integral to your research. So does your writing, which includes book notes and periodic research reports to discuss with your adviser.

These written reports blur the bright line between thesis research and thesis writing. Research is not something you do *after* you finish reading and *before* you start writing. It includes both, with a very happy result. It means that when you finally sit down to draft your thesis, you won't be starting from scratch. Large chunks will already be in place.

Beyond this focused reading and preliminary writing, what is your thesis research? It is the work needed to provide information, context, and contending perspectives about your topic—the work needed to answer the questions you have posed. You may acquire this basic information by reading primary documents, watching films, downloading survey data, conducting interviews, running tests, or finding still other sources to analyze. To provide a context for your work, you need to know the relevant secondary literature, that is, the analysis and interpretation scholars have already done on your topic.

These writers will not speak with one voice. They will ask different questions and often suggest different interpretations of the same basic data. They will offer varied perspectives and promote alternative theories. That's true no matter what your field is. To understand your topic fully, you need to understand these debates and then look beyond them to see what the debaters have in common and what their most fundamental differences are. Once you've grasped this literature, you may even choose to enter the debates yourself, adopting one stance and rejecting others, or perhaps finding a synthesis. In any case, you want to learn from the best work, engage it, and build on its findings.

Tip: Good research includes extensive reading about your subject. Learn the main questions, the common ground among experts, and the big debates.

Consider, for instance, a history thesis about African slaves arriving in South Carolina during the mid-1700s. Using primary documents such as ship manifests, bills of sale, and perhaps letters by slaveholders, you intend to study the slave ships and their human cargo arriving in the port of Charleston between 1740 and 1760. You would certainly want to read the best narrative histories about eighteenth-century slavery in general. That literature covers the triangular trade that brought slaves to America, the cotton plantations where they worked, and so on. These secondary works on slavery and Southern agriculture permit a richer interpretation of your primary documents because they situate the Charleston slave market within a wider social and economic context. As you read, you may discover gaps in the literature—questions not asked or topics not studied—which you can explore in your thesis. You may discover, for instance, that several articles deal with the size of slave families in Virginia and Louisiana, but rarely those in South Carolina and never for the decades you are studying. If that question interests you, you could fill an important gap in the scholarly literature *if* the primary documents reveal the data.

You also want to know which disputes surround your topic. What concerns the scholars who study your subject? Do some assert, for example, that the data for individual ships is not very good or that these ships are not representative? Is the most serious dispute about the number of slaves who died during the Middle Passage from West Africa to America? Are there brisk debates about the prices paid, the slaves' life expectancy, or their ultimate destination after sale in Charleston? Reading the secondary literature should alert you to these issues. You will learn which ones are well settled and which ones are hotly contested. Reading carefully should highlight the most interesting questions and the most vigorous debates. Some reflection about these issues and a little research may also reveal gaps in the literature, like the question about family size. When you discover questions and gaps like these, mention them to your adviser. She'll be a good source of feedback.

From your reading and conversations with faculty, you'll develop views on both primary and secondary sources. You'll learn which documents are trustworthy, which should be treated with considerable skepticism, and which are entirely worthless. You'll learn which secondary authors are reliable and highly regarded, and you'll want to compare their views to see where they agree and disagree. This critical assessment is vital to your research, and it applies to every field.

With this background in the literature and some guidance from your faculty adviser, you can narrow your topic to a few closely related questions on the slave trade and focus your research. You will continue to work with primary documents and secondary sources to find the answers and, quite often, to produce still more questions for investigation.

DIFFERENT KINDS OF RESEARCH FOR DIFFERENT KINDS OF QUESTIONS

Because theses differ so widely in substance and method, they require different kinds of research. Investigating slavery in South Carolina is radically different from interpreting Wordsworth's poetry or studying charter schools. For historians, research usually means analyzing primary documents such as the Carolina ship manifests, often supplemented by other historical data and writings from the period. For students of comparative literature, it means close reading and careful appraisal of novels, poems, and plays in their original languages. For social scientists, it often means refining theories and testing them against empirical evidence. Some do that by building and testing formal mathematical models, others by exploring specific cases in depth. Still others analyze large data sets. Demographers examine population statistics; voting specialists look at surveys and elections; psychologists compare experimental test results; economists consider statistics on trade, prices, capital flows, and savings. For many social scientists, research not only means finding this raw material, it means actually generating it through surveys, tests, experiments, and more.

This varied data reflects the equally varied aims of research. For students of literature and history, the aim is to interpret and compare primary texts. For most social scientists, the aim is to construct and test causal models reflecting their theories of social life. For interpretive social scientists, the goal is to make human action, symbols, and communication intelligible, at both the individual and collective levels. Their work seeks to explain, but rarely in the form of causal explanations. They are more interested in exploring how social meanings are constructed. In fields as diverse as education, social work, nursing, and public policy, the aim is not only to explain and interpret but also to evaluate current practices—and frequently to suggest more effective ones. Their audience reaches beyond the university to policy makers and working professionals.

Given these varied aims, what can be said about research in general? At least a few things, I hope, that can help students working on different kinds of thesis projects. Perhaps the most important is that your research should be tailored to your specific project and your individual skills. One size does not fit all. It does not fit all questions, and it does not fit all researchers.

> *Tip:* Your research method should meet two criteria. It should
> - Address questions posed in your thesis project (usually those in the proposal)
> - Use skills you currently have or can acquire during the project

Picking the method that suits *your questions* and *your skills* is a central element of the thesis project. Several factors will influence your decision whether to work mainly with primary documents or secondary sources, with detailed cases or large databases. First, what type of question are you investigating (and in which discipline)? Second, what kind of explanation are you trying to develop and evaluate? Are you trying to interpret a novel, painting, or movie, or perhaps compare several from the same genre? Are you trying to understand the meaning of an important event or offer a causal explanation for it? Are you evaluating one or two cases in depth, or are you trying to find broad patterns encompassing many cases? Could your explanation be rejected if you found some confounding data? If so, then you need to search for that crucial data to test your explanation.

Third, what research skills do you bring to the project? To build formal models, you need higher mathematics. To test large data sets, you need statistical training. To decipher primary documents, you need to know the languages and perhaps even the handwriting. Different topics and different approaches have their own distinct requirements. That's why you need to take advanced courses not only in your major but also in related fields. That's also why you should ask your thesis adviser for suggestions about courses to take during your senior year. Perhaps you can acquire some additional skills useful in your thesis research.

PLANNING FOR YOUR RESEARCH

The best time to start sorting out these research issues is soon after you've completed your proposal, while you are immersed in learning about your topic. By now, you've marked out your principal issues, compiled a working bibliography, and begun to read extensively. (Nag, nag!) The next questions to ask yourself are, "What kinds of research will best address my thesis questions? What will be most productive?" At a more personal level: "What kinds of research best fit my skills and training? What will be most rewarding and interesting to me?"

Your answers to these questions form your *research strategy*. Most likely, you've addressed some of these issues in your proposal. But you are further along now, and you can flesh out your answers. With your adviser's help, you should make some basic decisions about what information to collect and what methods to use in analyzing it. You will probably develop this research strategy gradually and, if you are like the rest of us, you will make some changes, large and small, along the way. Still, it is useful to devise a general plan early, even though you will modify it as you progress.

> *Tip:* Develop a tentative research plan early in the project. Write it down and share it with your adviser. The more concrete and detailed the plan, the better the feedback you'll get.

This research plan does not need to be elaborate or time-consuming. Like your bibliography, it is provisional, a work in progress. Still, it is helpful to write it down since it will clarify a number of issues for you and your adviser.

INFORMAL WRITING AS PART OF YOUR THESIS RESEARCH

You'll notice that I often urge you to write—even if it is brief and informal. Let me explain why. First, you learn as you write. We all do. Hard to believe, but true. It always surprises me, even though I've written for years. I sit down at the computer, fully expecting to write up what's in my notes, and—presto!—I always seem to discover something as I go along. I must be a slow learner because it's always a happy surprise to discover, once again, that I actually learn as I write. William Zinsser, a superb guide in this and all other writing issues, entitled one of his books *Writing to Learn*.[1] It's an apt title.

Second, a little writing sets the stage for more fruitful talks with your adviser. Bring it to your next meeting and you will have something concrete to talk about. That will improve the conversation since it not only tells your adviser *what* you are thinking about but also *how* you are thinking about it.

Third, these frequent little assignments encourage the welcome habit of writing down your ideas whenever they arise. Don't hesitate to do it, and don't delay until the end of the day. You have already set up some computer files for thesis ideas so you have the perfect spot to put any new thoughts. Writing them down not only preserves your ideas; it stimulates new ones. After all, ideas build on each other.

Jotting down your ideas and producing short documents also cracks the barrier between research and writing. Some of your informal writing—what we will later call "prewriting"—may wind up in your first draft, either as it stands or after some pruning. That will give you a big leg up on drafting the thesis. For all these reasons, it's valuable to write out items like your research plan and to amplify them when new ideas pop up later.

> *Tip:* Develop the writing habit early in your thesis project. Begin with book notes, research plans, and interim reports on work you are doing.

WRITING A RESEARCH PLAN

To write out your research plan, begin by restating your main thesis question and any secondary ones. They may have changed a bit since your original proposal. If these questions bear on a particular theory or analytic perspective, state that briefly. In the social sciences, for example, two or three prominent theories might offer different predictions about your subject. If so, then you might want to explore these differences in your thesis and explain why some theories work better (or worse) in this particular case. Likewise, in the humanities, you might consider how different theories offer different insights and contrasting perspectives on the particular

---

1. William Zinsser, *Writing to Learn* (New York: HarperCollins, 1993).

novel or film you are studying. If you intend to explore these differences, state your goal clearly in the research plan so you can discuss it later with your adviser. Next, turn to the heart of this exercise, your proposed research strategy. Try to explain your basic approach, the materials you will use, and your method of analysis. You may not know all of these elements yet, but do the best you can. Briefly say how and why you think they will help answer your main questions.

Be concrete. What data will you collect? Which poems will you read? Which paintings will you compare? Which historical cases will you examine? If you plan to use case studies, say whether you have already selected them or settled on the criteria for choosing them. Have you decided which documents and secondary sources are most important? Do you have easy access to the data, documents, or other materials you need? Are they reliable sources—the best information you can get on the subject? Give the answers if you have them, or say plainly that you don't know so your adviser can help. You should also discuss whether your research requires any special skills and, of course, whether you have them. You can—and should—tailor your work to fit your skills.

If you expect to challenge other approaches—an important element of some theses—which ones will you take on, and why? This last point can be put another way: Your project will be informed by some theoretical traditions and research perspectives and not others. Your research will be stronger if you clarify your own perspective and show how it usefully informs your work. Later, you may also enter the jousts and explain why your approach is superior to the alternatives, in this particular study and perhaps more generally. Your research plan should state these issues clearly so you can discuss them candidly and think them through.

If you plan to conduct tests, experiments, or surveys, discuss them, too. They are common research tools in many fields, from psychology and education to public health. Now is the time to spell out the details—the ones you have nailed down tight and the ones that are still rattling around, unresolved. It's important to bring up the right questions here, even if you don't have all the answers yet. Raising these questions directly is the best way to get the answers. What kinds of tests or experiments do you plan, and how will you measure the results? How will you recruit your test subjects, and how many will be included in your sample? What test instruments or observational techniques will you use? How reliable and valid are they? Your adviser can be a great source of feedback here.

> *Tip:* Your research plan should say
> - What materials you will use
> - What methods you will use to investigate them
> - Whether your work follow a particular approach or theory

There are also ethical issues to consider. They crop up in any research involving humans or animals. You need to think carefully about them, underscore potential problems, and discuss them with your adviser. You also need to clear this research in advance with the appropriate authorities at your school, such as the committee that reviews proposals for research on human subjects. Your adviser will know the ropes.

Not all these issues and questions will bear on your particular project. But some do, and you should wrestle with them as you begin research. Even if your answers are tentative, you will still gain from writing them down and sharing them with your adviser. That's how you will get the most comprehensive advice, the most pointed recommendations. If some of these issues puzzle you, or if you have already encountered some obstacles, share them, too, so you can either resolve the problems or find ways to work around them.

Remember, your research plan is simply a working product, designed to guide your ongoing inquiry. It's not a final paper for a grade; it's a step toward your final paper. Your goal in sketching it out now is to understand these issues better and get feedback from faculty early in the project. It may be a pain to write it out, but it's a minor sting compared to major surgery later.

> *Tip:* Your research plan is a working product. You will change and adapt it as you work on the thesis.

THE PERSONAL AND PRACTICAL SIDES
OF THESIS RESEARCH

So far, we have concentrated on the big issues: the questions you are posing, the theories and methods you are using, the explanations you are constructing. But there is also a personal, practical side to your plan, and it needs to be considered.

Your research strategy should rely on skills you have already acquired or those you can develop during the project itself. And it should be something you can do within the time available. These are reasonable—indeed, essential—considerations, and your research plan should not flinch from acknowledging them. If you can't read the Latin Vulgate Bible, then avoid research that absolutely requires it. You can still study the medieval church, but you will need to find a subject where the main documents have already been translated.

Similar issues arise in the quantitative social sciences. Some types of analysis require higher-level statistics or mathematics. Others do not. You can't skirt the issue simply by plugging in a high-powered statistics program. It will certainly crank out some results, but who knows what they mean? Unless you understand the methodological issues, you won't know how to interpret the results or, indeed, whether you have used appropriate procedures and produced any meaningful results at all. You'll be driving a Ferrari without a license. That's exhilarating . . . until you hit the first sharp curve.

If you are fortunate enough to have these skills—statistics, math, or languages—you have a wider range of research possibilities, and you can make good use of them. But even if you don't, you can still write a great thesis if you choose your questions and methods wisely.

Your research may depend on key documents. If it does, make sure they are readily available. Many historic documents are accessible in published collections, on microfilm, or online—but not everything is. A little reconnoitering early in your project can prevent some nasty surprises later on. You don't want to discover, several months into your thesis, that vital documents are available only in the basement of a Berlin museum. If you are studying U.S. foreign policy, you don't want to discover that crucial documents are still stamped "Top Secret." No matter that they deal with the Soviet Union and that this country is dead, deceased, expired, no longer among the living. The documents live on, still secret. Of course, you could try to declassify them, but there is no guarantee of success, and the process is glacial. After all, these are the people who run the U.S. Post Office.

Some problems like these always arise—it's a law of nature—and you need to cope with them, either by changing your questions (in big or small ways) or by tackling them differently. These are practical problems, and there are practical solutions. You just have to search for them.

CHECKLIST: CONDUCTING RESEARCH

- Familiarize yourself with major questions and debates about your topic.
- Devise a research plan that
  - Is appropriate to your topic;
  - Addresses the main questions you propose in your thesis;
  - Relies on materials to which you have access;
  - Can be accomplished within the time available;
  - Uses skills you have or can acquire.
- Divide your topic into smaller projects and do research on each in turn.
- Write informally as you do research; do *not* postpone this prewriting until all your research is complete.

6 USING CASE STUDIES EFFECTIVELY

Good data is the lifeblood of the social sciences. It is used to describe events, actors, and outcomes, to explain causes and interpret meanings. Before we can begin to explain why Thomas Jefferson High School is doing better academically than Millard Fillmore High, we need to be sure Jefferson really *is* doing better. That means we need a good measure of school performance and accurate data on the two schools. Likewise, before we can explain who voted for President Bush or why China's income has surged, we need solid data on American elections or Chinese economic growth. We don't want to spend time and effort trying to explain phantom "results."

Sometimes, the data needs to cover whole populations, like the U.S. Census, or vast activities, like trade, voting, or immigration. Demography, election studies, and most branches of economics rely on large databases like these. Analyzing them requires appropriate statistical techniques. Sometimes, however, the focus is on a small group, a single individual, or a revealing moment, such as how a family copes with unemployment. The data covers only a single case, but it needs to cover it in depth. Such detailed case studies are common in anthropology (for example, how a tribe lives in the South Sea Islands[1]), sociology (how a labor union[2] or urban gang[3] is organized), psychology (how a child's language and thought develops[4]),

---

1. Bronislaw Malinowski, *Argonauts of the Western Pacific: An Account of Native Enterprise and Adventure in the Archipelagoes of Melanesian New Guinea* (London: G. Routledge, 1922). Malinowski lived with his subjects and took detailed notes on all aspects of their lives. His work established the standard methodology for anthropological fieldwork.

2. Seymour Martin Lipset, Martin Trow, and James S. Coleman, *Union Democracy: The International Politics of the International Typographical Union* (Glencoe, IL: Free Press, 1956).

3. William Foote Whyte, *Street Corner Society: The Social Structure of an Italian Slum* (Chicago: University of Chicago Press, 1943).

4. Jean Piaget, "The Functions of Language in Two Children of Six," in *The Language and Thought of the Child,* trans. Marjorie Warden (New York: Harcourt, Brace, 1926).

political science (how an interest group operates[5]), education (how a pre-school class reacts to differences and disabilities[6]), and business (how a company channels workers into different jobs by gender[7]).

Because case studies like these are so common, I want to discuss them in more detail. What exactly are case studies? How can you use them effectively in your senior thesis?

Case studies are detailed investigations of individual events, actors, and relationships. They develop in-depth data on a single event or actor, or at most a few of them. They use that data to explore complex relationships, generate hypotheses, and test theories, to see how the actors understand their own situation, or to explain outcomes. The case may examine multiple facets of a single moment. Or it may trace the actors as they change over time, seeking to explain why those changes occurred and what impact they have had.

A good case study, then, offers more than rich description. Like other empirical work in the social sciences, it includes interpretation, conjecture, and explanation. Its aim is both to illuminate the specific case in depth and to suggest broader understandings and generalizations that can be drawn from it. In referring to these generalizations, I will use the term "argument," but my comments apply equally to hypotheses and other analytic approaches. Case studies can be used to evaluate all of them.

WHY USE CASES AT ALL?
WHY USE THESE PARTICULAR ONES?

Using case studies raises two fundamental issues that *must* be addressed in any study that relies on them:

- Why use case studies at all?
- Why use these particular cases?

---

5. Robert Dahl, *Who Governs? Democracy and Power in an American City* (New Haven, CT: Yale University Press, 1961). Dahl's study influenced a generation of scholarship on American politics.

6. Vivian Gussin Paley, *The Kindness of Children* (Cambridge, MA: Harvard University Press, 1999).

7. Rosabeth Moss Kanter, *Men and Women of the Corporation* (New York: Basic Books, 1977).

First, why use cases rather than some other method, perhaps a statistical analysis of many more cases? Once you have decided the case method is appropriate for your topic (*if* it is), you face a second question: Why choose these cases and not some others? A first-rate thesis should raise both questions explicitly and answer them convincingly before presenting the cases themselves. You should try answering both questions for yourself and then for your adviser *before* investing a lot of time in detailed case research.

> *Tip:* If you use case studies, you *must* explicitly answer two basic questions:
> - Why are you using cases and not some other method?
> - Why have you chosen these particular cases?

WHY USE CASE STUDIES AND NOT SOME OTHER METHOD?

Why use case studies at all? What kinds of questions do case studies answer especially well? What are they ill equipped to answer? What kinds of answers do they provide? The usual response—and the best one, I think—is that case studies are especially useful for exploring the subtle interaction among variables and observing causal processes at work, generating outcomes. It is revealing to see these details up close, in all their complexity.

Case studies are equally useful for exploring how actors see themselves and others, what values and interests they have, how they came to have them, and how they understand the choices they confront. In all these ways, case studies can be used not only to explain behavior but also to understand how the actors themselves are constituted.

Alexander George has made two important contributions to showing what case studies can do and showing how they can do it most effectively.[8] First, he advocates what he calls "structured, focused comparisons" between two nearly identical cases. Ideally, these cases differ in only one way: they have different values for one crucial variable—the causal variable we are interested in. With everything else held constant in this natural exper-

---

8. Alexander George, "Case Studies and Theory Development: The Method of Structured, Focused Comparison," in *Diplomacy: New Approaches in History, Theory, and Policy,* ed. Paul G. Lauren (New York: Free Press, 1979), 43–68.

iment, we can see how this single variable affects outcomes. George also suggests looking at individual cases as they develop over time. A careful researcher may observe causal relationships unfolding, something George calls "process tracing."

Whether you use George's methods or others, case studies are often valuable and manageable ways to explore arguments and evaluate them empirically. Closely examining the cases opens up several possibilities. You might be able to understand interactions among several variables; see how individual actors understand their own situation, communicate, and interact; or probe to see whether a new analytic approach is plausible.

WHY USE THESE CASES AND NOT OTHERS?

Besides justifying the use of case studies, you need to explain why you are using these particular cases. Well, why *have* you chosen them? Beware of the mountain climber's answer: "Because they are there." So are a lot of other mountains—and a lot of other recreations, for that matter. That answer may be fine for mountain climbers, who can pursue whatever challenge strikes their fancy. They can climb Mount Baldy or Mount Hairy. But it's not a very good rationale for defending your case selection. A stronger answer might be that you have chosen these cases because they are directly on point, well documented, and typical. "These five third-graders are similar to most students at Springfield Elementary School. They come from stable middle-class homes, with college-educated parents. . . ." The claim here is that these five students stand in for a much larger group: all the students at Springfield Elementary.

Before we proceed with this case study, however, we need to be sure these students really are typical. Or rather, we need to see if they are typical *in ways we care about for our study*. Let's say that most students at Springfield have mothers who stay at home to raise their children but that, as luck would have it, all five of our students have mothers with full-time paying jobs. Does that matter for our study? That depends on whether the mother's working status affects the specific question we are investigating. A quick review of the academic literature might show that it usually has no impact on TV watching, hyperactivity, computer use, or physical fitness. So, if we were studying any of those issues, these would still be "typical" kids at Springfield. No problem. However, the literature might also show that the mother's working status *does* affect reading achievement, self-image, and sociability. If we were studying those issues, these five students would be different from their peers. Big problem. The rationale for using these students in our case studies (that they are "typical") goes down in flames. Better to figure that out at the beginning, when you can adapt easily and choose different cases, than to carry out a fatally flawed study.

HARD CASES

Although our study of Springfield Elementary hinged on picking "typical" students, that's not always our goal. Some of the best studies are actually based on unusual cases or striking outliers because they throw a searching light on important problems. The hardest cases are those where your argument seems *least* likely to apply. The case is deliberately biased against you. If it works there, it's obviously a strong argument.

For example, if we wanted to show that Springfield does a great job educating students, we might pick several students who entered school with low test scores or other disadvantages. If these *atypical* students learned a lot at Springfield Elementary and left there performing well, we would have strong evidence that the school really does do a fine job. Note, however, that this study is designed, from the very outset, to be a hard case.

That's the point of a classic TV advertisement for Life cereal. Two older kids are sitting at the breakfast table, reluctant to try a cereal they've never eaten. "I'm not gonna try it. You try it," says each kid, sliding the bowl to the other. Finally, one of them hits upon a hard test, involving the little kid sitting quietly at the table. "Let's give it to Mikey. He hates everything." If the cereal passes this difficult test, the "Mikey test," then surely it is worth eating. One older kid reports the stunning results of this test—"He likes it!"—and, after that, they are happy to try it themselves.[9]

That's exactly how hard tests work. If your argument applies in hard cases, like Mikey, then surely it applies in many more cases, where the criteria are easier. That's why hard cases are such persuasive analytic tools.

---

9. The Mikey commercial for Life cereal, a gem of popular culture, was featured in a documentary film, *The World's Best Commercials of the Twentieth Century* (1999), screened at film festivals and venues like the Museum of Fine Arts in Boston.

They can convince readers that your argument is powerful and applies well beyond the few hard cases you have presented.

What if the cereal failed this hard test? The cereal still might be very tasty, and the skeptical kids might really have enjoyed it, if only they had been willing to try it. That, too, tells us something about hard tests. Failing them does not mean an argument is worthless. If an argument (or hypothesis) fails a hard test but passes an easier one, it might still be useful but limited in some important ways. We might determine, for example, that lots of kids like the cereal but that finicky eaters do not. Comparing the hard test with easier ones might also show how the specific context applies to the argument. That allows us to clarify the argument, show how it works in practice, and draw limits around its application.

> *Tip:* The cases you choose do not have to be typical or normal. They can be striking or unusual. But you must explain which kind of cases you have selected. That selection will also affect how you interpret your findings and how convincing they are.

To illustrate with something besides a cereal advertisement, let's say your argument is that career bureaucrats in the federal government have extensive power over policy outcomes, much more power than the public realizes. Based on your survey of the academic literature, you have already shown that this issue is important to voters and has attracted some scholarly interest. Now you turn to an empirical investigation. What's a hard case for your argument? Let's think it through. To begin with, high-level *elected* officials need to care about the issue. If they didn't care, then of course bureaucrats would control the outcome. Why wouldn't they? Nobody is competing with them for control. That's an easy case and not a very interesting one since you would expect bureaucrats to play a major role if nobody opposed them. It wouldn't prove much unless such issues were commonplace, all under the thumb of bureaucrats. It wouldn't be a hard case, either, if politicians and bureaucrats *preferred the same outcome*. In fact, we probably couldn't tell which one had the most influence since they would both be pushing in the same direction. So that wouldn't be a test at all. The interesting case is the hard one, where bureaucrats and politicians want different outcomes and where politicians care deeply about getting what they want. They are pushing hard in different directions. If you could show that bureaucrats profoundly affected outcomes in hard cases like these, then you would have strong support for your general proposition.

One of the most famous case studies in international relations—Graham Allison's investigation of the Cuban Missile Crisis—did exactly that.[10] It picked the hardest possible case and showed that his conjectures worked even there, in the harshest possible conditions. Allison wanted to show that bureaucracies and their standard operating procedures have a powerful impact on policy implementation and are difficult to dislodge. In choosing the Cuban Missile Crisis, he picked an issue where bureaucratic influence should have been minimal. Why? Because top policy makers thought it was a life-or-death matter, quite literally, and they were deeply involved in day-to-day decision making about it. The crisis totally consumed the attention of the president, his cabinet, and other senior officials. For thirteen days in October 1962, they were locked away in the White House, doing nothing but dealing with Russian nuclear missiles being installed in Cuba.

At first, U.S. officials favored a military attack on the missile sites. They eventually rejected that, fearing it would start World War III. Yet they also feared doing nothing. While inaction would avert an immediate confrontation, it would also allow the Soviets to build up a terrifying nuclear arsenal within easy reach of the United States. Top decision makers considered that unacceptable. Finally, President Kennedy made his momentous decision. He imposed a naval embargo on Cuba to force the Soviet Union to remove the missiles. There would be no direct U.S. attack—yet. The Soviets were informed that the U.S. Navy would stop their ships en route to Cuba, search them, and prevent any missiles or nuclear weapons from getting through. No one knew how the Soviets would respond. They might consider any attempt to stop their ships an act of war and launch an attack on the United States or its allies. It was a showdown on the high seas, and it risked global annihilation.

Allison showed that, despite a presidential order and close monitoring by the highest levels of American government, the U.S. Navy still implemented the embargo according to its own internal procedures. Now that's a hard case. That's why Allison's conclusions had such enormous impact on students of public policy and U.S. foreign policy.

---

10. Graham T. Allison, *Essence of Decision: Explaining the Cuban Missile Crisis* (Boston: Little, Brown, 1971).

WHAT KIND OF CASES ARE THESE?

Allison was tackling a hard case, and his readers knew it. Your readers deserve to know the same thing: what kind of cases are *you* using, and why? Telling them—before you present the cases themselves—should be standard procedure. You need to justify your research design when you use case studies just as you do when you use other methods. Justify it first to yourself and then to your adviser so you can justify it later to your readers.

Too many theses (and too many published articles, for that matter) don't bother to do that. They simply launch into their presentation of individual cases without saying why they are using cases at all or why they are using these particular ones, not some others. They almost always say that the cases are "important." Unfortunately, they don't say what "important" means, and they are silent beyond that. Are they supposed to be typical cases or hard ones? Are they supposed to be easy cases?

EASY CASES

Why would you ever use easy cases? For two reasons:

- To explore the logic and mechanisms of your argument; in an easy case, you expect the argument to work but you want to understand *how* it works.
- To set up a rudimentary test to see if your theory is plausible; if it cannot pass even an easy test, then the argument (or hypothesis or theory) should be rejected or seriously modified.

Both are useful exercises *as long as you understand you are exploring an easy case,* which has its own inherent limits. Easy cases can be useful for these two purposes, even though they won't convince a skeptic that your theory is powerful or far-reaching.

One valuable feature of easy cases is that they often provide an opportunity to show how your argument works in a real case. What is its logic? How do its mechanisms work in practice? The goal here is not to test a prediction. After all, we fully expect it to work in this easy case. Rather, the goal is to explore how a proposed causal mechanism works in practice. Of course, we still need to see if the prediction works. If it doesn't, it may be possible to show exactly why it failed and which mechanisms did not work as expected.

Such failures illustrate a second important use for easy cases. They set a low threshold to see if a theory is plausible. If an argument cannot pass a very simple test, then it probably cannot pass a much harder one. Without needing to go further, we will know if a theory should be tossed out or seriously modified. For example, if a student can't pass a simple algebra test, he's probably not ready for college-level calculus. Easy tests can show that without much strain. What they can't show is whether a student who *passes* the algebra test is really up to the challenge of calculus. For that, a better test is whether he can pass a difficult exam in trigonometry. In other words, easy tests can rule out weak candidates, but they can't show which passing candidates are strongest.

Easy tests of theories and conjectures work the same way. Passing them may mean a theory is plausible—it probably warrants more testing and exploration—but it does *not* mean it is powerful and applies widely. Maybe it is, maybe it isn't. At this point, we simply don't know. All we know is that it passes a low threshold. It may work when the stars are all perfectly aligned, but not in more typical cases. Easy tests are useful, then, but they have clear limits, and it's important to understand them.

Tip: Easy cases can be used to show a theory is plausible and that its mechanisms work in practice as they are posited in theory. Easy cases are not broadly convincing, however, and cannot show if a theory is powerful or applies widely.

THREE TYPES OF CASES

To summarize, you can analyze cases that are hard, typical, or easy. It's your choice. Each has its distinctive analytic uses; each can be valuable in its own way.

THREE TYPES OF CASES USED IN CASE STUDIES

Type of Case	Features of Case	Uses of This Type of Case
Easy	Instance where your argument, hypothesis, or approach is most likely to apply	Sets a minimum threshold and offers an opportunity to illustrate the logic and mechanisms of your argument in practice. If your argument fails here, it should be discarded or seriously modified. On the other hand, if the argument works well in an easy case, it is at least plausible, its mechanisms may be clearer, and it may deserve further testing.
Typical	Average circumstances, not biased in favor of your argument or against it	If your argument fails here, it needs to be discarded or modified. If it passes, it warrants further testing. Average cases are most useful for detailed exploration of relationships among variables, proposed causal mechanisms, and changes in variables over time.
Hard	Instance where your argument is least likely to apply	Sets a high threshold. If your argument applies here, it is convincing (though still unproven). It needs to be tested further to make sure it applies widely. Still, passing a hard test shows that the argument is a strong one. If an argument fails a hard test but passes an easier one, its mechanisms need to be specified further and the limits of the argument clarified.

TELL YOUR READERS WHICH TYPE OF CASE YOU HAVE CHOSEN AND WHY

Whichever type of case you choose, your readers need to know about it. What kind it is? Why you have chosen it? They won't know unless you tell them, plainly and directly. That's the only way they can size up your methods and draw reasonable conclusions from the studies you present. Is this supposed to be like the simple algebra test or the tough trigonometry one? Are the cases you present intended to be easy, typical, or hard? Not telling your readers leaves them in the dark and grumpy. And grumpy readers are definitely not what you want.

> *Tip:* Tell your readers exactly what kind of cases you have chosen and why. Are these cases supposed to be hard, typical, or easy?

Omitting the rationale for case studies is rarely a simple oversight, a paragraph the author somehow forgot to include. The trouble lies deeper. The rationale is probably missing because there really isn't one. The reader doesn't know because the author doesn't know, either. Yet this rationale is fundamental to good research design. That's why it should be part of any paper that uses case studies—including yours.

The larger point here is that you need to pick cases thoughtfully, after self-conscious reflection about their characteristics. Then you need to explain these criteria to your readers. If you do that well, case studies can be powerful tools for evaluating arguments and a valuable part of your thesis.

CHECKLIST: CASE STUDIES

If you decide to use case studies, you should explain to readers
- Why you are using case studies rather than some other method.
- Why you are using these particular cases.
- Whether these cases are supposed to be hard, typical, or easy.

---

7 EVERY THESIS SHOULD HAVE A THESIS

The core of your thesis should be your *argument*. An argument, in this sense, does not mean a dispute or a bald unsupported statement of views. It means a well-reasoned perspective on your subject, supported by logic or evidence, presented fairly.[1]

It's not your opinion, shouted to the whole bar. It's not a truckload of evidence, dumped in your poor reader's lap. It's not a debating game or legal proceeding, in which you present only the facts that help your side. It's not a public relations exercise, where you spin everything to fit some preconceived notion.

It's none of those. Rather, it is your distinctive viewpoint and your conclusions, backed by logical arguments and buttressed by evidence you have assembled, all of it presented honestly, without bias. *This reasoned viewpoint—this argument—is your thesis.*

> *Definition:* An argument is your reasoned perspective on the main subject of your paper, supported by logic or evidence, all presented fairly. The main argument of a book or paper is also called its "thesis."

A thesis (argument) is your take on the subject, and every thesis (paper) should have one.[2] You may also have some secondary arguments in your

---

1. This definition of "argument" is close to that of Anthony Weston, *A Rulebook for Arguments,* 2nd ed. (Indianapolis, IN: Hackett, 1992), x–xi.

2. Our ordinary language is confusing about some of the terms. An "argument" can mean either a shouting match in the parking lot or a scholarly statement of views, supported by logic or evidence (whether or not others disagree with it).

Similarly, a "thesis" has two meanings in daily usage. One is the culminating research paper for a BA, an MA, or a PhD. "He completed his thesis." The other is the main argument in any paper, article, or book. "Her book has an interesting thesis." My paper, covering subsidiary points. But for now, let's concentrate on developing your main argument.

STATE YOUR ARGUMENT CRISPLY

Your main argument should be brief and crisp. No matter how complicated and subtle your overall paper, your argument should be expressed in clear, pointed language. A reader should be able to say, "I agree with that" or "That just can't be right!" To frame an argument like this requires some serious thinking to boil down your views and some intellectual bravery to state them directly, without weasel words.

That won't happen overnight. It takes time to develop your viewpoint and the reasoning behind it, to turn a tentative thesis into a fully developed one. It demands careful thinking about how to support it and how to respond to skeptics. It often requires you to write better than the turgid academic articles you've plowed through, where ideas are cloaked in jargon. Let them be negative models of exposition. Don't let them mislead you into thinking this is the only way to sound intelligent or present research. It isn't. Clarity and simplicity are much better.

Once you have developed an argument, it's important to show how it fits into your field of study. You can do that by stating clearly which authors and which perspectives you are drawing on, and which ones you reject. It's helpful to readers if you differentiate your argument from others and identify these alternatives with specific scholars. For example: "Lipson is obviously wrong, once again, when he says . . . ." The emphasis, however, should be on developing your own position and evaluating it honestly and rigorously.

It takes weeks, sometimes months, to develop a compelling argument. That can be frustrating. But remember, if you knew exactly what you were

---

title for this chapter plays on these two meanings. "Every Thesis Should Have a Thesis" means every major research paper should have a coherent argument.

The meaning of "thesis" is usually clear from the context. When there might be confusion, I'll say either "paper" or "argument." When I'm referring to the thesis argument, I'll use the interchangeable terms "argument," "thesis argument," and "main argument." Of course, most papers also include secondary arguments about less important points.

going to say before you started, the whole project would be boring—to you and probably to your readers. Most of us begin with some general ideas and puzzling problems, hone the questions, find the right methods to investigate them, and then gradually work out some coherent answers. All this effort pays off in a well-grounded perspective, one that can persuade a skeptical reader.

> *Tip:* Nobody has a clear argument right away. It takes time and hard thinking to hone your perspective and distill it into a few sentences. But the effort is worth it. A succinct, well-reasoned argument is the heart of your thesis project.

What if you start your thesis project with a tentative argument already in mind? That's fine, as long as you keep an open mind. Ask yourself: "What could change my opinion? What evidence could effectively challenge my view?" If nothing could, then you don't have an argument, you have either a tautology or a theology. That's not what you are aiming for. You want a thoughtful perspective, not circular reasoning. You want a thesis, not a secular religion.

HOW TO DEVELOP A THESIS STATEMENT

How do you come up with a good thesis statement? The best way is to build on your proposal by writing a very brief paper proposing your slant on the subject. It only needs to be paragraph or so, plus a title. If you have more than one idea for the thesis statement, write down each one separately. They should be brief and to the point. If you can express it in a single sentence, so much the better.

This is not supposed to be a polished paper; it is merely a rough statement of your main idea, your prospective argument. There's no need to offer supporting evidence here. As long as this paragraph captures your basic thrust, it can prompt a useful discussion with your adviser.

Even a preliminary thesis argument is helpful because it will guide your research. That's why it is helpful to do it early in the process, perhaps in the third month, after you've completed your background reading.

Tip: Write a preliminary version of your thesis argument after you've completed your background reading. The argument only needs to be a paragraph, or perhaps even a sentence, capturing your main idea. Even this preliminary version will guide your research.

Both the discussion and the writing process will clarify your thinking and reveal more about your approach. That will lead to another round of brief writing and more discussion as you sharpen your focus and method.

Working on your thesis statement should not delay your research at all. As long as your proposal sends you in the right direction for reading and data collection, you can move ahead on that while you are still developing your argument. In fact, *you are likely to continue refining your main argument throughout the research and writing process.* Your final thesis statement may not be ready until you are near the end of the project.

Tip: To develop a clear thesis statement, you'll need to revise and update your paragraph as your research develops. You'll need to discuss it with your adviser. With revision, discussion, and research, your initial perspective can mature into your thesis argument.

That's one reason you will probably write the introduction and conclusion of your paper last. The introduction is where you will initially state your argument. The conclusion is where you will return to evaluate it, based on the research presented in the middle sections of the paper.

EXAMPLES OF THESIS STATEMENTS
FROM DIFFERENT FIELDS

What does a clear, strong thesis statement actually look like? You can see for yourself by reviewing the research articles you've been reading. Look at the best ones, the ones you really liked. Most will have a thesis statement (that is, their major argument) in the introduction or conclusion. To illustrate, let's consider some thesis statements from leading figures across a range of fields. They serve as academic models worthy of emulation.

Tip: As part of your thesis reading, look for clear arguments to serve as models. You find them in the best books and articles.

Here is Robert Nozick's introduction to *Anarchy, State, and Utopia,* one of the most influential—and controversial—works of philosophy in the past half century:

> Individuals have rights, and there are things no person or group may do to them (without violating their rights). . . . How much room do individual rights leave for the state? The nature of the state, its legitimate functions and its justifications, if any, is the central concern of this book . . . .
>
> Our main conclusions about the state are that a minimal state, limited to the narrow functions of protection against force, theft, fraud, enforcement of contracts, and so on, is justified; that any more extensive state will violate persons' rights not to be forced to do certain things, and is unjustified; and the minimal state is inspiring as well as right. Two noteworthy implications are that the state may not use its coercive apparatus for the purpose of getting some citizens to aid others, or in order to prohibit activities to people for their *own* good or protection.[3]

Here is Max Weber, summarizing his complicated analysis in *The Protestant Ethic and the Spirit of Capitalism:*

> What the great religious epoch of the seventeenth century bequeathed to its utilitarian successor was, however, an amazingly good . . . conscience in the acquisition of money, so long as it took place legally. . . . A specifically bourgeois economic ethic had grown up. With the consciousness of standing in the fullness of God's grace and being visibly blessed by Him, the bourgeois business man, as long as he remained within the bounds of formal correctness, as long as his moral conduct was spotless and the use to which he put his wealth was not objectionable, could follow his pecuniary interests as he would and feel that he was fulfilling a duty in doing so. The power of religious asceticism provided him in addition with sober, conscientious, and unusually indus-

---

3. Robert Nozick, *Anarchy, State, and Utopia* (New York: Basic Books, 1974), ix.

trious workmen, who clung to their work as to a life purpose willed by God.[4]

Friedrich Hayek wrote his influential *Road to Serfdom* in the midst of World War II, warning that increased planning by Western governments carried a profound hidden danger. Here is his thesis:

> For at least twenty-five years before the specter of totalitarianism became a real threat, we had progressively been moving away from the basic ideas on which Western civilization has been built. That this movement on which we have entered with such high hopes and ambitions should have brought us face to face with the totalitarian horror has come as a profound shock to this generation, which still refuses to connect the two facts. Yet this development merely confirms the warnings of the fathers of the liberal philosophy which we still profess. We have progressively abandoned that freedom in economic affairs without which personal and political freedom has never existed in the past.[5]

Some think that historical studies don't have such theses. After all, they are filled with detail and rarely seek to generalize their findings to other countries or other periods. Still, the best studies synthesize what they have found about their own time and place. They fuse the myriad details into a meaningful picture. Here is John W. Dower's eloquent summary argument from *Embracing Defeat: Japan in the Wake of World War II*:

> To understand the Japan that stands at the cusp of the twenty-first century, however, it is more useful to look not for the *longue durée* of an inexorably unfolding national experience, but rather at a cycle of recent history that began in the late 1920s and essentially ended in 1989. When this short, violent, innovative epoch is scrutinized, much of what has been characterized as a postwar "Japanese model" proves to [be] a hybrid Japanese-American model: forged in war, intensified through defeat and occupation, and maintained over the ensuing decades out of an abiding fear of national vulnerability and a widespread belief that Japan needed

---

4. Max Weber, *The Protestant Ethic and the Spirit of Capitalism* (1904–5), trans. Talcott Parsons (New York: Charles Scribner's Sons, 1958), 176–77.

5. F. A. Hayek, *The Road to Serfdom* (1944; reprint, Chicago: University of Chicago Press, 1972), 12–13.

top-level planning and protection to achieve optimum economic growth. This bureaucratic capitalism is incomprehensible without understanding how victor and vanquished embraced Japan's defeat together.[6]

Finally, here is David Bevington arguing that Shakespeare's plays have a visual dimension that reinforces their dialogue and contributes powerfully to their meaning:

> Shakespeare's texts demand visual realization. Ascents and descents, kneeling, ceremonial processions, joinings of hands, and the like are not only omnipresent but function as signs of hierarchical relationship, personal obligation, communal celebration, and a host of other meaningful qualities. Clothing betokens social rank or, conversely, a holiday inversion of it. Gestures often occupy the central moment of a scene or signal the reversal of dramatic action. My aim has been to study this unspoken language of the theater, and to see how Shakespeare regards both its capacity and its limitations.[7]

Bevington's thesis statement appears early—in the preface—but it really begins with the title of his book, *Action Is Eloquence: Shakespeare's Language of Gesture.* Dower's title, *Embracing Defeat,* captures his thesis, too, and Hayek's *Road to Serfdom* anticipates his argument. That's worth thinking about when you choose your own title. A great title does more than mark off your subject matter. It indicates your take on it. Your title effectively becomes the opening line of your thesis statement.

> *Tip:* The best paper titles do more than indicate the subject matter. They indicate your perspective on it.

WHAT GOOD THESIS STATEMENTS HAVE IN COMMON

The thesis statements shown here are vastly different in their subject matter. Yet all of them are concise, forceful, and original. As they stand,

---

6. John W. Dower, *Embracing Defeat: Japan in the Wake of World War II* (New York: W. W. Norton, 1999), 558.

7. David Bevington, *Action Is Eloquence: Shakespeare's Language of Gesture* (Cambridge, MA: Harvard University Press, 1984), viii.

however, they are little more than assertions. The authors spend most of their books developing these arguments, supporting them, defending them against likely objections, and showing their full implications. In the process, they build great books around interesting arguments.

In each case, the thesis statement shows that the project is coherent, that its multiple strands are bound together by a single aim. This aim, stated in the argument, is the focal point of the entire work.

That is exactly what you want to accomplish in your own thesis statement. In the first few months of thesis research, you'll take aim. As you move forward with your research and writing, you will adjust your sights. Revising your thesis statement is not a concession. It's learning. Finally, you will draw conclusions and try to show how your argument hits the bull's-eye.

> *Tip:* Don't worry if your argument changes during your research project. That's learning!

REVISING YOUR THESIS STATEMENT

It is common to revise a thesis argument as research goes forward. Revisions like this are welcome improvements. They don't mislead the reader unless you say (wrongly) that you have tested a proposition when you actually figured it out afterward, based on evidence revealed as you tested a different proposition.

Research 101 says *you cannot use the same evidence to generate a proposition and test it.* That's circular. But it's perfectly kosher to look at your evidence and revise your proposition or generate a new one. The revised proposition, you explain, fits the existing evidence but still needs to be tested on other evidence—perhaps another case or a different database. That's learning, too.

> *Tip:* Don't claim to have tested a proposition on evidence if you didn't, if what you really did was infer the proposition from the evidence you gathered.

You should consider revising the thesis statement in several ways as you work on the project. One, which we've just mentioned, is in response to testing and evaluation. If some predictions are wrong, then you need to take that into account and modify the argument. Having done that, test the revised predictions against *different* evidence (or at least say it needs to be done—by next year's seniors).

You may also discover that your argument is vague or cannot be evaluated in some circumstances. This problem may not be apparent until you've conducted some research, but, having discovered it, you should fix it. That means sharpening and clarifying the argument.

Another possibility is that your original argument is too broad. Your research may reveal it applies perfectly well to the United States but not to Canada, or vice versa. If your thesis statement incorrectly says it should apply to both countries, or perhaps to all democracies, then you need to delimit it. Put a fence around your argument, saying where it applies and where it doesn't. Don't do that in an arbitrary or ad hoc way. Specify the limits in clear, general terms, if possible—the same way you stated the thesis itself.

Similar problems can arise when you explore literary materials or historical documents. As you develop your analysis or narrative, you may discover that it no longer corresponds to your original argument. That's not uncommon as you move deeper into research and writing. But something's gotta give. Your broader argument should find support in the detailed analysis. Assuming you are more confident about the details (as most students are), then it's time to rework the thesis argument so it fits snugly.

Except for the comments about testing predictions, these observations apply to the humanities as well as the social sciences. Your analysis of Wordsworth may suggest some insights into his fellow Lake Poets and possibly into all Romantic literature. You may think this broad application is a promising possibility, although nothing more than a possibility at this stage. Or perhaps you are certain the comments apply only to Wordsworth or, even more narrowly, to only a few of his poems. Say that. Tell your readers how widely your analysis applies and what its limits are.

Beyond exploring these limits, review your work to make sure the argument corresponds to the detailed research. If gaps remain, consider how best to explain them and discuss these issues with your adviser.

Sharpening and refining your argument like this not only improves your paper; it improves your understanding. It's a learning experience well beyond most course work.

CAN YOU PASS THE "ELEVATOR TEST"?

How do you know when you have finally developed a clear-cut argument to call your own? Take the elevator test. As you start to ascend from the lobby, a visiting professor turns to you and says: "So, I see you are writing a thesis. What's it about?" First, take off your headphones. Then describe your subject and your basic slant on it. If you can explain both in a straightforward, accessible way, you pass with flying colors. If you can do it before you reach the fourth floor, you are well on your way to a great thesis.

> *Tip:* Once you have a clear, sharp argument, you should be able to state it in a few sentences. In fact, it should be brief enough to explain on an elevator ride. That's a great test, unless the elevator is in the Empire State Building.

CHECKLIST: THESIS ARGUMENT

- Write a preliminary version of your main argument or "thesis statement" after you have completed background readings.
- Revise this argument as you continue researching and writing.
- Discuss your argument periodically with your adviser.
- Work toward a briefer, sharper statement of your argument (the elevator test).

IV

Writing
Your Best

8 PLANNING AND PREWRITING: HOW DO THEY HELP YOUR THESIS?

A strong thesis is well written and convincingly argued. Over the next four chapters, I will offer some suggestions about how to do that: how to write a lucid and persuasive thesis.

Why take four chapters? Because good writing is so important to your thesis and because it's helpful to distinguish several aspects of thesis writing, even if they overlap in practice. In fact, I'll argue that these elements of writing *should* overlap as you work on your thesis. More about that later in this chapter.

The first task is to devise a general plan for your writing. For short papers, like so many you've written in the past, these plans can be simple and informal. You may not even need to write them down. You just think over what you plan to say and then write a short essay. Or you might jot down a brief outline, covering a few main points, before you start writing. Your thesis is different. You have more material to organize and more pages to write. To do that effectively, you need a more detailed plan. Of course, you will modify it as you write, adding new items and shifting old ones. Still, it's helpful to sketch out a general route before you grab a backpack and begin a long hike. Our first task, then, is to sketch out an effective plan for writing your thesis. That's the goal of this chapter.

In the next chapter (9), I'll focus on writing the first draft. How can you make it more readable, taking the reader smoothly from one point to the next in a logical order? After that, in the third chapter (10), I'll turn to the two most important sections in your paper: the opening and closing. I'll also discuss how to make effective transitions between sections.

Finally, in the fourth chapter (11), I'll discuss how to edit your material. That's much more than just checking punctuation;?.! It's also reviewing the language, tone, and overall structure of your paper. That's an essential part of all good writing, although for too many writers it is a mere afterthought. To put it bluntly: Good writing *is* rewriting. There's no way around it. A good editing job makes your thesis easier to understand and more persuasive. Of course, I'll pass along some suggestions about how to do that.

These chapters on writing are united by one overriding message: Effective writing is more than just "presenting the material," as important as that is. It is also about making your argument clearly and making it stick. That's what these chapters will help you do.

The same basic approach is equally valuable with maps, charts, graphs, and tables. The aim of these visual presentations is identical to that of good writing: to present your evidence clearly and make your argument persuasively. I'll illustrate some ways of doing that in chapter 12, "Presenting Information Visually."

WHAT IS PREWRITING? AND WHY BOTHER DOING IT?

Good thesis writing begins with good planning.

As important as planning is, the topic is usually treated in dry and somber tones. You are given one big, grim message: Make a long, detailed outline and follow it. The thin finger of a Victorian grammar teacher reaches out from the grave to warn you: Every item in the outline must have exactly the same form; you cannot have only one subpoint under an item, and on and on. You are cast in the role of Bob Cratchit, dipping your quill in the inkpot and scratching out tiny Roman numerals in Scrooge's ledger.

If that works for you and Tiny Tim, fine. But it doesn't need to be done that way. Christmas future can be different. Your goal, after all, is not to write a dazzling outline but to write your best thesis.

A better way to plan your thesis is to work back and forth between your research notes and "prewriting." What is prewriting? It is the basic work of organizing your materials, writing informally about them, and preparing to write a first draft, based on these notes and writings.[1]

Prewriting starts with reviewing your research notes and personal com-

---

1. Some experts take a wider view of prewriting. For them, it also includes brainstorming and freewriting. Brainstorming is a freewheeling effort to generate ideas, usually in small-group discussions. Freewriting is a special technique to generate ideas and overcome writer's block. Freewriting is discussed in chapter 13, as part of the section on writer's blocks. Students are told to write rapidly for ten minutes or so, without interruption, ignoring spelling or grammar. Sometimes they are told to write about anything and not bother staying on topic. Other times, they are told to stay loosely on topic,

ments. You've been accumulating them for just this purpose. The goal of this review is straightforward: You want to group similar materials together and then put these materials in a logical order. You need to organize them so you can present them coherently in your paper.

Tip: Instead of detailed outlining, try prewriting. Prewriting involves sorting through your book notes and comments, amplifying them with sentences and paragraphs, and then putting them in a logical sequence.

Organization is essential because you've got a lot of material—more than you've ever dealt with before. There is simply too much to keep straight in your head, too much to make up the organization as you ramble along. If the material is disorganized, your thesis will be difficult to write and equally difficult to read. Your argument will be muddled, rather than transparent. That's not what you want. You want a paper that moves through your research logically, without detours or dead ends. You want it to unfold sensibly to your readers, buttressing your basic argument, showing its logic and presenting key evidence. Prewriting is designed to help you accomplish that.

FOUR STEPS TO EFFECTIVE PREWRITING

If you were writing a book or dissertation, the first step would be to organize your research material into chapters. That's what I did for this book. Senior theses are shorter—they are more like academic articles than

---

but not to worry if they veer off. Just keep writing without pause. They may be encouraged to repeat the process, focusing on the ideas they liked in previous rounds. The result is still a *very* loose draft, which may become part of the paper's first draft or may stimulate ideas for it. The benefits are (1) striking, original language because the writer is less constrained by convention, less able to staunch the flow of original ideas, and (2) "words on paper," overcoming writer's block. The leading proponent and innovator is Peter Elbow. See his *Writing without Teachers,* 2nd ed. (New York: Oxford University Press, 1998); and *Writing with Power,* 2nd ed. (New York: Oxford University Press, 1998). Joan Bolker advocates it as a therapeutic technique for students with writer's block. Joan Bolker, *Writing Your Dissertation in Fifteen Minutes a Day: A Guide to Starting, Revising, and Finishing Your Doctoral Thesis* (New York: Henry Holt, 1998).

books—so they generally use sections rather than chapters. But the organizing principle is the same: Start by focusing on the biggest building blocks. In this case, the biggest blocks are the sections of your paper. Figure them out first since they are the key to transforming a shapeless file of notes into a well-ordered thesis.

Here we come to the one part of traditional outlining you really can use. Every good outline begins with the biggest categories, the capitalized Roman numerals I, II, III, IV . . . . That's exactly what you need to establish here. Do it first. Don't worry about getting them in the right order, at least not yet. We'll do that *after* we nail down the categories. Right now, just think about what the categories should be. These Roman numerals will become the main sections of your paper. At this point, however, you should think of them as *categories into which you will place your research.*

> *Tip:* The first step in prewriting is to decide on the main sections of your paper. These are the big Roman numerals in a traditional outline. In our prewriting, we will call them the *main categories.*

Since a lot of research will go in these categories, you need to sort through it in several steps. You can do that by asking—and answering—four questions *in this order:*

1. What are the appropriate categories (or paper sections), given my argument and evidence? (These are the capitalized Roman numerals in an outline.)
2. What is the best order in which to line up these categories and present them to readers?
3. Into which category should I put any particular piece of research, such as a book note or personal comment?
4. Did I inadvertently leave any gaps in my argument, either by missing a category entirely or by doing too little research on one?

So you want to take these four steps in order: (1) set up the main categories; (2) line them up in a logical order; (3) file individual items in the right category; and (4) check for any holes in the sequence.

FOUR STEPS IN PREWRITING

| Set Up Main Categories | → | Line Up Categories in Order | → | File Items in Individual Categories | → | Check for Holes (Missing Categories or Missing Evidence) |

GETTING THE MAIN CATEGORIES RIGHT

Determining the main categories is job number one because they are the foundation stones for your paper. Do *not* let your research files decide these categories by default. That's backward. You should decide the categories self-consciously in light of your thesis question and argument. Impose some intellectual order. Then, once you have set up the categories, use them to sort the evidence.

It's sometimes hard to figure out the main categories and their sequence. After all, you've been wrapped up in detailed research, and it's easy to lose sight of the big questions and big answers. Now is the time to step back from the evidence and mull over your questions, answers, and argument. Review your argument (or main point) so you can state it clearly and simply. Then, ask yourself, "What does the reader absolutely need to know for my argument to make sense?"

Your response should concentrate on the major elements, not the details, so you can nail down the most reasonable progression. What you want to do is take your readers through your argument in large steps, tracing a path to your destination. You want to mark out this path for yourself first, before drafting the paper and filling in the supporting details. Staking out this path is your first major goal in prewriting.

Each big step along the path will become one of your main categories, and you will parcel out your research among them. Naturally, the categories and their order are tightly linked, so you need to keep one in mind when you're thinking about the other.

Tip: To determine the main categories (or sections) of your paper, ask yourself, "What are the essential building blocks of my argument?"

GETTING THE ORDER RIGHT

Aside from the introduction and conclusion, there are usually about four or five main categories, although there could be more. These are the middle sections of your paper, the sections where you do the heavy lifting to explain your project in detail and make your argument convincing. It's where you actually interpret Whitman's poems, critique Kurosawa's films, explain why the European Union was formed, or analyze how Dell manufactures so efficiently. In these sections, you describe your methods, interpret your materials, and analyze your evidence.

Your first prewriting task is to figure out what these sections (or categories) should be. Your second task is to line them up in order. The order is important because it captures the logic of your argument. That is how you will present your materials in the paper. Your choice finally boils down to your judgment about the best sequence for setting out your research and supporting your argument so readers can understand it.

> *Tip:* Once you have set the paper's main categories, determine the best order for them.

For history papers, the sequence is almost always chronological. For others, it depends on the particular process you are exploring. In this book, for instance, it makes sense to discuss how to pick a thesis topic before discussing prewriting. Both of them should come before a chapter on editing. So that's how I laid out my categories. For other projects, the order might depend on the fundamental logic of the argument.

To see how it's done in your field, simply look at a few articles you've read for thesis research. Look closely at how they are organized and see how each section builds on the ones that came before. The best articles will give you ideas about how to organize your own work.

> *Tip:* For examples of how to organize your thesis, look at articles in your field. See how they divide their general topic into sections and how they order the sections and evidence.

Whatever sequence you choose, you should explain it briefly to your readers in the introduction, where you first present the argument. (The introduction and conclusion are not major elements of prewriting. I will discuss them separately in chapter 10.) For now, let's concentrate on the middle sections of the paper, the ones where you develop your argument and present your evidence.

Getting the Order Right: An Example

Let's say your argument has this basic form: "If A and B, then C." In this case, your first category should establish the logical underpinnings of the argument. Is it really true that "if A and B, then C"? You need to demonstrate that your logic is sound, and you need to defend it against any obvious objections.

That done, your second main category should present empirical evidence that A, B, and C exist (or that they exist in the specific case you are studying). You might also insert a methodological section here to explain how you acquired your evidence, how reliable it is, and how you will analyze it.

The final category supports your causal claim that A and B actually do lead to C, not just in theory but in practice. Your evidence might focus on the statistical relationship, the causal process, or both. The goal here is to show how the causal mechanism works in the real world and to show that it works exactly like you said it would in your argument. (If, as it turns out, the evidence *contradicts* your initial argument, present it honestly. Never fudge. Explain what the problem is, what it means, and how your argument should be modified. That's not a failure. Showing how an argument should be changed is important in its own right.)

Your adviser can help immensely at this stage, when you are setting up the main categories. *I recommend a meeting specifically to discuss your categories and the order in which you intend to present them.* As with all your meetings, you should do a little writing first. In this case, simply bring in a page or so, listing the main categories in order. It might help to add a few sentences next to each category saying what it is supposed to accomplish. That will facilitate a conversation with your adviser.

> *Tip:* The categories and their order form the basic architecture of your paper. Spend time on them. Hold a special meeting with your adviser to discuss them.

Although this paper is brief, you will profit from discussing it fully. Your adviser has undoubtedly read many papers and developed a practiced eye for what kind of organization works best. Then, too, thinking about structure is what she does every time she writes articles and conference papers herself. So she knows the territory and can give you some valuable guidance when it's most useful. And it is very useful indeed to get the basic architecture right. You don't want to start building without a solid plan.

To get this valuable advice, though, you have to ask. Advisers are busy, and, in any case, it's your job, not theirs, to keep your thesis on track. When you need help or feedback from faculty advisers, you need to ask. Always remember that it's your responsibility. That's true about the thesis as a whole—you own it.

> *Tip:* It's your responsibility to keep your thesis project on track. Your adviser can help in many ways, but the ultimate responsibility is yours. When you need help, ask.

Having asked for this meeting with your adviser, you should arrive with a very simple agenda. It boils down to two questions:

- Are these the right categories?
- Do I have them in the right order?

If you take the initiative, your adviser can help you answer these questions and contribute a lot at this critical moment.

Workshops and tutors can help, too, for exactly the same reasons. This is a great opportunity to take advantage of them. You will learn from discussing your categories and explaining how you arranged them. The give-and-take with fellow students and workshop leaders can be a valuable learning experience. That learning will show up in a better thesis.

PUTTING EVIDENCE INTO THE RIGHT CATEGORY

After you have decided on the main categories and their sequence, it's time to decide what evidence you need to ground each step along the way. Go through your research reports, book notes, and personal comments and place each one in the appropriate category. Nearly all your material should fit into one of the categories you have formulated. To take an example from this book, I separated my notes on prewriting, which I am using now, from those on refining the thesis topic, which I used earlier.

As you review these materials, some may prompt ideas you want to explore further. Terrific. Take some time to jot down your thoughts before anything gets in the way. Then file them away for use later. You *will* use them later. They're an important part of your prewriting.

> *Tip:* Once your categories are in place and in order, sort your research notes into the appropriate categories.

Sorting your research and commentary always presents a few problems. If an item fits into several spots, make a provisional choice now and a final determination later. If a lot of material fits in several places, then your categories are too broad or too vague. Reduce the confusion by defining your categories more narrowly and precisely. If some notes don't fit anywhere (and that always happens), you can park them temporarily in a miscellaneous category. But eventually you either need to add a new category, fit them into an existing one, or scrap this material. After all, there isn't going to be a section in your thesis called "Miscellaneous."

Don't worry about scrapping some material. Everybody needs to. Some research always turns out to be unnecessary or repetitive. It's a bit like preparing for an exam question that isn't asked. Much better to leave it out than to squeeze it in, pointlessly. Be brave and cut. The excess doesn't strengthen your argument. It detracts and confuses.

As you categorize, you may discover that your research is compelling in several categories, but thin or uneven in one or two others. Perhaps you have only one source on a particular topic. Or you may have several but they're all on the same side of a controversial issue. That wasn't apparent while you were doing the research because you were working on so many things at once. Now, as you sort the material into categories, it shows up clearly.

This kind of setback is common, but, fortunately, it's only minor. The remedy is simply a little more focused research, designed to strengthen a weak category or balance a lopsided one. To apply this quick fix, though, you first have to catch it. So keep your eyes open for glitches as you sort through your research.

> *Tip:* As you sort through your research, you will probably discover some unnecessary work on a few topics and not enough on others. That's par for the course. The best response: Cut the unnecessary material and do the fill-in research.

You may also need to make some small adjustments in the categories themselves. If your evidence about A or B or C is extensive and you want to present a lot of it, then give each one a separate category. Just make sure the size of the categories is balanced—relative to each other and relative to your overall paper. It would be odd and a little misleading if you presented three times as much material about B as you did about A and C, *unless* you had already convinced the reader of its outsized importance.

As you sort through your research, you should shuttle back and forth between your assessment of the overall argument, the research to support it, and the order in which to present it most convincingly. That's why, when you begin sorting the evidence, you may return to fine-tune the categories or their order. You are working back and forth, fitting the research materials into the categories and arranging the categories into a presentation, making sure it all bears directly on the development of your thesis.

> *Tip:* Work back and forth among your categories, their order, and your evidence. You may need to adjust the categories, change their order, or do more research in some.

Don't rush this prewriting process because you are anxious to start "real writing." The urge to get going is understandable—you want to finish the thesis—but rushing at this point is self-defeating. Work steadily on your prewriting and take the time to do it well. It will pay off handsomely by making your paper better organized and more interesting. Keep adding ideas and writing paragraphs to extend your notes. If you see links between different parts of your research, write those down, too. This preliminary work will make the writing process much more comfortable and efficient.[2]

Organizing Your Thesis by Prewriting: Another Example

Let's take another example to show how this organizing process works, this one from public policy. The topic concerns suburban transportation, which was narrowed to three Sun Belt counties. (Remember how useful it is to narrow the topic.) The central argument is that transportation needs are growing rapidly in the suburbs and have not been addressed adequately, at either the state or federal level. Given this thesis, what categories would work best?

There are undoubtedly several ways to organize this research, but here's one that makes sense to me: (1) Evidence that the problems are serious and increasing, and that these particular counties are good examples of them. After all, if you can't show the problems are serious, there's nothing to explain. (2) Evidence that existing transportation policies are not working well, focusing on the three Sun Belt counties. (3) Projections, inevitably speculative, that the problems won't solve themselves but will gradually worsen if current policies are continued. Taken together, items 1–3 show that these are serious problems and that they are not being solved by current policies. (4) Survey of alternative policies, based on a literature review, followed by analysis of one or more alternatives that have actually been implemented. (5) Evidence that some of these alternatives are superior to current policies, according to criteria you have explicitly set out and defended in the paper.

Another way to organize this would be to take the first three categories (the problem is serious, existing policies aren't working, and things are getting worse) and discuss only the national problems, based on your reading of the literature. Then turn to case studies of the three Sun Belt counties

---

2. This emphasis on prewriting and not rushing yourself is underscored in the work of Robert Boice. He advocates a calm, steady approach, and his writing conveys that very feeling. He offers wonderful suggestions for dealing with writer's block, binge writing, and other problems. Robert Boice, "Strategies for Enhancing Scholarly Productivity," in *Writing and Publishing for Academic Authors*, ed. Joseph M. Moxley and Todd Taylor (Lanham, MD: Rowman & Littlefield, 1997); and Robert Boice, *How Writers Journey to Comfort and Fluency: A Psychological Adventure* (Westport, CT: Praeger, 1994).

and show how profoundly the problems affect them. You could use the cases to illustrate the problems in detail and make the policy issues more tangible. Then the last two categories (which show that alternatives are available and would work better than existing policies) could be developed using data from the nation as a whole or from your three counties.

Either organization would work well in this paper, and there may be others. Notice how the categories in both versions are closely tied to the development of the argument itself. That's exactly how it should be. That's what you are aiming for: close integration between your argument and your paper's organization.

FILLING IN THE GAPS

Now that your research is sorted into categories and the categories are lined up properly, it may seem like your prewriting is done. It nearly is, but there is one more important question to ask: "Have I skipped some crucial element of the sequence, leaving a gap in my argument?" If you have, then now is the time to identify it and do the fill-in research.

Here, once again, your adviser can help. Besides her experience with paper organization, she gives you another set of eyes to glimpse what you might have overlooked. In the transportation example, you or your adviser may realize that you have only reviewed hypothetical alternatives. You haven't really reviewed any alternatives that have been implemented in the real world, and your argument would be stronger if you did. It's understandable that you missed this point; you were preoccupied with lots of other research.

Tip: Double-check for gaps in your argument and supporting evidence. Then fill them with targeted research.

Finding a gap like this is not a crisis. It happens to everybody who does research, professors as well as students. It only becomes a crisis if you *don't* find it, or if you don't find it until you are polishing your final draft. Then it's much harder to repair. If you find it early, you only need to make minor adjustments, the equivalent of installing a missing water pipe when you begin building a new room. It's cheap and easy to fix. If you overlook it, though, you face a major overhaul and a major bill. To install the pipe later, when the room is nearly complete, you have to rip out the kitchen sink and the wall cabinets. That's painful, dusty, and expensive. Saving yourself this pain is why you are doing all this planning and prewriting. It will produce a more coherent, persuasive thesis and save a lot of aggravation later. I know. I've ripped out quite a few sinks.

PUTTING THE WRITING IN PREWRITING

Where is the writing in all this prewriting? Actually, there should be quite a lot of it, and I'll explain how to fit it in. The goal here is to avoid the stultifying sequence of completing a detailed outline first, then writing a first draft from scratch, and finally, after the draft is finished, revising the entire paper.

TRADITIONAL APPROACH TO THESIS WRITING

| Create Detailed Outline | Write First Draft | Revise Entire Draft |

For most people, including me, that's not the most productive way to move through the process. It's awkward and difficult to write a detailed outline before writing any prose at all. It creates problems down the line, too, because the outline should respond to discoveries made during the writing process itself. Believe me, you *will* make discoveries as you write. But you'll stymie them if you set up rules that prevent changes. An overly detailed outline can block the flexibility you need to make these discoveries and incorporate them in your thesis.

Second, the rigid sequence of "outline → draft → revise" poses an unnecessary roadblock to writing in areas where you are ready to go. That blockage can calcify and make it difficult to begin drafting the paper, even after the outline is finished.

Finally, the emphasis on completing a full outline puts too much weight on what the outline does best: putting the details into the right subcategory. The initial emphasis should be on getting the main categories right— the capitalized Roman numerals in an outline—and putting them in the right order. After that, it's more fruitful to flesh out your notes and ideas within each category than to figure out where minor subpoints should go in your outline. It's more important to develop your key arguments and find imaginative connections between the major elements. That's what prewriting does.

Some authors advocate making detailed outlines; others simply urge prewriting without much attention to overall organization. My approach suggests a middle way, one that combines the two and, I hope, captures the best features of both. The most important part of outlining is that it gives you structure so you can organize your materials. The most important part of prewriting is that it coaxes you to start writing and thinking, to connect the elements in your research and make new discoveries as you write.

The way to combine these two approaches is to set up the main categories (I, II, III, IV, and V in a normal outline) and then fill them in with extensive prewriting. That's more useful than determining the subcategories A, B, C, and D under each Roman numeral, and 1, 2, and 3 under each letter. Setting up the main categories emphasizes structure and sequence, which are essential. Prewriting within each category encourages you to build on your research where you can and to begin making discoveries and connections as you write.

> *Tip:* The most effective way to prewrite is to
> - Set up the main categories
> - Line them up in order
> - Sort evidence into the categories
> - Expand on your evidence and start writing sentences and paragraphs for various categories—the more, the better
>
> This approach combines clear organization for the paper as a whole (the capital Roman numerals) with lots of informal exploratory writing.

START WRITING!

There are a couple of complementary ways to begin this writing. First, as you put items in categories and shuffle them around, go beyond simply listing them. Periodically, switch over to writing comments about them. Jot down a few paragraphs about specific items that interest you or perhaps about the connections you see between them.[3] The aim is to blur the line,

---

3. Boice wisely urges writers to look for these connections between items and categories during prewriting. Boice, *How Writers Journey*, 54–56.

quite deliberately, between prewriting and writing, between organizing and drafting. I did that as I prepared for this book, and it will work in your thesis project, too.

> *Tip:* You should write as part of prewriting. Begin by adding sentences and paragraphs to your research notes. Look for connections between different parts of your research and write that down, too. File these expanded notes in your main categories so you can use them later.

Second, after you have established the main categories and sorted the relevant research, *consider writing a short paper on one of these categories.* For the moment, it can be treated as a small stand-alone topic. You don't need to connect it to any of the other categories, at least not yet. I've often suggested this approach to my BA (and MA) thesis students, and they say it works well. We discuss these smaller papers at their regular weekly meetings. After you write a paper for one category, you can do the same for another. Later I'll show how to connect them.

> *Tip:* Write an informal stand-alone paper covering one section of your thesis. Begin by choosing one of your categories and reviewing your research and expanded notes. Use them to draft an informal paper for that category alone. Don't worry about connecting it to the other categories (that is, to the rest of your thesis). That will come later.

To illustrate how you can write small stand-alone papers as part of your larger project, let's consider the thesis mentioned earlier on suburban transportation problems. The first two prewriting categories were

1. Evidence that the problems are serious and increasing, and that these particular counties are good examples of them;
2. Evidence that existing transportation policies are not working well, focusing on the three counties.

Either topic (or the other three categories, for that matter) would be a perfectly fine subject for a short paper, exactly like the ones you've written countless times for classes. Let's concentrate here on category 2, which says that suburban transportation policies are ineffective and that our selected counties are good illustrations. If you've already assembled a fair amount of research on this topic, there's no reason why you can't write a short paper on that topic alone, running perhaps two to five pages. You don't have to touch on issues that arise later in the thesis, such as potential alternatives. You don't have to say how it relates to topics that come before or after it. You simply concentrate on category 2 and write a short paper on that, using your research.

In fact, you can start writing about category 2 before you have finished sorting and organizing your materials for categories 3 and 4. You don't even need to write these small papers in order. You could write about 2 before you've finished 1, although I personally find that difficult. It might be easy for you, though. Everybody's different. In any case, it is not hard to do *some* productive writing for these later sections, even before you've "reached them." You can write a few paragraphs, here and there, to expand on specific issues in those categories. Then just file them away for a later day. When you finally reach that category and are ready to begin drafting, you'll have some important work already in place.

As you write these short rough drafts on individual sections, bring them in to discuss with your adviser. You only need to polish them a little. Out of respect for your reader, check spelling and basic grammar. If you want to do more polishing and refining, that's great and it will pay off later, but it's not essential. These short papers and discussions will produce a better thesis, made up of stronger parts.

DIFFERENT APPROACHES TO PREWRITING AND DRAFTING

You don't have to write short papers on all the sections, and you don't have to write them in any particular order. You don't need to polish them at this stage, unless, like me, you prefer to work that way. You can write them while you are still assembling research for other sections. You've got options. You can exercise your preferences.

Mine are stuck in the mud. I generally work on the sections in order, editing and polishing one while I'm drafting others. I edit intensively and go back to each section time and again. Of course, I return to work on the whole manuscript after all the sections are complete. By then, the sentences and paragraphs are already glittering gems that move readers to tears or laughter, but some parts may be in the wrong place. It may finally dawn on me that I've left out some working parts entirely. So I trudge back, rearrange the text, and add what's missing. Then I read it again and work on it some more.

Other writers do it differently. Some would rather produce a very rough draft (often called a "messy draft" or "zero draft") and then revise and edit the whole thing. Like a blacksmith, they keep reheating and forging the whole ingot, beating their manuscript into shape with successive revisions. The process makes for the finest swords, and it can make for fine manuscripts, too.

These choices are entirely matters of personal preference. Over the years, you have written enough papers to know what works best for you. The only difference with your thesis is its scale. Because there is more research and more text, you have to spend more time at every stage: prewriting, drafting, and rewriting. But you have choices about the best ways to do it. You can edit and polish these small sections as you go along, or you can do it later. You can write them in sequence, or you can do it out of order.

Whatever approach you take, *don't hesitate to write some paragraphs on any aspect of the thesis whenever you happen to think about it.* Do it whenever the ideas pop up. That might be when you are reading, reviewing your notes, or puzzling over the right order for the categories. Any of these tasks can stimulate new ideas and new writing. Write down your ideas and file them so you can use them later, when you reach that section. Don't push it aside to do more research right now. That can wait. Write—that's what's crucial—write when ideas strike you. You'll always be able to use this writing later, either as part of your prewriting or in an actual draft of the paper.

I'm skeptical, then, of the traditional approach of "outline → write → revise." I recommend doing things differently. But my objections are purely practical. If *you* work best by first writing a detailed outline, then by all means charge ahead that way. If your adviser prefers to see a full outline before you start drafting, then write one (and feel free to do some prewriting, too).

For most writers, though, it is more productive to use what I call an "overlapping approach," in which you (a) prewrite instead of outlining in detail (b) write sentences, paragraphs, and fragments as you go through each section, (c) turn this prewriting into draft sections, and (d) refine some earlier sections while you start drafting later ones.

OVERLAPPING APPROACH TO THESIS WRITING: A BETTER WAY

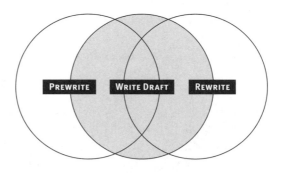

> *Tip:* Prewriting, draft writing, and rewriting should overlap. As you prewrite, expand your notes into paragraphs and then use those notes and paragraphs to write drafts for that category (or paper section). You can revise while you work on other sections.

Even the overlapping sequence "prewrite → draft → rewrite" is a bit deceptive since it refers to individual sections (or categories), not to the paper as a whole. As you continue to sort your research and organize the categories, you can begin writing some portions and adding a few paragraphs to others. You could be revising section 1 while you are drafting section 2 and prewriting section 5. Whenever ideas come up about sections 3 or 4, you could drop paragraphs about them into your notes, too. As the diagram indicates, it's a three-ring circus.

The happy result is that, when you are ready to begin drafting your thesis, you won't have to start from scratch, with nothing more than a detailed outline. You won't be staring at a blinking cursor on a blank screen. In fact, you will have a great deal more than the main categories and their sequence. You will also have several sections well under way, either in a rough draft or a little more refined. You will have draft paragraphs for other sections, too.

It is not too difficult to write these individual paragraphs and sections. They are small well-defined tasks, the kind you've done so often before. That means you do not face the daunting, unprecedented job of writing a thirty- or forty-page paper all at once. You can learn from your writing while you are still doing research. You can get feedback on the individual sections and modify your approach, in ways big or small. Most of all, you can draw on the ideas and writing you've completed when you sit down to "write your first draft." It will be a lot more like draft 1.5.

MEET REGULARLY WITH YOUR ADVISER AS YOU PREWRITE

Prewriting these middle sections is the middle stage of your thesis project. In my experience, *one of the most common mistakes students make at this stage (roughly months 3–5) is failing to meet their advisers regularly*. That contrasts with the first and last month of the thesis project. In the early weeks, students come to meetings often as they refine their topics and build reading lists. They welcome a chance to talk as they launch the project. In the intense final weeks, they return often as they pull their project together. But during the middle months, while students are busy researching and writing, they meet their advisers more sporadically. I think that's a mistake.

Even brief meetings—ten or fifteen minutes—will keep you on track and working steadily. They give you a chance to talk about your work, listen to feedback, and make midcourse corrections when they are still easily accomplished. My advice: Keep meeting regularly with your adviser at every stage of the thesis project. Don't go AWOL.

> *Tip:* Set up regular brief meetings with your adviser during the middle phase of your thesis project, while you are researching and prewriting. Keep your adviser up-to-date on what you have accomplished and what you plan to do next. Bring in some questions to each meeting and, if possible, a little writing.

TIME SCHEDULE FOR PREWRITING, DRAFTING, AND REWRITING

How does this prewriting and drafting process fit into your thesis work schedule? It should be your central focus beginning in about week 8, after you've completed general background reading and produced a workable proposal. If you finish your background reading sooner, you can begin this new stage sooner, too. The point is to spend the middle three or four months of your thesis project doing directed research, organizing your notes, prewriting, and then drafting sections of the thesis.

If you and your adviser prefer to work from a more detailed outline, then do that (or, better yet, do that plus some prewriting). Just be sure to update your outline as you draft the thesis and discuss the updated version with your adviser. Give yourself every opportunity to learn and adapt as you research and write.

Whichever approach you take, don't worry about the introduction and conclusion at this stage. You will tackle them toward the end of the drafting process, but not until then. I'll discuss that in chapter 10.

**TIME SCHEDULE FOR MONTHS 3–5
(OR MONTHS 3–6, DEPENDING ON YOUR SCHOOL SCHEDULE):
RESEARCH AND WRITING**

Reading: Focused research and planning

Writing: Prewrite middle sections of thesis
Write and revise middle sections
Prewrite the introduction and conclusion

CHECKLIST: PLANNING AND PREWRITING

- Establish main categories for your paper (similar to Roman numerals in an outline).
- Line up categories in a logical order—the building blocks of your argument.
- Sort your research and notes into these categories.
- Amplify your work in each category by writing sentences and paragraphs (prewriting).
- Build on this prewriting and research to draft brief stand-alone papers for categories.
- Look for gaps in your research and begin filling them.

9 WRITING YOUR BEST

You are not only a researcher; you are a writer. The two tasks are intimately bound together. Good organization and crisp language are the high road to engaging your readers and persuading them.

Early in the paper, you should lay out your major argument—that is, your thesis statement. That's important for you *both as a writer and a researcher*. It will guide your readers through the entire paper and give them a clear sense of your main points. That's why it should be placed prominently in the introduction, where it can orient readers for the journey to come.[1]

The thesis statement's importance does not mean it has to appear at the top of page 1. That's a very visible spot, and you might commandeer it for a compelling story or quote to engage readers. (For an example, see how I begin chapter 11.) Or you might prefer to give a general introduction to your topic, with a little caffeine kick. That's what I try to do in most chapters of this book, including this one. But whatever your opening is, use it effectively and then turn to the main questions you want to raise and the argument of your thesis. State them clearly, briefly, and early. Don't bury them. Don't try to be overly subtle and indirect in presenting them. State them directly.

> *Tip:* Your argument and your main questions should appear early in the paper, stated as simply and clearly as possible.

This sets the stage for you to explain

- Why your topic is important—in practical terms, in theory, or in both
- What methods you will use to investigate it
- What texts or evidence you will rely on

---

1. The importance of your thesis statement, or main argument, is discussed in chapter 7. In chapter 10, I will discuss how to place it prominently in your introduction.

If you are using some key terms (such as the term "argument" in the last few chapters), introduce them as they arise and define them in simple, precise language, perhaps reinforced by an example or two. Using these terms consistently will establish a *core vocabulary* for your project, one you share with your readers and then use repeatedly throughout your thesis.

> *Tip:* Define key terms simply and precisely. Then use them consistently as a core vocabulary throughout your thesis.

Of course, you can't cover everything in the first few pages—certainly not in any detail—but you should at least pose your central questions and explain your argument. Beyond that, you should briefly introduce some other major elements of your thesis to prepare the reader for a full discussion later. You might mention what kinds of evidence you will use, for example, or which theories you will consider. There's no need to offer many details at this point, but flagging these topics will orient your readers. All this should unfold smoothly, giving your readers confidence that your analysis will proceed in a sensible, orderly way.

REMEMBERING YOUR AUDIENCE

Always remember you are writing for others, as well as yourself. You want readers to understand the topic and your ideas about it. You want to persuade them that your analysis offers useful insights into an important issue. It's helpful to assume they are open-minded and receptive but need a little convincing. Show them that your topic is well worth their time, your approach is fruitful, and your conclusions are logical and well-grounded.

> *Tip:* Always remember you are writing for an audience. Think of them as intelligent peers you want to educate and persuade.

Thinking of your readers as peers encourages a more natural conversational tone. And it avoids a cardinal sin: talking down to your audience. Never, ever do it. You might tell a friend, for example, that you consider Einstein the most important scientist of the twentieth century or that he revolutionized physics while still a young clerk in a Swiss patent office. But you would never say, "Einstein, the well-known scientist . . . ." That's not just starched language; it assumes you are talking to a moron. "Hold on, I thought you were talking about Einstein the bagel maker."

A thesis that begins, "William Shakespeare, in his play *Hamlet*," is in trouble before it reaches the first verb. We're just fortunate Shakespeare didn't have a middle name, or it would be included, too. Yes, we may need to be told that *The Cherry Orchard* is a play or *The Wasteland* is a poem, but *Hamlet* is the most famous play by the most gifted writer in the English language. It is part of our common cultural heritage. Better to say: "In *Hamlet's* opening scene, Shakespeare writes . . . ."

Assume your readers are intelligent and well educated; they're just not experts in your field. They want useful information, clear ideas, and compelling analysis. Give it to them in simple, lucid prose, without ever talking down to them.

> *Tip:* Never talk down to your readers. Let me repeat that slowly. . . .

To write like that, you need to keep your readers constantly in mind. Most of all, you need to show them genuine courtesy. Since we research and write alone, it is all too easy to ignore this world of readers, to think we are writing only for ourselves. We *should* write for ourselves, but not for ourselves alone. We should remember that we are also writing for others who want to understand the subject. Give them clear language and convincing arguments.

> *Tip:* Good thesis writing is clear, convincing, and courteous to readers.

Presenting your draft work to advisers, tutors, and workshops is a continuous reminder that somewhere out there, lurking behind the computer screen, are actual readers. Thinking about them and their needs will improve your writing. The moral of this tale: Respect your audience. It worked for the very famous English playwright, the Bard of Avon, William R. Shakespeare. It will work for you, too.

TIGHT, CLEAR WRITING

Aim for taut presentation. Your writing and editing should eliminate fat wherever you find it, without severing muscle or bone. That means following the wise advice of Strunk and White: no extraneous words, sentences, paragraphs, or sections.[2] They weigh down your prose, distracting readers and obscuring your ideas.

> *Tip:* Write as clearly as you can, with unaffected prose. Prune the excess words so your ideas can shine through.

Compliment your readers, says John Trimble, "by writing as if they preferred unaffected, unsolemn, conversational prose to the pretentious Formal variety."[3] Trimble is not just saying which words to use. He is saying how to treat your readers. Respect their intelligence and acknowledge their quest for understanding, their sense of humor, and their desire for graceful language with an occasional snap of surprise.

This combination of clarity, simplicity, and courtesy is the opposite of dumbing down or oversimplifying. It's the enemy of jargon and pretentious blather. It's the bodyguard of obscure ideas that are, at bottom, hiding from honest debate. This kind of bloated prose is all too common in academic journals, I'm afraid. It is not modeled on great science or humanistic scholarship. It is modeled on the Wizard of Oz, where heavy curtains and the Wizard's booming voice conceal a tiny, fearful man and a fundamental fraud. That's no model for you.

PRACTICAL ADVICE ABOUT WRITING YOUR BEST

This spare viewpoint on writing yields practical advice for your thesis. Let me hit the high points and add some explanations or illustrations where I think they might help:

---

2. Strunk and White is the bible of clear, concise writing. William Strunk Jr. and E. B. White, *The Elements of Style,* 4th ed. (New York: Longman, 2000).

3. John R. Trimble, *Writing with Style: Conversations on the Art of Writing,* 2nd ed. (Upper Saddle River, NJ: Prentice Hall, 2000), 87.

- *Write courageously.* Present your ideas as clearly as possible so others can understand and engage them.

    When readers understand you, they may agree or disagree, but at least they know where you stand and why you hold the views you do. You have launched an honest discussion, and that is a contribution in its own right, even if others disagree. That is how knowledge advances.

- *Use plain, unadorned language.*

    Don't use long words when short ones will do. Don't use Latinate words when Anglo-Saxon ones carry the same meaning. Avoid pretentiousness. "Short words are the best," Churchill said, "and old words when short are best of all."

    On the other hand, never simplify to improve readability *when it would distort your meaning.* It's fine to trot out elaborate words and complex sentences occasionally when you need them to convey your precise meaning. Just think hard before you do it.

    T. S. Eliot pointed the way to combining plain language with (occasional) more elaborate forms:

    > The common word exact without vulgarity,
    > The formal word precise but not pedantic,
    > The complete consort dancing together[4]

- *Write in the active voice.*

    The passive voice is not only weak and clumsy; it often conceals the main player—the one who is doing the acting. That's why it is so beloved of politicians and public figures in deep trouble. Their mantra is "Mistakes were made." That language intentionally obscures the crucial question: "Who made the mistakes?" They say, "Revenues should be enhanced," not "I want to raise taxes." George Orwell drives home this point in his classic essay "Politics and the English Language."[5] It is a rallying cry against the deadening language of bureaucratic control. Don't fall into that trap yourself. Write in compact, transparent language. Tell your readers exactly who is doing what to whom and why. Write in the active voice.

---

4. T. S. Eliot, *Little Gidding* (London: Faber and Faber, [1942]).

5. George Orwell, "Politics and the English Language," in *Shooting an Elephant and Other Essays* (New York: Harcourt Brace Jovanovich, 1946).

Along the same lines, avoid weak verbs like "is," "was," and other forms of "to be." We all have to use them sometimes, but don't overdose.

Let strong verbs carry the heavy load, without flowery modifiers. This follows the advice of my friend, a chef, who told me how to read a menu: "You can't eat adjectives."

- *When editing, cut deeply and cut often to get rid of extra words and stray thoughts.*

It's easy to fall in love with our own words. It's partly self-love— the story of Narcissus enchanted by his own reflection—and partly the memory of how long it took to hammer out that particular sentence or paragraph. Remember, instead, your reader's needs. They are paramount.

To make the cuts less painful, set up a "scrap file." The file should be organized to reflect the different sections of your paper. When you delete a sentence or paragraph you might wish to reinstate, just put it in the appropriate section of the scrap file. That way, you can always put it back in.

Chances are you won't reuse any of these sentences. That's certainly been my experience. In fact, the main reason for this scrap file is psychological. It's easier to remove a paragraph that took an hour to write if you know you are "just moving it to another file," not murdering it with an ice pick. Occasionally, you'll return to the scrap graveyard and revive a sentence you want to use. It's amazing how rarely that happens. ~~That proves you were right: you really could cut it out.~~

- *When in doubt, break long sentences into shorter ones, as long as the result is not choppy.*

There is nothing inherently wrong with long sentences. At their best, they are graceful, rolling, and elegant. The Declaration of Independence, a masterpiece of persuasive writing, begins with one: "When in the course of human events it becomes necessary for one people to dissolve the political bands which have connected them with another . . . ." That sentence runs for seventy-one words. The next one is even longer and equally famous.

So why do nearly all writing teachers say, "Avoid them"? Because most of us are not Thomas Jefferson. Long sentences, with their elegantly framed subordinate clauses, were integral features of good writing in the eighteenth century. Jefferson, Edward Gibbon, and Samuel Johnson mastered them. But developing that mastery took years and always required a deft hand.

Long, complex sentences are more difficult to control and more likely to contain unneeded words. They can meander through vast, prickly fields of verbiage and tangential thoughts. Compact prose is more powerful, more likely to drive home your point.

Short sentences do pose some risks, though. They can be choppy, monotonous, and singsong: "See Spot run. Run, Spot, run." Tedious. At their worst, they talk down to readers. To avoid these problems, simply vary the length and construction of your sentences. Change their rhythm from time to time. You can also try one more trick; occasionally join some short sentences with a semicolon.

- *Write brief, coherent paragraphs, each with a single topic sentence.*

Paragraphs, not sentences, are the building blocks of your prose. Well-constructed paragraphs develop your questions and answers in orderly ways. Building them is like any other craft. It is improved by attentive practice and mentoring, just like pottery or woodworking, but with less heavy machinery.

Each paragraph should have a single idea, captured in a topic sentence. The topic sentence is usually the first or second in the paragraph, though that's not a hard-and-fast rule.

Paragraphs should be relatively short and focused. If any run over five or six sentences, check to see if you are cramming too much into them. But don't chop them in half just "because." Divide a group of sentences when you realize it actually contains *two* paragraphs, with two topic sentences. That's why you are checking.

Occasionally, you may want to write a one-sentence paragraph. That's not illegal or fattening, as long as you don't do it too often. Used carefully, they can change the pace of your writing, create surprise, and, most of all, highlight a point. That's why they are valuable.

That's also why they should be used sparingly.

- *Rewrite any sentences that string together prepositions.*

If you find three or four prepositions in a sentence, perform emergency surgery. Compare these examples, the first with several prepositions strung together, the second without them.

(1) <u>In</u> defense <u>of</u> his theory <u>of</u> the beginning <u>of</u> World War II, Gerhard Weinberg states . . . .

(2) Defending his theory of how World War II began, Gerhard Weinberg states . . . .

The revised version is easier to read, with no loss of meaning. That's exactly what you should aim for.

- *When you mention a person for the first time, use the full name, unless it is Aristotle, Shakespeare, or a rock diva.* After that, use a shortened form, and be consistent.

  "Toni Morrison's *Beloved* explores the deep, continuing wounds of slavery through a powerful narrative and complex characters. Morrison writes that . . . ."

- *Check to see if you are repeating yourself or using the same words too often.*

  Check to see if you are repeating yourself or using the same words too often. Check to see . . . .

  Let me take an example from this book. When I reread an early draft, I realized I had used the adjective "key" far too often. Everything seemed to be a "key idea" or "key point." The repetition was boring. So I lost the *key*s and replaced them with synonyms. Variety engages your readers.

  There is one important exception, one area where you should avoid variety: core vocabulary terms. *Don't use synonyms for core terms* since they may confuse your readers. Analytic terms like "argument" should be defined early and used consistently so readers become familiar with them.

- *Use direct quotations sparingly and name the person being quoted.*

  I'll discuss quotations below and show how to use them effectively.

- *Review your opening and closing paragraphs, and edit them with special care.* They are the most important in the paper.

  The opening lines have the most difficult task in the entire thesis: they need to announce your subject while enticing the reader to continue.

  The closing paragraphs are almost as important since they offer your principal conclusions.

  I'll discuss both in the next chapter.

- *Know the rules of grammar, but don't be an ayatollah.* When the rules produce stiff, awkward language, bend the rules not the reader.

Grammatical rules make communication easier and more reliable. That's why you should know them, and why you should use them correctly . . . most of the time. Bend the rules—knowledgeably, self-consciously—when they damage your conversational tone or interfere with sensible speech. Churchill clinched the point with ridicule, the sharpest of all rhetorical tools. The target was a proofreader, who had primly corrected his manuscript, striking out a sentence that ended with a preposition. Churchill responded: "This is an impertinence up with which I will not put."

- *Use examples, stories, quotations, hypothetical cases, and anecdotes to enliven your abstract language and theoretical presentation.*

They vary the tone, quicken the pace, illustrate your points, and make your paper more accessible. They are not out of place in a thesis, as long as they actually make a point and you don't run them into the ground.

- *Read aloud as you edit, or read silently but hear the words.*

One of the best ways to improve your writing is to read it aloud to yourself. I know it seems silly, but it really works, and all good writers know it. If your sentences sound leaden when you read them aloud, then you've struck lead, not gold. As a practiced reader, you can hear when your own prose sounds wrong or even a little off. If your roommate complains, read silently but listen for the words. Or get a new roommate.

- *Edit, edit, and edit some more.*

I will discuss editing in the next two chapters, but it can't be postponed entirely. After all, editing begins the moment you choose one word instead of another. Mark Twain, who knew something about these matters, said, "Use the right word and not its second cousin."

It's impossible to write well without editing continuously. One or two editorial passes through the text is not enough. Your first draft and even your second may not produce the clear argument and graceful prose you want. Persist. Careful editing is *the* way to make your thesis sharper, deeper, and more readable. Keep going through your text, and keep editing each time you do. That's the surest way to produce your best work.

As you begin work each day, read what you wrote the day before. That's an excellent way to edit because you approach the cold text with a fresh attitude. Be sure to do it with a pen in hand so you can smooth out your sentences and shuffle paragraphs to the right spot.

None of this is rocket science. Mostly, it's a matter of caring about your prose and caring about your readers. That, plus some practice, will make you a more lucid writer and a more persuasive one.

You certainly get a lot of practice, whether you like it or not, as you write your thesis. You are constantly preparing notes, short papers, and draft sections, and receiving faculty comments on them. You can use this drafting and editing to grow as a writer *if you make it your goal.*

Contrary to the old adage, practice does not make perfect. Sometimes, it just perpetuates the same old problems. That's as true of writing as it is of other endeavors. To improve, you have to make improvement your goal, monitor your work, and, above all, edit your writing with a good ear as well as a sharp pen. If you do that, then practice *will* make perfect.

FORMAL VERSUS INFORMAL LANGUAGE

As you've probably noticed, I use conversational language throughout this book. I don't hesitate to use contractions or begin sentences with personal references. That doesn't make the analysis any less thoughtful or rigorous, I hope, but it does change the tone.

You and your adviser may prefer a different tone. In fact, most theses use more formal language, as do most books and articles. They avoid contractions and rarely use personal references. The writing is more reserved and professional. That should *not* mean it is starched, dull, and dry.

The differences between formal and informal styles are easy to see by comparing sentences that say essentially the same thing:

Formal	Informal
That is a compelling argument.	I certainly agree with that argument.
Do not use contractions.	Don't use contractions.

So, which language should *you* use? That depends on several things: which feels most comfortable to you as a writer and a reader, which style your adviser prefers or requires, and whether your field avoids informal language.

To make your choice, think about the articles that have impressed you, especially those you consider well written. Think, too, about how you prefer to write. Review your work to see which style you use and whether you do so consistently. Of course, your style can differ from assignment to assignment, but an individual paper shouldn't wobble back and forth.

After you've done this homework, ask your adviser's opinion about one of your early drafts. Is your style suitable and effective? Working from a writing sample like this, you can go beyond an abstract discussion about "how to write." You can talk concretely about how well you express your views, the tone you strike, and whether your adviser thinks it is appropriate for your thesis.

Whichever style you choose, you can write well that way. Formal sentences do not have to be stiff. Informal ones don't have to be sloppy. You can write powerfully and precisely using either style.

USING QUOTATIONS

Quotations are a great resource and an important element in thesis writing. But don't overuse them. Avoid them when you are simply presenting data or well-known opinions. It's better to rephrase those quotes in your own words and cite the sources in a note.

Don't use any quotes without explaining, in the text itself, who is talking. Sometimes quotes simply stagger in, out of nowhere. They arrive with no name tag and no introduction, and the reader stumbles over them. "That's absolutely true." Citations don't correct this particular problem. You need to introduce quotes first.

Tips on quotations:
- Use them judiciously.
- Name the speaker.
- Introduce long quotes so your text makes sense even if readers skip the quote.

Use the *exact* words whenever you quote. If you leave something out, add an ellipsis (which is simply three dots with spaces before and after each one). If the omission comes in the middle of a sentence, then an ellipsis . . . is all you need. If the omission comes at the end, then you need a period and an ellipsis. . . . If you insert a word to make a sentence understandable, put it in [brackets].[6] If the writer misspells or makes a grammatical error, reproduce it exactly and add the bracketed term [*sic*] where the mistake occurs, unless your addition would sound fussy. If you add *italics* for emphasis, the footnote or endnote should say "italics are my own."

> *Rule:* Use the exact words when you quote, along with quotation marks and proper citation. If you omit words, use ellipses . . . and use [brackets] if you add them.

TWO TIMES WHEN YOU SHOULD USE QUOTES

When are quotes most useful? In at least two instances. First, some quotations capture a speaker's striking, memorable language. For example:

In President John Kennedy's ambitious phrase, "We will pay any price, bear any burden."[7]

"Politicians *are* interested in people," P. J. O'Rourke observes. "Not that this is always a virtue. Fleas are interested in dogs."[8]

As George Bernard Shaw put it, "Assassination is the extreme form of censorship."[9]

What sensible person would want to paraphrase those words?

Second, well-chosen quotes can illustrate the viewpoint—and sometimes even the character—of a scholar, policy maker, or participant. The

---

6. These points are covered in more detail in chapter 3.

7. John F. Kennedy, "Inaugural Address," January 20, 1961, in *The Public Papers of the Presidents of the United States: John F. Kennedy, 1961* (Washington, DC: Government Printing Office, 1962), 1.

8. P. J. O'Rourke, *Parliament of Whores* (New York: Vintage Books, 1991), 58.

9. George Bernard Shaw, "The Rejected Statement," in *The Doctor's Dilemma, Getting Married, and The Shewing-up of Blanco Posnet* (London: Constable, 1911), at http://www.gutenberg.net/dirs/etext04/shwbp10.txt (accessed August 9, 2004).

words may not be memorable in their own right, but they reveal the speaker. For example:

> Senator Joseph McCarthy did more than call his opponents misguided; he repeatedly damned them as "communists" or "fellow travelers."

> Lenin, who understood dictatorships since he ran a brutal one himself, called them "authority untrammeled by any laws, absolutely unrestricted by any rules whatever, and based directly on force."[10]

Lenin's quote does not just tell us about dictatorships. It tells us about Lenin. The McCarthy quotes are examples of his demagoguery.

Tip: Use quotes to capture distinctive language or reveal the speaker's viewpoint. Avoid them for more pedestrian materials, which you should paraphrase.

USING LONG QUOTES

What about much longer quotes, running several sentences? Use them sparingly unless your project is mainly a textual analysis, such as the study of a novel. When you do use longer quotes, set them off from the text, indent them, and place citations in their usual spot, at the end of the quotation. When you use indents like this, you should omit the quotation marks. They are implied; your readers will understand this is quoted material.

Because long quotes interrupt the narrative flow, it is important to introduce them with one or two summary sentences. A fortunate by-product of this introduction is that your text will still make sense if readers skip over the quotes, which they sometimes do. Here, for example, is my introduction to a longer quote from Mahatma Gandhi:

In 1922 Mohandas Gandhi was convicted of sedition. His crime: writing magazine articles that opposed British rule in India. Before sentencing, Gandhi was allowed to address the court. It was a highly charged moment, and Gandhi made the most of it, defending his actions and explaining his strategy of nonviolent resistance:

---

10. Quoted in J. M. Roberts, *Twentieth Century: The History of the World, 1901 to 2000* (New York: Viking, 1999), 294.

> Nonviolence is the first article of my faith. . . . But I had to make my choice. I had either to submit to a system which I considered had done an irreparable harm to my country, or incur the risk of the mad fury of my people bursting forth, when they understood the truth from my lips. . . . I do not ask for mercy. I do not plead any extenuating act. I am here, therefore, to invite and cheerfully submit to the highest penalty that can be inflicted upon me for what in law is a deliberate crime and what appears to me to be the highest duty of a citizen.[11]

This example shows how to handle a longer quotation. First, it is introduced with a sentence or two, followed by a colon before the quote itself. Because Gandhi's comments run several sentences, they are indented rather than included in a normal paragraph. The indentation signals a quote, so there is no need for quotation marks. Finally, the note reference appears at the end of the quoted material.

PUTTING QUOTATION MARKS AROUND "ORDINARY WORDS"

Sometimes, students use quotation marks around "ordinary words" in the middle of a sentence. Be careful. It's fine to say: He went downtown wearing "casual Friday" clothes. You are putting quotation marks around a characteristic term to call attention to it. Or you might say:

> What the military often calls "collateral damage" is really killing and maiming innocent civilians, smothered in the numbing language of bureaucracies.

The quotation marks around "collateral damage" are fine because they refer to specific words used by government officials.

What is irritating, however, is to see quotation marks used to make sly arguments, a passive-aggressive way of showing the writer is superior to the subject. Compare these two sentences:

- France is a civilized country.
- France is a "civilized" country.

---

11. "Gandhi Defends His Beliefs," in *Lend Me Your Ears: Great Speeches in History*, ed. William Safire (New York: W. W. Norton, 1992), 323.

In the second one, the writer is striking a snide, ironic pose. Sarcasm like this rarely works, although you've certainly got a better shot if the target is France. It won't work at all unless you lay the proper groundwork or follow the quote immediately with supporting evidence. These, for example, meet the rules:

- France is said to be a "civilized" country, but it certainly treats its immigrants, religious minorities, and allies in uncivil ways.
- Many call France a "civilized" country, and after visiting the Louvre and lingering over a demitasse at a nearby café, who could deny it?

If you don't offer such explanations, then you are trying to sneak your viewpoint in the backdoor, hoping nobody's guarding it. Don't. Say what you mean and argue openly for your view. My advice is to use this kind of "in-line quote" only when you want to flag a word's use (or misuse) and have made your purpose clear.

> *Tip:* Be careful using quotation marks around "ordinary words." They are fine to highlight a word or phrase people are saying. Don't use them as sarcastic put-downs.

HE SAID, SHE SAID

Finally, a few words about identifying the speaker in the text. "Most of the time, his name should go at the beginning or end," according to Dr. Lipson, "but it adds variety to put it in the middle occasionally."

Be consistent about using the present tense or past tense to identify when someone spoke or wrote. If you say, "Mark Twain writes frequently about small-town life," then don't lapse into "Henry James *wrote* about cities." This consistency is important not only for identifying quotations but for the rest of your text as well.

> *Tip:* Don't wobble between present tense and past tense in your text or in introducing quotes.

Most quotes are best introduced with straightforward words like "said," "wrote," "noted," or "observed." Don't spend too much effort trying to add variety here. Plain words are usually the best choice. Steer clear of frilly modifiers. "Go easy on the adverbs," he opined emphatically.

**TIME SCHEDULE FOR MONTHS 3–5
(OR MONTHS 3–6, DEPENDING ON YOUR SCHOOL SCHEDULE):
WRITING AND REVISING THE MIDDLE SECTIONS**

Reading:	Focused research and planning
Writing:	Prewrite middle sections of thesis
	Write and revise the middle sections
	Prewrite the introduction and conclusion

CHECKLIST: EFFECTIVE WRITING

- Write with plain, unaffected language.
- Use the active voice.
- Cut excess words.
- Write brief, coherent paragraphs, each based on a topic sentence.
- Use examples, stories, and quotes to enliven your text.
- Proofread each version of your text for spelling and grammar.
- Above all, make sure your ideas come through clearly.

Now that we've discussed writing in general, let's consider two areas where good writing is vital: the introduction and conclusion. They are the most important pages in your thesis, and they should be the best written. The opening section should entice readers and pose your main questions directly; the final section should state your answers firmly and clearly. The next chapter discusses how you can write strong introductions and conclusions—and drive home your major ideas.

10 EFFECTIVE OPENINGS, SMOOTH TRANSITIONS, AND STRONG CLOSINGS

Now that we have covered some general writing issues, let's turn to a couple of specific tasks: writing your paper's introduction and conclusion. (We dealt with the middle sections in chapter 8, on prewriting.) Your opening and closing sections will be read more carefully than any others, so it's crucial to make them your best. Begin by taking control of the subject matter. Raise the questions *you* want to raise, say why they are important, and state your argument. Then, after developing your argument and evidence in the middle sections, bring your paper to a strong conclusion by drawing together your answers, insights, and judgments.

GOALS OF YOUR INTRODUCTION

The introductory section of the paper should do three things:

- Entice the reader into the subject matter, beginning with a compelling anecdote, concrete example, real-life puzzle, or powerful overview, which should come in the first paragraph.
- Explain the topic you are studying, the material you will cover, and your argument about it; this overview of the project should come soon after the opening paragraphs.
- Orient your reader by giving a "road map" for the overall paper, explaining briefly the order of upcoming sections and what each will do; this should come at the end of the introductory section.

Let's see how these goals are accomplished. How can you do them well? How can you avoid the pitfalls?

YOUR OPENING PARAGRAPHS

The first page of your thesis should draw the reader into the text. It is the paper's most important page and, alas, often the worst written. There are two culprits here and effective ways to cope with both of them.

First, the writer is usually straining too hard to say something terribly BIG and IMPORTANT about the thesis topic. The goal is worthy, but the aim is unrealistically high. The result is often a muddle of vague platitudes rather than a crisp, compelling introduction to the thesis. Want a familiar example? Listen to most graduation speakers. Their goal couldn't be loftier: to say what education means and to tell an entire football stadium how to live the rest of their lives. The results are usually an avalanche of clichés and sodden prose.

The second culprit is bad timing. The opening and concluding paragraphs are usually written late in the game, after the rest of the thesis is finished and polished. There's nothing wrong with writing these sections last. It's usually the right approach since you need to know exactly what you are saying in the substantive middle sections of the thesis before you can introduce them effectively or draw together your findings. But having waited to write the opening and closing sections, you need to review and edit them several times to catch up. Otherwise, you'll putting the most jagged prose in the most tender spots.

> *Tip:* Edit and polish your opening paragraphs with extra care. They should draw readers into the paper.

After you've done some extra polishing, I suggest a simple test for the introductory section. As an experiment, chop off the first few paragraphs. Let the paper begin on, say, paragraph 2 or even page 2. If you don't lose much, or actually gain in clarity and pace, then you've got a problem.

There are two solutions. One is to start at this new spot, further into the text. After all, that's where you finally gain traction on your subject. That works best in some cases, and I occasionally suggest it. The alternative, of course, is to write a new opening that doesn't flop around, saying nothing.

What makes a good opening? Actually, they come in several flavors. One is an intriguing story about your topic. Another is a brief, compelling quote. When you run across them during your reading, set them aside for later use. Don't be deterred from using them because they "don't seem academic enough." They're fine as long as the rest of the paper doesn't sound like you did your research in *People* magazine. The third, and most common, way to begin is by stating your main questions, followed by a brief comment about why they matter.

> *Tip:* Good openings take several forms. Some use illuminating stories or quotes. Some raise hard questions. Others simply state the subject matter and the argument, saying why they are important and worth studying.

Whichever opening you choose, it should engage your readers and coax them to continue. Having done that, you should give them a general overview of the project—the main issues you will cover, the material you will use, and your thesis statement (that is, your basic approach to the topic). Finally, at the end of the introductory section, give your readers a brief road map, showing how the paper will unfold.

EXAMPLES OF EFFECTIVE OPENINGS

Quotes, anecdotes, questions, examples, and broad statements—all of them have been used successfully to begin academic books and articles. It's instructive to see them in action, in the hands of skilled academic writers.

Let's begin with David M. Kennedy's superb history, *Freedom from Fear: The American People in Depression and War, 1929–1945*. Kennedy begins each chapter with a quote, followed by his text. The quote above chapter 1 shows President Hoover speaking in 1928 about America's golden future. The text below it begins with the stock market collapse of 1929. It is a riveting account of just how wrong Hoover was. The text about the Depression is stronger because it contrasts so starkly with the optimistic quotation.

> *"We in America today are nearer the final triumph over poverty than ever before in the history of any land."*—Herbert Hoover, August 11, 1928

Like an earthquake, the stock market crash of October 1929 cracked startlingly across the United States, the herald of a crisis that was to shake the American way of life to its foundations. The events of the ensuing decade opened a fissure across the landscape of American history no less gaping than that opened by the volley on Lexington Common in

April 1775 or by the bombardment of Sumter on another April four score and six years later.

The ratcheting ticker machines in the autumn of 1929 did not merely record avalanching stock prices. In time they came also to symbolize the end of an era.[1]

Kennedy has exciting, wrenching material to work with. John Mueller faces the exact opposite problem. In *Retreat from Doomsday: The Obsolescence of Major War,* he is trying to explain why Great Powers have suddenly stopped fighting each other. For centuries they made war on each other with devastating regularity, killing millions in the process. But now, Mueller thinks, they have not just paused; they have stopped permanently. He is literally trying to explain why "nothing is happening now." That may be an exciting topic intellectually, it may have great practical significance, but "nothing happened" is not a very promising subject for an exciting opening paragraph. Mueller manages to make it exciting and, at the same time, shows why it matters so much. Here's his opening, aptly entitled "History's Greatest Nonevent":

On May 15, 1984, the major countries of the developed world had managed to remain at peace with each other for the longest continuous stretch of time since the days of the Roman Empire. If a significant battle in a war had been fought on that day, the press would have bristled with it. As usual, however, a landmark crossing in the history of peace caused no stir: the most prominent story in the *New York Times* that day concerned the saga of a manicurist, a machinist, and a cleaning woman who had just won a big Lotto contest.

This book seeks to develop an explanation for what is probably the greatest nonevent in human history.[2]

In the space of a few sentences, Mueller sets up his puzzle and reveals its profound human significance. At the same time, he shows just how easy it is to miss this milestone in the buzz of daily events. Notice how concretely he does that. He doesn't just say that the *New York Times* ignored this record-

---

1. David M. Kennedy, *Freedom from Fear: The American People in Depression and War, 1929–1945* (New York: Oxford University Press, 1999), 10.

2. John Mueller, *Retreat from Doomsday: The Obsolescence of Major War* (New York: Basic Books, 1989), 3.

setting peace. He offers telling details about what they covered instead: "a manicurist, a machinist, and a cleaning woman who had just won a big Lotto contest." Likewise, David Kennedy immediately entangles us in concrete events: the stunning stock market crash of 1929. These are powerful openings that capture readers' interests, establish puzzles, and launch narratives.

Sociologist James Coleman begins in a completely different way, by posing the basic questions he will study. His ambitious book, *Foundations of Social Theory*, develops a comprehensive theory of social life, so it is entirely appropriate for him to begin with some major questions. But he could just as easily have begun with a compelling story or anecdote. He includes many of them elsewhere in his book. His choice for the opening, though, is to state his major themes plainly and frame them as a paradox. Sociologists, he says, are interested in aggregate behavior—how people act in groups, organizations, or large numbers—yet they mostly examine individuals:

> A central problem in social science is that of accounting for the function of some kind of social system. Yet in most social research, observations are not made on the system as a whole, but on some part of it. In fact, the natural unit of observation is the individual person . . . . This has led to a widening gap between theory and research . . . .[3]

After expanding on this point, Coleman explains that he will not try to remedy the problem by looking solely at groups or aggregate-level data. That's a false solution, he says, because aggregates don't act; individuals do. So the real problem is to show the links between individual actions and aggregate outcomes, between the micro and the macro.

> The major problem for explanations of system behavior based on actions and orientations at a level below that of the system [in this case, on individual-level actions] is that of moving from the lower level to the system level. This has been called the micro-to-macro problem, and it is pervasive throughout the social sciences.[4]

Explaining how to deal with this "micro-to-macro problem" is the central issue of Coleman's book, and he announces it at the beginning.

---

3. James S. Coleman, *Foundations of Social Theory* (Cambridge, MA: Harvard University Press, 1990), 1–2.

4. Coleman, *Foundations of Social Theory*, 6.

Coleman's theory-driven opening stands at the opposite end of the spectrum from engaging stories or anecdotes, which are designed to lure the reader into the narrative and ease the path to a more analytic treatment later in the text. Take, for example, the opening sentences of Robert L. Herbert's sweeping study *Impressionism: Art, Leisure, and Parisian Society:* "When Henry Tuckerman came to Paris in 1867, one of the thousands of Americans attracted there by the huge international exposition, he was bowled over by the extraordinary changes since his previous visit twenty years before."[5] Herbert fills in the evocative details to set the stage for his analysis of the emerging Impressionist art movement and its connection to Parisian society and leisure in this period.

David Bromwich writes about Wordsworth, a poet so familiar to students of English literature that it is hard to see him afresh, before his great achievements, when he was just a young outsider starting to write. To draw us into Wordsworth's early work, Bromwich wants us to set aside our entrenched images of the famous mature poet and see him as he was in the 1790s, as a beginning writer on the margins of society. He accomplishes this ambitious task in the opening sentences of *Disowned by Memory: Wordsworth's Poetry of the 1790s:*

> Wordsworth turned to poetry after the revolution to remind himself that he was still a human being. It was a curious solution, to a difficulty many would not have felt. The whole interest of his predicament is that he did feel it. Yet Wordsworth is now so established an eminence—his name so firmly fixed with readers as a moralist of self-trust emanating from complete self-security—that it may seem perverse to imagine him as a criminal seeking expiation. Still, that is a picture we get from *The Borderers* and, at a longer distance, from "Tintern Abbey."[6]

That's a wonderful opening. Look at how much Bromwich accomplishes in just a few words. He not only prepares the way for analyzing Wordsworth's early poetry; he juxtaposes the anguished young man who wrote it to the self-confident, distinguished figure he became—the eminent man we can't help remembering as we read his early poetry.

---

5. Robert L. Herbert, *Impressionism: Art, Leisure, and Parisian Society* (New Haven, CT: Yale University Press, 1988), 1.

6. David Bromwich, *Disowned by Memory: Wordsworth's Poetry of the 1790s* (Chicago: University of Chicago Press, 1998), 1.

Let me highlight a couple of other points in this passage because they illustrate some intelligent writing choices. First, look at the odd comma in this sentence: "It was a curious solution, to a difficulty many would not have felt." Any standard grammar book would say that comma is wrong and should be omitted. Why did Bromwich insert it? Because he's a fine writer, thinking of his sentence rhythm and the point he wants to make. The comma does exactly what it should. It makes us pause, breaking the sentence into two parts, each with an interesting point. One is that Wordsworth felt a difficulty others would not have; the other is that he solved it in a distinctive way. It would be easy for readers to glide over this double message, so Bromwich has inserted a speed bump to slow us down. Most of the time, you should follow grammatical rules, like those about commas, but you should bend them when it serves a good purpose. That's what the writer does here.

The second small point is the phrase "after the revolution" in the first sentence: "Wordsworth turned to poetry after the revolution to remind himself that he was still a human being." Why doesn't Bromwich say "after the *French* Revolution"? Because he has judged his book's audience. He is writing for specialists who already know which revolution is reverberating through English life in the 1790s. It is the French Revolution, not the earlier loss of the American colonies. If Bromwich were writing for a much broader audience—say, the *New York Times Book Review*—he would probably insert the extra word to avoid confusion.

The message "Know your audience" applies to all writers. Don't talk down to them by assuming they can't get dressed in the morning. Don't strut around showing off your book learnin' by tossing in arcane facts and esoteric language for its own sake. Neither will win over readers.

Bromwich, Herbert, and Coleman open their works in different ways, but their choices work well for their different texts. Your task is to decide what kind of opening will work best for *yours*. Don't let that happen by default, by grabbing the first idea you happen upon. Consider a couple of different ways of opening your thesis and then choose the one you prefer. Give yourself some options, think them over, then make an informed choice.

USING THE INTRODUCTION TO MAP OUT YOUR PAPER

Whether you begin with a story, puzzle, or broad statement, the next part of the introduction should pose your main questions and establish your argument. As earlier chapters noted, this is your thesis statement—your viewpoint along with the supporting reasons and evidence. It should be articulated plainly so readers understand full well what your paper is about and what it will argue.

After that, give your readers a road map of what's to come. That's normally done at the end of the introductory section (or, in a book, at the end of the introductory chapter). Here's John J. Mearsheimer presenting such a road map in *The Tragedy of Great Power Politics.* He not only tells us the order of upcoming chapters, he explains why he's chosen that order and which chapters are most important:

THE PLAN OF THE BOOK

The rest of the chapters in this book are concerned mainly with answering the six big questions about power which I identified earlier. Chapter 2, which is probably the most important chapter in the book, lays out my theory of why states compete for power and why they pursue hegemony.

In Chapters 3 and 4, I define power and explain how to measure it. I do this in order to lay the groundwork for testing my theory. . . .[7]

As this excerpt makes clear, Mearsheimer has already laid out his "six big questions" in the introduction. Now he's showing us the path ahead, the path to answering those questions.

> *Tip:* At the end of the introduction, give your readers a road map of what's to come. Tell them what the upcoming sections will be and why they are arranged in this particular order.

MAKING TRANSITIONS BETWEEN SECTIONS OF THE PAPER

After the introduction come the substantive middle sections of the thesis. In them, you explain your methods, present your data or textual materials, and interlace it all with your analysis and interpretation. We discussed these sections in chapter 8.

Here, I only want to mention a few more items to include as you write

---

7. John J. Mearsheimer, *The Tragedy of Great Power Politics* (New York: W. W. Norton, 2001), 27.

these middle sections. First, give each section a title, or subhead. It provides a useful guidepost to readers. If you want some examples, look at any chapter in this book. The sections within them all have descriptive subheads. Second, introduce each new section as you reach it. You can do that briefly, saying why it is important to your overall argument and why it comes next. A sentence or two will do the trick, usually at the beginning of the new section. Third, ease the transition between sections. Most should conclude with a few summary remarks and a transition, smoothing the way for the next section. Occasionally, it makes more sense to put this transition material at the beginning of the new section. Wherever it goes, the transition should lead comfortably into the next topic. It should tell the reader why you are tackling the upcoming topic, how it matters to your overall argument, and why it logically comes next in your paper.

Tip: Give each section a subhead (that is, a descriptive title). As you reach each new section, introduce it and explain why it is important. Later, as you edit, create smooth transitions between sections.

TWO ISSUES IN MAKING TRANSITIONS

There are two distinct issues in making strong transitions:

- Does the upcoming section actually belong where you have placed it?
- Have you adequately signaled the reader why you are taking this next step?

These issues correspond to the two types of editing discussed in the next chapter.

The first is the most important: Does the upcoming section actually belong in the next spot? The sections in your paper need to add up to your big point (or thesis argument) in a sensible progression. One way of putting that is, "Does the architecture of your paper correspond to the argument you are making?" Getting this architecture right is the goal of "large-scale editing," which focuses on the order of the sections, their relationship to each other, and ultimately their correspondence to your thesis argument.

It's easy to craft graceful transitions when the sections are laid out in the right order. When they're not, the transitions are bound to be rough. This difficulty, if you encounter it, is actually a valuable warning. It tells you that something is wrong and you need to change it. As one experienced thesis adviser told me: "If the points in the paper do not in fact add up to the big picture that the student wants to draw, then the transitions will be very hard to write and will likely look sloppy. Forcing students to make the transitions stronger is an important step in forcing them to be clear about what they really mean. This pays off . . . ." That's exactly right, and it's wise advice. If the transitions are awkward and difficult to write, warning bells should ring. Something is wrong with the paper's overall structure.

After you've placed the sections in the right order, you still need to tell the reader when he is changing sections and briefly explain why. That's an important part of line-by-line editing, which focuses on writing effective sentences and paragraphs.

Tip: Good transitions between sections of your paper depend on
- Getting the sections in the right order
- Moving smoothly from one section to the next
  - Signaling readers that they are taking the next step in your argument
  - Explaining why this next step comes where it does

EXAMPLES OF EFFECTIVE TRANSITIONS

Effective transition sentences and paragraphs often glance forward or backward, signaling that you are switching sections. Take this example from J. M. Roberts's *History of Europe.* He is finishing a discussion of the Punic Wars between Rome and its great rival, Carthage. The last of these wars, he says, broke out in 149 B.C. and "ended with so complete a defeat for the Carthaginians that their city was destroyed . . . ." Now he turns to a new section on "Empire." Here is the first sentence: "By then a Roman empire was in being in fact if not in name."[8] Roberts signals the transition with just

---

8. J. M. Roberts, *A History of Europe* (London: Allen Lane, 1997), 48, for both quotations.

two words: "By then." He is referring to the date (149 B.C.) given near the end of the previous section. Simple, smooth.

Michael Mandelbaum also accomplishes this transition between sections effortlessly, without bringing his narrative to a halt. In *The Ideas That Conquered the World: Peace, Democracy, and Free Markets,* one chapter shows how countries of the North Atlantic region invented the idea of peace and made it a reality among themselves. Here is his transition from one section of that chapter discussing "the idea of warlessness" to another section dealing with the history of that idea in Europe.

> The widespread aversion to war within the countries of the Western core formed the foundation for common security, which in turn expressed the spirit of warlessness. To be sure, the rise of common security in Europe did not abolish war in other parts of the world and could not guarantee its permanent abolition even on the European continent. Neither, however, was it a flukish, transient product . . . . The European common security order did have historical precedents, and its principal features began to appear in other parts of the world.

> PRECEDENTS FOR COMMON SECURITY

> The security arrangements in Europe at the dawn of the twenty-first century incorporated features of three different periods of the modern age: the nineteenth century, the interwar period, and the Cold War.[9]

It's easier to make smooth transitions when neighboring sections deal with closely related subjects, as Mandelbaum's do. Sometimes, however, you need to end one section with greater finality so you can switch to a different topic. The best way to do that is with a few summary comments at the end of the section. Your readers will understand you are drawing this topic to a close, and they won't be blindsided by your shift to a new topic in the next section.

Here's an example from economic historian Joel Mokyr's book *The Lever of Riches: Technological Creativity and Economic Progress.* Mokyr is completing a section on social values in early industrial societies. The next section deals with a quite different aspect of technological progress: the role of property rights and institutions. So Mokyr needs to take the reader across

---

9. Michael Mandelbaum, *The Ideas That Conquered the World: Peace, Democracy, and Free Markets* (New York: Public Affairs, 2002), 128.

a more abrupt change than Mandelbaum did. Mokyr does that in two ways. First, he summarizes his findings on social values, letting the reader know the section is ending. Then he says the impact of values is complicated, a point he illustrates in the final sentences, while the impact of property rights and institutions seems to be more straightforward. So he begins the new section with a nod to the old one, noting the contrast.

> In commerce, war and politics, what was functional was often preferred [within Europe] to what was aesthetic or moral, and when it was not, natural selection saw to it that such pragmatism was never entirely absent in any society. . . . The contempt in which physical labor, commerce, and other economic activity were held did not disappear rapidly; much of European social history can be interpreted as a struggle between wealth and other values for a higher step in the hierarchy. The French concepts of *bourgeois gentilhomme* and *nouveau riche* still convey some contempt for people who joined the upper classes through economic success. Even in the nineteenth century, the accumulation of wealth was viewed as an admission ticket to social respectability to be abandoned as soon as a secure membership in the upper classes had been achieved.

INSTITUTIONS AND PROPERTY RIGHTS

The institutional background of technological progress seems, on the surface, more straightforward.[10]

Note the phrase, "on the surface." Mokyr is hinting at his next point, that surface appearances are deceiving in this case.

WRITING THE CONCLUSION

Your paper should have a strong, succinct concluding section, where you draw together your findings. Think of it as a conclusion, *not* a summary. The difference is that you are reaching overall judgments about your topic, not summarizing everything you wrote about it. The focus should be on

---

10. Joel Mokyr, *The Lever of Riches: Technological Creativity and Economic Progress* (New York: Oxford University Press, 1990), 176.

- Saying what your research has found, what the findings mean, and how well they support the argument of your thesis
- Establishing the limits of your argument: How widely does it apply? What are the strengths and weaknesses of your method? How clear-cut are your findings?
- Explaining how your findings and argument fit into your field, relating them to answers others have given and to the existing literature

You may also want to add some concise comments about possible future developments or what kind of research should come next, but don't lay it on too thick.

Tip: Your final section should offer conclusions and major findings, not a summary of all that came before it. The section should
- Highlight your main findings
- Show how they support your argument
- Say how your argument and findings bear on larger issues

The place of honor goes to your own explanation. Don't spend too much of your final section criticizing others. Don't introduce any big new topics or ideas. You certainly don't expect to see new characters in the last scene of a movie. For the same reasons, you shouldn't find any big new topics being introduced in the last paragraphs of a thesis.

Your concluding statement should focus on what your findings mean. How do you interpret them? Are they just as easily explained by alternative theories or other perspectives? Here, you are returning to the questions that first animated you and answering them, based on your thesis research. You not only want to give the answers; you also want to explain their significance. What do they mean for policy, theory, literary interpretation, moral action, or whatever? You are answering the old, hard question: "So what?"

Be wary of overreaching. You really need to do two things *at the same time:* explain the significance of your findings and stake out their limits. You may have a hunch that your findings apply widely but, as a social scientist, you need to assess whether you can say so confidently, based on your current research. Your reader needs to know: "Do these findings apply to all college students, to all adults, or only to white mice?" White mice don't come up much in the humanities, but the reader still wants to know how far your approach reaches. Does your analysis apply only to this novel or this writer, or could it apply to a whole literary genre?

> *Tip:* In your conclusion, explain both the significance of your findings and their limits.

Make it a priority to discuss these conclusions with your adviser. In my experience, the main danger here is that students finally reach this final section with only a week or two left before the due date. They don't have enough time to work through their conclusions and revise them. That leaves the paper weakest at the end, precisely where it should be strongest, nailing down the most significant points.

The solution: Begin discussing your major findings with your adviser while you are still writing the heart of the paper. Of course, your conclusions will be tentative at that stage, but it helps to begin talking about them. As always, a little writing helps. You could simply list your main findings or write out a few paragraphs about them. Either would serve as a launching pad for meetings with your adviser. You will find these discussions also shed light on the research that leads to these findings. That, in turn, will strengthen your middle sections. Later, when you draft the conclusion, review your notes on these talks and the short documents you wrote for them. They will serve as prewriting for the final section.

> *Tip:* Discuss your conclusions with your adviser well before the paper is due. It helps to write down a few major conclusions for these preliminary discussions.

EXAMPLES OF STRONG CONCLUSIONS

As an example of how to end your paper, let's turn again to John Dower's splendid book on postwar Japan, *Embracing Defeat: Japan in the Wake of World War II*. In the final pages, Dower pulls together his findings on war-ravaged Japan and its efforts to rebuild. He then judges the legacies of that period: its continuing impact on the country's social, political, and economic life. Some insights are unexpected, at least to me. He argues that Japan has pursued trade protection as the only acceptable avenue for its persistent nationalism. America's overwhelming power and Japan's self-imposed restraints—the intertwined subjects of the book—blocked any political or military expression of Japan's nationalist sentiment. Those avenues were simply too dangerous, he says, while economic nationalism was not. Dower ends with these paragraphs:

> The Japanese economists and bureaucrats who drafted the informal 1946 blueprint for a planned economy were admirably clear on these objectives [of "demilitarization and democratization"]. They sought rapid recovery and maximum economic growth, of course—but they were just as concerned with achieving economic demilitarization and economic democracy. . . . Japan became wealthy. The standard of living rose impressively at every level of society. Income distribution was far more equitable than in the United States. Job security was assured. Growth was achieved without inordinate dependence on a military-industrial complex or a thriving trade in armaments.
>
> These are hardly trivial ideas, but they are now being discarded along with all the deservedly bankrupt aspects of the postwar system. The lessons and legacies of defeat have been many and varied indeed; and their end is not yet in sight.[11]

Remember the anecdotal opening of Herbert's book *Impressionism: Art, Leisure, and Parisian Society,* with Henry Tuckerman's 1867 arrival in a much-changed Paris? Herbert strikes a completely different tone in his conclusion. It synthesizes the art history he has presented, offers a large judgment about where Impressionism fits among art movements, and suggests why exhibitions of Monet, Manet, and Renoir are still so popular. He manages to do all that in a few well-crafted sentences:

> Although we credit [Impressionism] with being the gateway to modern art, we also treat it as the last of the great Western styles based upon a perception of harmony with natural vision. That harmony, long since lost to us in this century of urbanization, industrialization, and world

---

11. John W. Dower, *Embracing Defeat: Japan in the Wake of World War II* (New York: W. W. Norton, 1999), 563–64.

wars, remains a longed-for idea, so we look back to Impressionism as the painting of a golden era. We flock into exhibitions of paintings that represent cafés, boating, promenading, and peaceful landscapes precisely because of our yearning for less troubled times. The only history that we feel deeply is the kind that is useful to us. Impressionism still looms large at the end of the twentieth century because we use its leisure-time subjects and its brilliantly colored surfaces to construct a desirable history.[12]

Robert Dallek offers similarly accessible, powerful judgments in his conclusion to *Flawed Giant: Lyndon Johnson and His Times, 1961–1973:*

> [Johnson's] presidency was a story of great achievement and terrible failure, of lasting gains and unforgettable losses. . . . In a not so distant future, when coming generations have no direct experience of the man and the passions of the sixties are muted, Johnson will probably be remembered as a President who faithfully reflected the country's greatness and limitations—a man notable for his successes and failures, for his triumphs and tragedy.
>
> Only one thing seems certain: Lyndon Johnson will not join the many obscure—almost nameless, faceless—Presidents whose terms of office register on most Americans as blank slates. He will not be forgotten.[13]

Some writers not only synthesize their findings or compare them to others; they use the conclusion to say what their work means for appropriate methods or subject matter in their field. That is what Robert Bruegmann does in his final statement in *The Architects and the City: Holabird & Roche of Chicago, 1880–1918.* His conclusion goes beyond saying that this was a great architectural firm or that it designed buildings of lasting importance. Bruegmann tells us that Holabird & Roche helped shape modern Chicago and that its work, properly studied, helps us understand "the city as the ultimate human artifact":

> Traditional architectural history has tended to see the city less as a process than as a product, a collection of high art architectural objects in a setting dominated by mundane buildings of little interest. This tended

---

12. Herbert, *Impressionism,* 306.

13. Robert Dallek, *Flawed Giant: Lyndon Johnson and His Times, 1961–1973* (New York: Oxford University Press, 1998), 628.

to perpetuate a destructive and divisive attitude about the built environment, suggesting that only a few buildings are worthy of careful study and preservation while all others are mere backdrop. I hope that these explorations in the work of Holabird & Roche have shed light on parts of the city rarely visited by the architectural historian and on some little explored aspects of its history. If so, perhaps it has achieved its most basic goal: providing an insight into the city as the ultimate human artifact, our most complex and prodigious social creation, and the most tangible result of the actions over time of all its citizens.[14]

These are powerful conclusions, ending major works of scholarship on a high note.

What concluding paragraphs should *never* do is gaze off into the sunset, offer vague homilies, or claim you have found the meaning of human existence. (If you discover it, please write me directly.) Remember the perils of the Very Import Graduation Speech as you write your conclusion as well as your introduction. Be concrete. Stick to your topic. Make sure your conclusions stand on solid ground.

Tip: Avoid vague platitudes in your conclusion. Your goal should be reaching strong, sound judgments, firmly grounded in your readings and research.

Better to claim too little than too much. Best of all, claim what you've earned the right to say: what your research really means.

TIME SCHEDULE FOR WRITING THE INTRODUCTION AND CONCLUSION

You should begin drafting the introduction and conclusion only after you have written at least a rough draft of most of the thesis. That will probably be the fifth or sixth month of your thesis project, although (naturally) individual schedules vary. By then you'll have a full overview of the project,

---

14. Robert Bruegmann, *The Architects and the City: Holabird & Roche of Chicago, 1880–1918* (Chicago: University of Chicago Press, 1997), 443.

so you can give it a sharp, clear opening and draw together your major findings in the conclusion. As you write these crucial sections, you'll return to other sections and revise them in light of your introduction and conclusion. Working back and forth like this will produce a stronger, more tightly integrated work.

TIME SCHEDULE FOR MONTHS 3–5
(OR MONTHS 3–6, DEPENDING ON YOUR SCHOOL SCHEDULE):
WRITING THE INTRODUCTION AND CONCLUSION

Reading: Focused research and planning

Writing: Prewrite middle sections of thesis
            Write and revise middle sections of thesis
            Prewrite the introduction and conclusion

CHECKLIST: OPENINGS, TRANSITIONS, AND CONCLUSIONS

Remember to edit your introduction and conclusion several times. They are the last written but the most carefully read.

In the introduction do the following:
- Entice your reader into your subject.
- Explain
  ◦ Why your topic is important;
  ◦ What methods you will use to investigate it;
  ◦ What texts or evidence you will rely on.
- Define your key terms and use them consistently as a "core vocabulary."
- State your thesis argument.
- Provide a road map for the overall paper.

In the middle sections of your paper
- Make sure the order of the sections is right, matching your argument;
- Smooth the transitions between sections;
- Show (briefly) why the next section comes where it does.

In the conclusion
- Highlight your main findings;
- Show how they support your thesis statement;
- Explain the range and limits of your findings and any generalizations;
- Connect your findings to larger issues.

11 GOOD EDITING MAKES GOOD WRITING

In 1776 the Continental Congress made a fateful decision to issue a statement declaring America's independence and explaining its reasons. To draft it, they formed a small committee, including John Adams, Benjamin Franklin, and Thomas Jefferson. The committee asked Jefferson to produce an initial version. He worked quickly to convey their common ideas, thinking of himself more as a draftsman than as an original author.

Jefferson borrowed freely from the Virginia Constitution he had written earlier and from George Mason's draft of a Virginia Declaration of Rights, both based on the English Bill of Rights (1689). It was Mason, for example, who had declared that "all men are born equally free and independent" and "all power is vested in, and consequently derived from the people."[1] If those phrases are familiar, it's because Jefferson borrowed them. If they don't sound quite right, it's because Jefferson edited them to make them more compact and resonant.

Jefferson's version is the one we know. Mason had written: "standing armies, in time of peace, should be avoided." Jefferson dropped the passive voice: "There shall be no standing army but in time of actual war."[2] Mason had written that all men had natural rights to "the enjoyment of life and liberty, with the means of acquiring and possessing property, and pursuing and obtaining happiness and safety." Jefferson cut it once and then a second time, producing one of the most compelling lines in American history: "life, liberty and the pursuit of happiness."[3] He returned with a powerful, eloquent document, fusing reason and passion. All in all, good enough for government work.

Now it was the Drafting Committee's turn to edit. Most of the changes

---

1. I have modernized the spelling. Jefferson also drew heavily on Locke's *Second Treatise on Government*. Quoted in Pauline Maier, *American Scripture: Making the Declaration of Independence* (New York: Alfred A. Knopf, 1997), 104, 124–27.

2. Quoted in Maier, *American Scripture*, 128.

3. Quoted in Maier, *American Scripture*, 134.

were small cuts, and it is not always clear who initiated them. It was probably Benjamin Franklin—although we cannot be sure—who changed the
second line. Jefferson had written: "We hold these truths to be sacred and
undeniable." That's a ringing phrase as it stands. Wise editing made it im-
measurably stronger: "We hold these truths to be self-evident." The new
word, "self-evident," is modest, but it packs a punch. This change did more
than quicken the language and buttress America's claims. It made them virtually unassailable.

If careful editing can improve Jefferson's Declaration, then surely it can
help you and me. Nobody's first draft is their best, and editing is the only
way to make it better—*the only way.* As you cut, paste, and rewrite, focus
on communicating to readers as well as expressing yourself. Engage your
readers by letting your ideas emerge clear, strong, and uncluttered.

> *Tip:* Editing your work again and again is the way—*the only way*—to
> produce your best writing.

Your goal should be lucid, persuasive writing, aimed squarely at your
reader. Communicate, inform, persuade. That means writing with your
readers in mind. It means tightening your language, scrapping needless
words and sentences, and deleting tangents. It means building paragraphs
around central ideas, and then arranging them in a sensible order within
each section. It means reconsidering the sections themselves, making sure
they are in the right order, and moving them if they're not. Above all, it
means writing with courtesy and respect for your readers.

No matter how profound your argument, your language should be
unaffected and unpretentious, leavened with pointed examples, choice
quotes, occasional humor, and unexpected phrases. Clarity, simplicity, and
persuasiveness—the values I have spoken of so often—come through pa-
tient revision. That's partly the patina of repeated rubbing, partly the effect
of putting yourself in the reader's chair, something you do each time you
read the text to edit.

REVISE EARLY AND OFTEN

Revising is not something you do only once, after you have finished your
"real" writing. Nor is it grunt work, cleaning up loose ends. It should be an

integral part of your writing, fully as important as prewriting and rough drafting. The aim is to step back from what you've written, remember your readers, and then tighten your language so your ideas come through cleanly and smoothly. Your language and ideas are intertwined. Editing should bind them close.

Don't wait to revise until you have completed all your writing. Do it as you complete each section of the paper, or even a meaningful part of it. Later, after you have completed a full draft with these revised sections, you can return to work on the document as a whole. That may mean more buffing and polishing, or it may mean moving walls and doors, shifting whole portions of the document to different spots so your argument unfolds more logically and persuasively. Whether the changes are big or small, editing your drafts is the key to making your thesis sharper, deeper, and more readable. Doing that requires you to edit the text several times.

Tip: As you finish drafts of each section, you can begin editing them. You don't have to wait until you've completed a draft of the entire paper.

GOALS IN REWRITING

Rewriting is the best place to think about

- Reinforcing your argument and adding evidence at any weak points
- Anticipating objections to your approach
- Including examples, analogies, and compelling details to illustrate your points
- Cutting excess words
- Ensuring continuity between paragraphs and sections
- Adding variety to your sentences, so they don't all have the same form and length
- Maintaining a consistent tone (or voice) in your writing

These elements may get short shrift in a first draft. That's understandable. You are concentrating on your argument and evidence. Now, as you revise, you can include more illustrations, more variety in your sentences, and more continuity between paragraphs and sections. Play around with different options and pick the ones that work best.

Don't be afraid to cut extraneous material and marginal points, even if they took a long time to write. Remember, you are not being paid by the hour or by the word. What matters is the quality of the final product. It should be taut and clear. It is painful to cut your own hard-wrought prose. I know, believe me, I know. But your paper will be much better for it.

> *Tip:* Cut bravely! Tighten your paper by lopping off excess words, sentences, and paragraphs.

This pruning has a purpose: it clears the ground for your main themes to flourish. As you edit, decide if these themes need reinforcement or additional evidence. If they do, now's the time to add them. That might mean nothing more than adding a sentence or paragraph. Or it might mean doing a little targeted research and then writing.

Consider what objections might be raised to your argument and address the most important ones directly. Don't be too subtle here. If there is a standard objection to your viewpoint, state it plainly and tackle it squarely. If you didn't do that in the original draft, now is the time. Your adviser can help here by discussing these counterarguments and suggesting responses. Confronting these alternatives effectively is one mark of an outstanding thesis.

> *Tip:* Clearly state the main objections to your viewpoint or argument. Then meet them head-on.

This editorial work is essential for every thesis, but it needs to be more extensive for writers who produce a loose, quick first draft. (Some writers call this a "zero draft" to indicate that it is not yet a first draft.) There's nothing wrong with writing drafts quickly, and some writers prefer it. They think it produces more original, less constricted work and prevents writer's block.[4] Often, they are more comfortable and productive when they have a

---

4. Some writing teachers advocate these "messy first drafts" as good ways to overcome inertia and produce innovative ideas. Peter Elbow and Joan Bolker are among the leading proponents. Another option would be to produce a messy draft of each section, rather than the whole thesis, and then begin editing that section.

loose draft already in hand and can begin editing. If that's how you work best, fine. Just remember: if your first draft is very loose, you need to spend more time editing the next versions.

TWO TYPES OF REVISION

When you revise, work over your draft at all levels, from individual words to the planned order of your sections. Think about potential changes, small and large.

> *Tip:* Editing should be done at two levels:
> - Small-scale changes, focusing on words, sentences, paragraphs
> - Large-scale changes, focusing on the architecture of the paper: the order of the sections and their relationship to each other

Small-Scale Revisions

Small-scale changes are designed to increase readability: line by line, paragraph by paragraph. You can work on them after you've completed an entire draft or, if you prefer, after you've finished a particular section. Either way, the more you polish, the more your text will shine.

The best way to make sure your text flows smoothly—sentence after sentence—is to read it aloud (or read silently but "hear" the words). Listen for the tone and cadence and shades of meaning. If a sentence sounds awkward, it *is* awkward. Rewrite it, and listen to the new version.

Make sure you have well-defined paragraphs, each built around a single idea. Check on transitions so each paragraph sets up the next and flows into it. Vary your sentences. If three or four in row are long, make the next one short and punchy. That's hard to do while drafting; it's easy to do while editing. If several paragraphs are abstract and theoretical, consider adding an example or two. Your readers will welcome the change of pace, and you will find it reinforces your abstract points. Conversely, if you've written several pages with detailed empirical materials, consider adding some more general analysis or flagging some larger issues.

Large-Scale Revisions

Large-scale revisions focus on the paper's organization. They are designed to improve the overall structure of your project. They give you a chance to reconsider the way you are making your argument and the order in which you are presenting the materials.

You are, in effect, reimagining your initial thesis plan. That plan was always meant to be a work in progress, and now is the time to reassess it, after you've learned so much about the subject. Maybe you will modify your original plan, maybe not. In any case, think it over. It's easy enough to cut and paste if it will strengthen your thesis.

The individual sections of your paper are like small chapters in a book. You can easily rearrange them. It might help to add a new section, divide an existing one, or drop one you had planned or even drafted. You can subdivide a long section or combine several because you now realize they are more closely related than you expected. Be flexible, be thoughtful, and be ready to change what you have written.

As part of this revision, consider the order of the sections. It is easy enough to move them around, once you actually give yourself permission to think about it. Feel free to drag-and-drop, or to stay with the order you currently have. Whatever your choice, line up the sections so your presentation develops logically and sensibly.

Once you have reviewed the sections and arranged them as you want, look over the transitions between them. They need to show the reader why you are taking the next step. If that's hard to explain, then maybe the next section is in the wrong spot.

This sequence of large-scale revision is illustrated in the following figure:

EDITING SEQUENCE: MIDDLE SECTIONS OF PAPER

After you have done this large-scale revision—putting the sections in your preferred order and creating smooth transitions—sit down in a quiet place and disconnect yourself from the electronic world. Turn off your cell phone, instant messaging, two-way pager, and PDA. Then read through the *entire* thesis uninterrupted, at a single sitting. That's the best way to double-check your editorial judgments. This attention to the paper's over-all organization pays off in a stronger, more coherent, more readable thesis.

EDIT OCCASIONALLY ON PRINTED COPIES

Do this "read-through" on paper rather than on-screen. It's much easier to read the manuscript as a whole and capture its rhythms.

As you work through the manuscript, mark it for changes such as "foot-note needed here" or "awkward wording here, redo," but don't pause too long to correct these problems. Signal these changes with a red pen so they stand out. Later, go back and actually make the alterations. But right now the main task is to get a full overview of the project as you steer it onto the final glide path.

After you've made these corrections, and certainly before you turn the thesis in, repeat this uninterrupted reading and markup. The more times you do it, the better. This extra editing will ensure a successful landing, with no fire trucks on the runway.

EDIT THE YOUR SECTION SUBHEADS
AND THE THESIS TITLE

Your sections should all have clear titles, or subheads. As you move the sections around and change their content, some old subheads may not fit anymore. Or you might simply come up with better ones. Reviewing these section subheads is part of the editing task, too. (By the way, you should print these subheads in boldface. That way, they'll stand out clearly and show readers how your paper is organized.)

Tip: Don't forget to edit section subheads and the thesis title.

The most important title of all is for the thesis itself. You already have a working title. Keep a running list of other ideas. A good title can convey your subject matter and even your argument. Most of all, it can attract readers to your work, not least by showing them you are a good writer. F. Scott Fitzgerald gave a dreary name to one of his manuscripts: *Among the Ash-Heaps and Millionaires.* His editor, Maxwell Perkins, casually remarked, "I always thought that *The Great Gatsby* was a suggestive and effective title."[5] Good idea.

One approach is to pick a straightforward title that accurately and briefly describes your subject, such as

- Wayne Booth, *The Rhetoric of Fiction*
- Alicia F. Lieberman, *The Emotional Life of the Toddler*
- Richard Rhodes, *The Making of the Atom Bomb*
- Raymond Williams, *The Sociology of Culture*[6]

Some titles go beyond that. They give an evocative description of their subject and sometimes anticipate the argument of the book. The books I used to illustrate introductions, conclusions, and thesis statements—by Dower, Mandelbaum, and the rest—all have strong titles. Here are a few more, which may guide you as you search for your own title. See if you find the titles intriguing and descriptive.

- Fouad Ajami, *The Dream Palace of the Arabs: A Generation's Odyssey*[7]
- Allan Bloom, *The Closing of the American Mind: How Higher Education Has Failed Democracy and Impoverished the Souls of Today's Students*[8]

---

5. A. Scott Berg, *Max Perkins: Editor of Genius* (New York: E. P. Dutton, 1978), 62.

6. Wayne Booth, *The Rhetoric of Fiction* (Chicago: University of Chicago Press, 1961); Alicia F. Lieberman, *The Emotional Life of the Toddler* (New York: Free Press, 1993); Richard Rhodes, *The Making of the Atom Bomb* (New York: Simon & Schuster, 1986); Raymond Williams, *The Sociology of Culture* (New York: Schocken Books, 1982).

7. Fouad Ajami, *The Dream Palace of the Arabs: A Generation's Odyssey* (New York: Pantheon, 1998).

8. Allan Bloom, *The Closing of the American Mind: How Higher Education Has Failed Democracy and Impoverished the Souls of Today's Students* (New York: Simon & Schuster, 1987). This is another title that improved with editorial assistance. The original title was "Souls without Longing." That would have sold six hundred copies to confused students in divinity school. Bloom's editor urged him to come up with something better and more descriptive. Bloom did so, and *The Closing of the American Mind* sold hundreds of thousands of copies. Nathan Tarcov, literary executor for Allan Bloom, personal communication, July 14, 2003.

- Patrick Brantlinger, *Who Killed Shakespeare? What's Happened to English since the Radical Sixties*[9]
- Larry Cuban and Michael Usdan, eds., *Powerful Reforms with Shallow Roots: Improving America's Urban Schools*
- Norman Golb, *Who Wrote the Dead Sea Scrolls? The Search for the Secret of Qumran*
- Nathan Rosenberg and L. E. Birdzell Jr., *How the West Grew Rich: The Economic Transformation of the Industrial World*
- Richard A. Shweder, *Why Do Men Barbecue? Recipes for Cultural Psychology*
- William J. Wilson, *The Declining Significance of Race: Blacks and Changing American Institutions*[10]

Notice that none of the book titles include the word "and," and only two include it in the subtitle. That's because "and" is usually a weak placeholder, saying only that two topics are connected without saying how. Compare the vague title *Boys and Play* with *Why Boys Play Rough*. Which title looks more interesting?

Good titles don't just lie there comatose, blandly stating the subject matter. They pose intriguing questions, entice readers into their topic, or advance a strong position. Take the title of Joseph S. Nye's recent book, *The*

---

9. Patrick Brantlinger, *Who Killed Shakespeare? What's Happened to English since the Radical Sixties* (New York: Routledge, 2001). A similar title in the classics turned out to be confusing. True story: The book *Who Killed Homer?* disappointed many readers who expected it to be about *The Simpsons*. They forgot to read the full title. Victor Davis Hanson and John Heath, *Who Killed Homer? The Demise of Classical Education and the Recovery of Greek Wisdom* (New York: Free Press, 1998). D'oh!

10. Larry Cuban and Michael Usdan, eds., *Powerful Reforms with Shallow Roots: Improving America's Urban Schools* (New York: Teachers College Press, Columbia University, 2003); Norman Golb, *Who Wrote the Dead Sea Scrolls? The Search for the Secret of Qumran* (New York: Scribner, 1995); Nathan Rosenberg and L. E. Birdzell Jr., *How the West Grew Rich: The Economic Transformation of the Industrial World* (New York: Basic Books, 1986); Richard A. Shweder, *Why Do Men Barbecue? Recipes for Cultural Psychology* (Cambridge, MA: Harvard University Press, 2003); William J. Wilson, *The Declining Significance of Race: Blacks and Changing American Institutions* (Chicago: University of Chicago Press, 1978).

Paradox of American Power: Why the World's Only Superpower Can't Go It Alone.[11] The first half of the title is intriguing: we want to know, "What's the paradox?" The answer is not obvious since America is the most powerful state in the modern world, perhaps in world history. The subtitle shows how Nye will resolve that paradox in the book. He will argue that even though the United States is extraordinarily powerful, it still needs allies to accomplish its foreign-policy goals.

Here's a title so good that I bought the book even though I seldom read about evolutionary biology. *Why Is Sex Fun? The Evolution of Human Sexuality* by Jared M. Diamond.[12] The chapter titles are great, too. They ask fundamental—but often overlooked—questions and pose them in provocative ways, just as the book title does. Here are a couple: "Why Don't Men Breast-feed Their Babies? The Non-Evolution of Male Lactation" and "The Animal with the Weirdest Sex Life." (Diamond's guess: Your dog probably thinks it's you.)

SOME NUTS-AND-BOLTS TIPS ABOUT REVISING

Since you have written and edited a lot of class papers, you probably have your own way of doing it, your own tricks of the trade. I've got mine, too, and I'll pass them along, hoping they make your task easier and more efficient. I've already mentioned a couple in passing.

First, do some of your editing *off the computer*. It's fine to do most of your editing on-screen. It's very efficient, especially for making small-scale changes. But you should occasionally work with a printed copy. After all, that's how everybody else will read it. It puts you in their shoes. That's a good place to be as you edit. It also allows you to read through the whole paper easily. That gives you a better overall perspective, which is crucial for making large-scale changes.

---

11. Joseph S. Nye Jr., *The Paradox of American Power: Why the World's Only Superpower Can't Go It Alone* (New York: Oxford University Press, 2002).

12. Jared M. Diamond, *Why Is Sex Fun? The Evolution of Human Sexuality* (New York: HarperCollins, 1997). Diamond has a knack for good titles, as evidenced by his best-selling *Guns, Germs, and Steel: The Fates of Human Societies* (New York: W. W. Norton, 1997).

> *Tip:* Most of your editing will be at the computer screen, but do at least
> some from a printed copy. It will give you a better overview.

Second, as you read and mark the printed copy with changes, use red pens. Bright red ink stands out from the printed text, and that's important when you return to the computer to type in your modifications. It is easy to miss changes if you mark them in black or blue ink. Those markings fade into the existing text. So, buy a box of red pens.

Even with red ink, it's sometimes hard to find small changes. To make sure you catch them later, circle them and put a red line (or arrow) in the right or left margin.

> *Tip:* Use red pens to edit printed copy. The color pops out from the text.
> Circle small changes so you catch them later when you enter the changes
> on your computer.

Since I print my drafts as single-spaced texts (to prevent widespread deforestation), it's sometimes hard to read the changes I insert between the lines. Mind you, I'll be retyping them myself, but I still may not understand what I wrote. If an insert is hard to read, I write it a second time in the margin.

Sometimes, I strike out a word, write in a new one, and then realize the original one was better. Now, unfortunately, the original has a red ink line through it. Here I reach for a standard proofreading mark, "stet." It means "leave the original words in place." I sometimes put that in the margins, too, as I do with "ital" to add italics. I usually circle them to make sure I notice them later.

Just as I use red pens, I use red fonts on the computer screen to highlight notes about changes I need to make later. I even use **boldface** and CAPS—I'm a belt-and-suspenders guy about this. The capital letters and boldface make it easy to catch these notations when I'm reading a printed black-and-white copy.

I don't use these computerized notations often since I usually enter the changes as I think of them, at least when I'm editing on-screen. But I do sometimes need to remind myself to find a citation or quotation later, either with a computer search or a trip to the library. The notations need to be standard (so I can search for them), and they need to be easily noticed as I read them on-screen. Here are a few I use:

SOME NOTATIONS I USE FOR EDITING

Notation	Meaning
CITE	Get a citation.
	If I need some citation materials to include in the text itself, I put the red notation in the normal text, along with some reminder of what I need. If I've completed the relevant text and just need to complete the footnote, I begin the footnote and then include the word CITE in the footnote. In this chapter, I completed the text and began a footnote about the Declaration of Independence. But I needed some information to complete the footnote so I wrote: (CITE, Maier, page?).
19xx or 20xx	Find the year of a publication or event.
EXAMPLES	Insert examples at that spot.
EXPAND	Add some text at this point.
	Sometimes I include a notation saying what I need to add, such as "EXPAND: Jefferson's role in Continental Congress."
??? or CHECK???	Review the text or check a fact.
	In this chapter, I wanted to double-check the date of the English Bill of Rights.
AWKWARD	Get out the chisel and fix my prose at that location.
STOP	Ended the day's work here.
	Perhaps I really should write START since that's where I'll begin tomorrow.

Word processors have standard features to simplify these tasks. One is auto-correct, which I use to recognize these phrases. When my computer program sees a designated phrase typed in ALL CAPS, it automatically changes it to red boldface. (Honestly, that made it quite an adventure to type the previous paragraph, kind of like naming your dog "Fetch.")

It also helps to have a separate computer folder dedicated to your thesis and a regular "to do" file within it. When I start a writing project like this book, I always set up a new folder so I can keep my bibliography, notes, and draft chapters in one place and back them up easily. I include a "to do" file for each new writing project and find it especially useful when I'm editing.

I jot down tasks such as finding citations and keep the list handy when I work at the library.

> *Tip:* Keep a "to do" file for your thesis and keep it up-to-date.

DOUBLE-CHECK YOUR DEPARTMENT REQUIREMENTS

As you complete your thesis editing, check with your department about formatting requirements. A departmental administrator will know them. Double-check the due date and find out how many copies you need to turn in (and where!). Most departments simply ask for one or two clean, easy-to-read copies. Others have more detailed rules, such as double spacing, twelve point fonts, and standard cover pages. Even if you don't have to meet these requirements, it's a good idea to double-space your copy and use a twelve-point proportional font such as Times New Roman.

Some departments require that you cite references a particular way, such as APA or MLA citations (see appendix 2, "Footnotes 101"). You might discover some other requirements, too, such as printing on twenty-pound bond paper or using standard margins. (The most common margins are 1 inch on top and bottom, and between 1 and 1.5 inches on the left and right.) All these requirements are easy to handle, but you need to check on them a few days before printing your final copy.

> *Tip:* Ask a department administrator if there are specific formatting requirements for the thesis. They might include page margins, line spacing, type of citations, cover page, bond paper, and binding. None are difficult, but you need to check.

Speaking of checking, be sure to proofread the final version of the paper *very* carefully. Your trusty spell-check will catch some errors, of course, but you still need to review grammar, punctuation, and formatting. Be sure each section subhead appears on the same page as the first sentence of the new section. It shouldn't be orphaned at the bottom of the previous page. If you have a bibliography or reference list, be sure it includes all the works you've cited and all the necessary information about them. Make sure the pages of the thesis are numbered. Finally, don't forget to back up the final copy. One good way to do that is to send an electronic version to your adviser, along with a note saying that you will be dropping off a hard copy.

> *Tip:* Proofread the final version of the paper very carefully. Check spelling, grammar, punctuation, and formatting. Back up the final copy.

A FINAL THOUGHT

Editing is about persistence and perspective. It's about sticking with your writing and your ideas until you've refined them, making them sharp and clear. Stopping short is like pulling a cake from the oven fifteen minutes early. After all that work, it's still not quite a cake. It's more like goo. Editing is also about seeing your work from a different perspective, from the reader's chair as well as the writer's desk. It requires attention to individual sentences as well as to the paper's overall organization. If you pay close attention and stick with it, you'll make good choices and your work will be much stronger. We hold these truths to be self-evident.

CHECKLIST: EDITING

- Edit your drafts again and again.
- Focus on
  - Strengthening your argument;
  - Adding evidence and examples at weak points;
  - Anticipating objections.
- Read aloud as you edit, or read silently but hear the words.
- When editing line by line, eliminate extra words, add variety to sentences, and ensure continuity between paragraphs.
- When editing the overall structure of your paper, concentrate on the section order and how the sections relate to each other.
- Give each section a descriptive title, or subhead, printed in boldface.
- Remember to edit the subtitles of each section and the paper title.
- Keep an up-to-date "to do" list for your thesis, including research you need to complete.
- Check with your department about formatting requirements for the final version of the thesis.

CHECKLIST: FINAL PROOFREADING

Proofread the final version of your thesis very carefully before turning it in. Check
- Spelling
- Grammar
- Punctuation
- Formatting
- Section subheads (which should appear on the same page as the new section's text, not orphaned at the bottom of a page)
- Bibliography (which should include every item cited in your paper)

Be sure to back up the final proofread version of your paper.

12 PRESENTING INFORMATION VISUALLY

Many theses, especially in the social sciences, need to present substantial amounts of information, usually empirical data. How can you do that most effectively?

The answer is usually a well-designed chart or graph. Tables work well enough for a few numbers but rarely for large data sets, where readers need to visualize vast quantities of data and grasp patterns within it. Well-designed visual presentations are powerful because they can present these data sets without overloading readers.

What's best for your readers is also best for you. Clear presentations will enrich your analysis. They will help you think about the data and explore its meanings.

In this chapter, I'll discuss some ways of presenting data effectively. I'll also consider other kinds of visual presentations, from maps to paintings, which may be important in your thesis.

There are four main types of visual presentations, and I will discuss each in turn.

- *Maps* for geographic and spatial information
- *Verbal tables and figures* for arguments and concise analysis
- *Pictures, posters, and drawings* for illustration of important points
- *Charts and graphs* for numerical data

A couple of important points apply to all of them. You need to cite the source, and you need to introduce these visual elements in the text, just as you would a long quotation.

Whenever you use graphs, maps, tables, photographs, or any visual materials, cite the original sources, just as you do for other kinds of information. Give credit where credit is due, whether it's for words, ideas, drawings, or other work.

Giving that credit is simple: list the source immediately below the image. After a graph, for instance, you might say, "*Source:* Data and graph from Book X, 153, fig. 3." Or you might say that you constructed the chart yourself, based on "population statistics from database Z and economic statistics from article W." If you have modified an existing visual image, say that, too. For a map entitled "The Western Front in World War I, 1918," you might say, "*Source:* Philip J. Haythornthwaite, *The World War One Source Book* (London: Arms and Armour Press, 1993), 41, casualty figures added." Later in this chapter, I'll show examples of these various citations.

> *Tip:* Cite the source for each visual presentation. The best way to do that is usually a credit line immediately below the presentation, with full citation information.

Don't assume that visuals speak for themselves. You should introduce them just as you would a long quotation and give each one a title. You may also need to add labels that identify crucial information. The information that's crucial depends on your paper topic and argument. It's your job to guide the reader to the significant points in any map, picture, chart, or graph. A picture may be worth a thousand words, but it will be worth more if you use another ten words to introduce it.

> *Tip:* Introduce each visual item in the text and give a title to each one. On maps, charts, and graphs, add labels and arrows to highlight points of interest.

MAPS

If your thesis contains important geographical information, you should include maps tailored to your needs. Spatial dimensions are crucial to many topics: war, nationalism, immigration, urban studies, environmental changes, and more. If you are studying one of these topics, look for good maps to download or scan. When you find one during your research, make a special note of it so you can use it later (with proper citation, of course). In most cases, you don't need to create your own maps from scratch. Existing maps are perfectly fine, although you may wish to add a few labels and arrows to highlight points of special interest.

Students are reluctant to include maps. Too much like middle-school geography, I guess. In fact, maps can complement your text and orient your readers. And they can do more. They can show what you are trying to analyze, and, in some cases, they can help you explain it.

These multiple uses are why classicist Donald Kagan includes some thirty maps in his book on the Peloponnesian War, intended for a wide audience. His narrative refers to numerous city-states, and it's important for intelligent lay readers to know exactly where they are, and where they are relative to one another.[1] By contrast, Kagan's monumental four-volume history of the Peloponnesian War, intended solely for scholars of ancient Greece, contains no maps.[2] These specialists already know the geographical information. Kagan is not only a great scholar; he knows his different audiences.

Because maps force us to think spatially, they sometimes produce startling insights. Consider the 2000 Bush-Gore presidential election. The map televised on election night showed a mixture of red and blue states. Some large states were colored blue (for Gore) because he carried their cities by substantial margins, offsetting his losses in suburban and rural areas. This state-by-state map obscured deep divisions between cities and less populated areas, between the Atlantic and Pacific coasts and the vast midsection of the country. When a county-by-county map of the vote was finally published, it was virtually all red (for Bush) in the middle of the country.[3] The blue was concentrated in three areas: cities, counties with large minority populations, and the East and West coasts. Bush won about 80 percent of the country's territory, a vast swath of red, startling even experienced observers. (In the maps below, blue is shown as dark gray, red as light gray.)

This county-by-county map reconfigured our perspective, shifting it away from individual voters, states, or electoral votes. That's because the county-by-county map dramatically underweights cities, where many

---

1. Donald Kagan, *The Peloponnesian War* (New York: Viking, 2003).

2. See, for example, his first volume: Donald Kagan, *The Outbreak of the Peloponnesian War* (Ithaca, NY: Cornell University Press, 1969).

3. The best known maps were published by *USA Today*. Electoral map: http://www.usatoday.com/news/vote2000/electfront.htm. County-by-county map: http://www.usatoday.com/news/vote2000/cbc/map.htm. For clarity, I have used a county-by-county map by Steven Hill, Center for Voting and Democracy, at http://www.fixingelections.com/map.html (accessed May 5, 2004) (converted to gray scale). Hill's map is less confusing because it omits the overlay of state and county boundaries.

ELECTORAL MAP, 2000

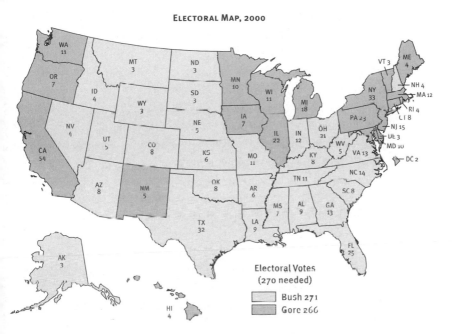

Electoral Votes
(270 needed)

Bush 271
Gore 266

Source of electoral vote information: http://www.archives.gov/federal_register/electoral_college/
votes/2000.html (accessed August 29, 2004).

COUNTY-BY-COUNTY ELECTION MAP, 2000

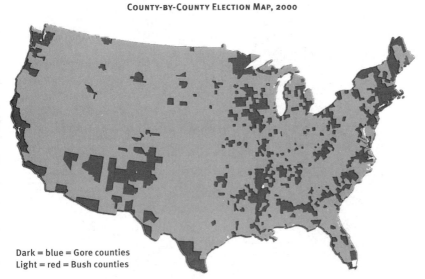

Dark = blue = Gore counties
Light = red = Bush counties

Source: Steven Hill, Center for Voting and Democracy, http://www.fixingelections.com/map.html
(accessed May 5, 2004) (converted to gray scale).

voters are squeezed into little space, and overweights suburbs and rural areas. If we focus only on square miles, Cook County (Chicago) is the same size as a downstate county without a Starbucks or an orthodontist. This map is not "right" and the others "wrong," or vice versa. They are simply different perspectives on the geography of the election.

For some analyses, a detailed geographic perspective is essential; for others it only confuses and detracts. Consider two very different maps, both dealing with international politics. One, by Chaim Kaufmann, deals with forced population transfers, which sometimes reduce violence and sometimes increase it. The main point, Kaufmann says, is that antagonistic groups are sometimes so intermingled that an *incomplete* separation leaves one group vulnerable. These details explain the prevalence of violence after incomplete population transfers and explain why some, anticipating the problem, oppose separation in the first place. To make this argument, he needs detailed maps showing the geographical distribution of ethnic groups and their intermingling in different regions. His map of "Muslim and Sikh Populations in Punjab, 1941" (shown below) includes these crucial details.

MUSLIM AND SIKH POPULATIONS IN PUNJAB, 1941

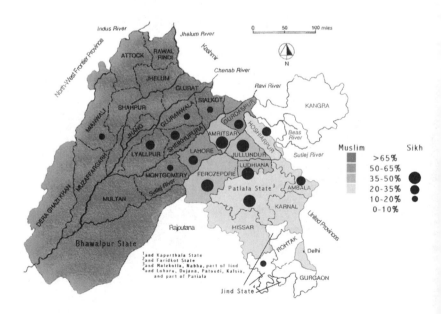

Source: Chaim D. Kaufmann, "When All Else Fails: Ethnic Population Transfers and Partitions in the Twentieth Century," *International Security* 23 (Fall 1998): 137, map 2.

Daryl Press, on the other hand, wants to show how the United States deployed its forces against Iraq in the 1991 Gulf War. Presenting geographic details would overload his readers with useless information and shift the focus away from where he wants it, on powerful military groups poised to attack. So Press uses highly stylized maps, such as the one below on "Coalition Forces and Deployment Plans, Iraq, 1991." Later in the article, he adds details—but *not* details about physical geography. He uses stylized symbols to show invasion routes and locations of major battles.

COALITION FORCES AND DEPLOYMENT PLANS, IRAQ, 1991

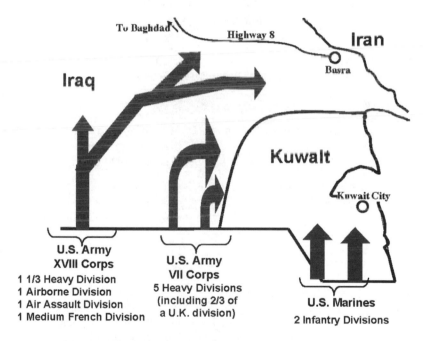

Source: Daryl G. Press, "The Myth of Air Power in the Persian Gulf War and the Future of Warfare," *International Security* 26 (Fall 2001): 17, fig. 2.

Both Press and Kaufmann need maps for their arguments, but they need different kinds of maps because they are making different kinds of arguments.

VERBAL TABLES

Verbal tables contain written information, such as lists of wars and dates, rather than numbers. They are valuable tools and, in my opinion, should be used more often in theses, articles, and books. Let me give a couple of examples and show how they present material in compact, accessible ways and often promote succinct analysis.

Consider a thesis dealing with German nationalism in the mid-nineteenth century. It would surely include Prussia's successful wars in the 1860s and 1870s, which created the German Empire. Before analyzing these wars and their relationship to German nationalism, it helps to orient readers with a simple table, naming the wars, dates, opponents, and results. A verbal table can do that easily, in a few phrases, without clogging the text itself. (Your word processor can produce such tables easily.) A map of Prussia's expansion would nicely complement this table.

Name of War	Years	Opponent	Result
Schleswig-Holstein War	1864	Denmark	Schleswig-Holstein is brought into the German Confederation after conquest by Prussia and Austria.
Austro-Prussian War	1866	Austria	Prussia defeats Austria quickly and replaces it as the dominant state within Germany; a lenient peace encourages Austria to become Prussia's junior partner internationally.
Franco-Prussian War	1870–71	France	Prussia defeats France quickly and imposes a punitive peace, including the reparations and seizure of the French provinces Alsace and Lorraine; south German states are incorporated into new Prussian-led German Empire.

Tip: Keep the entire table on the same page, if possible.

Tables like this are valuable *before* or *after* your main presentation in the text. Before the presentation, they orient the reader. Afterward, they summarize your findings. It is challenging to summarize your findings in only a few words, as tables require, and that is precisely why they are so useful for you and your readers.

> *Visual Tip:* Avoid clutter in your tables. A good way to do that is to eliminate any horizontal or vertical lines that aren't necessary to separate data. Remember: The simpler your presentation, the more your information stands out. That's a good rule for visual presentations, just as it is for prose.

Cluttered

	Column 1	Column 2	Column 3	Column 4
Row 1	aaaa	bbbb	cccc	dddd
Row 2	eeee	ffff	gggg	hhhh
Row 3	iiii	jjjj	kkkk	llll

Better

	Column 1	Column 2	Column 3	Column 4
Row 1	aaaa	bbbb	cccc	dddd
Row 2	eeee	ffff	gggg	hhhh
Row 3	iiii	jjjj	kkkk	llll

Best

	Column 1	Column 2	Column 3	Column 4
Row 1	aaaa	bbbb	cccc	dddd
Row 2	eeee	ffff	gggg	hhhh
Row 3	iiii	jjjj	kkkk	llll

Here's an example of an incisive verbal table from John Mearsheimer's *Tragedy of Great Power Politics,* which we mentioned earlier for its introduction and road map to the rest of the book. Mearsheimer also shows how verbal tables can be used to present concise, powerful analysis as well as facts. In the first chapter, Mearsheimer develops a "Realist" theory of international politics. This theory has a long tradition and several branches, which academic specialists know from years of study. Mearsheimer, however, wants to reach a wider public, and he wants to show all his readers, specialists and general readers alike, exactly what's right and wrong with existing theories. The disagreements are especially important because they underscore what is original about his theory. Mearsheimer accomplishes all this in a brief table near the end of his introduction. It summarizes his analysis thus far and prepares the ground for the rest of his book.

THE MAJOR REALIST THEORIES

	Human Nature Realism	Defensive Realism	Offensive Realism
What causes states to compete for power?	Lust for power inherent in states	Structure of the system	Structure of the system
How much power do states want?	All they can get. States maximize relative power, with hegemony as their ultimate goal.	Not much more than what they have. States concentrate on maintaining the balance of power.	All they can get. States maximize relative power, with hegemony as their ultimate goal.

Source: John J. Mearsheimer, *The Tragedy of Great Power Politics* (New York: W. W. Norton, 2001), 22, table 1.1, reproduced exactly.

The last column, "Offensive Realism," is the author's theory, and the table offers a clear contrast between it and the alternatives. In the process, Mearsheimer succinctly states his central thesis—eighteen words—passing the elevator test before the doors have closed.

Verbal tables can also be used to summarize findings. I do that in my book on democracies and war, *Reliable Partners: How Democracies Have Made a Separate Peace*. One chapter begins with a list of conjectures to evaluate. I am particularly interested in analyzing relationships between two democracies (called "joint democracy"). These relationships are different, I argue, from relationships that include one or more non-democratic states. Here are the first three conjectures from a long list:

**TABLE OF CONJECTURES: IMPLICATIONS OF RELIABLE CONTRACTING
BETWEEN DEMOCRACIES**

- *Self-protective mechanisms:* Self-protective mechanisms [in treaties and agreements] are stronger and more extensive when agreements involve non-democracies.
- *Alliance duration:* Alliances are more durable when only democracies are members.
- *Learning effects:* Because of learning effects, longer periods of joint democracy should produce more stable peace.

Source: Charles Lipson, *Reliable Partners: How Democracies Have Made a Separate Peace* (Princeton, NJ: Princeton University Press, 2003), 140, table 6.1, excerpts.

After a chapter evaluating these conjectures, I present the findings in another table.

EVIDENCE FROM THE CONJECTURES

Conjecture	Findings
Self-protective mechanisms: Self-protective mechanisms are stronger and more extensive when agreements involve non-democracies.	Generally supported, although the evidence is not systematic.
Alliance duration: Alliances are more durable when only democracies are members.	Strongly supported in large empirical studies.
Learning effects: Because of learning effects, longer periods of joint democracy should produce more stable peace.	Strongly supported in large empirical studies.

Source: Charles Lipson, *Reliable Partners: How Democracies Have Made a Separate Peace* (Princeton, NJ: Princeton University Press, 2003), 172, table 7.1, excerpts.

A findings table like this gives readers a quick, comprehensive overview of your research. To produce one requires some intellectual effort to distill your findings. And it requires some fortitude to state the findings plainly, where others will have a clear shot at refuting them. That's exactly why it's so valuable.

FIGURES

Figures are rather like free-form tables and are equally useful. In chapter 8, on prewriting, I used figures to distinguish the traditional outline-based approach from my own "overlapping approach" to prewriting, drafting, and rewriting. The figure with overlapping circles contrasts sharply with separate boxes for the traditional approach.

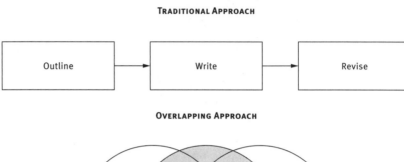

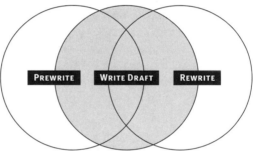

If you borrow figures like these from another author, remember that you need to cite them, just as you do maps, paintings, photographs, architectural drawings, and any other visual materials. The rule is simple: If you use others' work, give them credit.

Figures are also useful for presenting causal analysis. Let's say we found an intriguing correlation among three variables, A, B, and O. They vary together, and we want to see whether one of them causes this joint variation. We are particularly interested in explaining the outcome, O. (Since the labels are arbitrary, why not use intuitive ones like O for outcome instead of the meaningless letter C? If the variables were height and weight, why not use H and W?) Can we figure out the underlying causal relationship, if there is one?

Many possible relationships could produce this correlation, aside from chance, and it's helpful to show the ones we want to investigate, and to show why we are ruling out others. There are quite a few *possible* relationships. Simple figures with causal arrows are the easiest way to show them. Later, you might use some of these figures to describe the findings and explain why one relationship fits the data better than others.

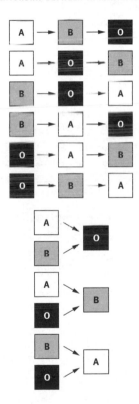

RELATIONSHIP BETWEEN THREE VARIABLES

There is one additional way figures and verbal tables can serve as orienting tools. They can orient the researcher herself. I often suggest that students produce such visual aids for weekly sessions, as part of their prewriting. They are simple, effective ways to summarize work in progress. Of course, some parts of the figures or tables may be incomplete since the research is ongoing. That's fine. They will be completed later as the research progresses.

Figures and verbal tables are valuable learning tools because they demand brief, direct presentation—exactly what good thesis writing should be. That makes them excellent prewriting devices, as well as useful elements of the final paper.

> *Tip:* Use figures and verbal tables to present ideas and findings concisely.

PICTURES

Unless you are studying art, cultural history, or consumer marketing, your thesis probably doesn't need pictures. Never use them for decoration, and think twice before using them to illustrate. They may distract, not enhance. Follow the usual rule: Use nothing extraneous. There's no need to plop a picture of Otto von Bismarck into your analysis of nineteenth-century German nationalism. He's a mammoth man and would plop heavily. We don't need a picture to show he's a central player in the German story.

When should you use pictures, then? When you are analyzing the pictures themselves or when they convey something vital to advance your narrative or analysis. If you were writing about social conformity in the 1950s, for instance, a picture of people walking down Madison Avenue would be striking and effective. If you've ever seen one of these photos, you'll remember. They show a sea of identically dressed white men, all wearing gray suits, white shirts, dark ties, and hats. It's like a corporate-executive marching band. There are few women in the picture because they were not yet part of the white-collar workforce. Few blacks or Latinos, either. If you buttressed this photo with a full description, it could add zip and detail to your thesis. Juxtaposed to modern photos of the same area, this vintage picture could aid a discussion of social change.

Speaking of Madison Avenue, why write about advertising without including some pictures of print advertisements? Pictures are perfectly appropriate for studies of mass media, propaganda, popular culture, and the like. But, again, don't use them for atmosphere, like soft music and scented candles. Save that for your social life. Make sure any pictures or posters you include actually advance your analysis and that you say something informative about them. And, again, give proper credit to the sources.

Tip: Don't use pictures to decorate. Use them only if they
- Aid your explanation, or
- Illustrate what you want to explain.

CHARTS AND GRAPHS

If your thesis includes substantial data, you'll need to think about the best ways to present it—ways that are accurate, clear to your readers, and well integrated into your paper. For small data sets, say ten or twelve numbers, tables are usually the best solution. But for larger data sets, tables have serious drawbacks. It's hard for readers to absorb a dense array of numbers, hard to discern the key features and major trends. You'll do better using well-designed charts or graphs.

Charts is the more general term, referring to any display of information, whether it's a pie chart or an organizational chart. *Graphs* are simply charts that display quantitative information on axes, such as the x- and y-axes on graph paper.

You may be reluctant to use these visual tools, fearing they are less "accurate" or "professional" than numerical tables. There's no need to worry. Charts and graphs are an excellent way to present empirical materials. Because they are so efficient, they can convey much more data than tables. If you think a table's detailed numbers are essential, then include them in an appendix, as selected labels on the graph itself, or, as a last resort, as a table alongside the graph. All these alternatives preserve the narrative flow of your paper. Whichever format you choose, cite the data source.

Tip: For large data sets, use charts and graphs instead of tables for presentation and analysis. Be sure to cite the original source for the data, just as you would for a table.

Let me illustrate these points with a couple of simple examples, beginning with a list of widget prices, calculated annually from 1970 to 2004. Looking at the table below, it's hard to discover the basic features of the data, even with close inspection. A simple graph, on the other hand, shows the trends and patterns. The thirty-five annual data points in the graph could easily have been extended to several thousand (say, daily prices on the London widget market) without making the graph hard to read.

Placing a couple of comments on the graph makes it even stronger. One label gives the exact price of widgets at their high point. That's a significant data point, and you might want to underscore it for your readers. You can do that without having to insert the entire table. A small text box in the graph is sufficient. I have inserted another text box giving the average price of widgets in recent years. That average is not included in the table (although it is calculated from it) and would not be visible to anyone reading the table alone. The graph, then, is not only more readable than the table; it actually includes more information.

WIDGET PRICES, 1970–2004

1970	$12.27	1979	$14.05	1988	$12.38	1997	10.30
1971	11.23	1980	15.75	1989	13.07	1998	11.01
1972	13.04	1981	23.90	1990	11.79	1999	9.21
1973	13.57	1982	35.06	1991	12.02	2000	9.01
1974	11.00	1983	20.00	1992	10.40	2001	10.00
1975	9.05	1984	16.04	1993	9.35	2002	9.79
1976	8.00	1985	13.05	1994	9.82	2003	10.05
1977	8.35	1986	10.00	1995	8.90	2004	10.83
1978	11.55	1987	11.34	1996	9.59		

WIDGET PRICES, 1970–2004

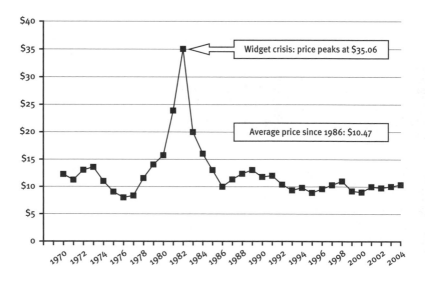

Widget crisis: price peaks at $35.06

Average price since 1986: $10.47

Similarly, it is usually easier to follow a multi-step process with a flow-chart rather than tabular data. Flowcharts are diagrams designed to show how a procedure (or system) moves forward, step-by-step. When you are explaining a multi-step process, that's exactly what you want to show your readers.

Here, for instance, is an evaluation for an actual job-training program, presented first as a table and then as a flowchart by Edward A. Parker and Louis J. Mortillaro in their article "Graphical Presentation of Multilevel Data." See which presentation is more informative and easier to understand.

JOB TRAINING PROGRAM, PRESENTED AS TABLE

	Completed Training Program and Got a Job	Completed Program but Did Not Get a Job	Did Not Complete Program
At 30–90-day follow-up			
Same job	94 (39%)		
New job	4 (2%)		
Unknown	35 (14%)	10 (4%)	
Reasons for termination			
Administrative separation			21 (9%)
Exceeded program duration			19 (7%)
Refused to continue			14 (6%)
Unable to locate			12 (5%)
Did not complete basic skills			2 (1%)
Miscellaneous			33 (13%)
Totals, $n = 244$	133 (55%)	10 (4%)	101 (41%)

Source of data and table: Edward A. Parker and Louis J. Mortillaro, "Graphical Presentation of Multilevel Data: Table versus Flowchart Format," in "Creating Effective Graphs: Solutions for a Variety of Evaluation Data," ed. Gary T. Henry, special issue, *New Directions for Evaluation* 73 (Spring 1997): 26, table 3.1, reproduced exactly.

Here is the same data, presented as a flowchart, showing the reader exactly what happened to job trainees at each stage of the process.

JOB TRAINING PROGRAM, PRESENTED AS A FLOWCHART

Source of data and chart: Edward A. Parker and Louis J. Mortillaro, "Graphical Presentation of Multilevel Data: Table versus Flowchart Format," in "Creating Effective Graphs: Solutions for a Variety of Evaluation Data," ed. Gary T. Henry, special issue, *New Directions for Evaluation* 73 (Spring 1997): 27, fig. 3.1.

In the remainder of this chapter, I will discuss how charts and graphs like these can be used in your thesis, and I'll offer some ideas about how to make the best choices for your particular project.

VISUAL PRESENTATIONS AND TEXTS SHOULD MEET THE SAME STANDARDS

Although visual presentations are distinctive, the basic standards are the same as those for writing. The goal is to communicate effectively to readers. Your figures, charts, and graphs should

- Focus on your readers' needs
- Emphasize simplicity, presenting information with as little clutter as possible

Just as you learn while writing, you learn while graphing—and while creating maps, figures, and charts. Don't think of yourself as simply "presenting" your data and findings. Think of yourself as "visualizing the data," in the words of Edward Tufte, and then helping your readers to visualize it.

The process is similar to one I emphasize for writing. First, use the drafting process to *think about the data yourself,* and then share your insights with readers. "At their best," says Tufte, "graphics are instruments for reasoning about quantitative information. Often the most effective way to describe, explore, and summarize a set of numbers—even a very large set—is to look at pictures of those numbers. Furthermore, of all methods for analyzing and communicating statistical information, well-designed data graphics are usually the simplest and at the same time the most powerful."[4] Just as writing leads to a deeper understanding and unexpected discoveries, so does visualization and analysis of data.

Generally speaking, then, charts and graphs are more effective than tables for thinking about data and for sharing your thoughts with readers. The real question is *what types* to use and *what options* to include within them.

A few points apply to all charts and graphs. All of them should have

- Descriptive titles and explanatory captions (or explanations in nearby text)
- Clearly labeled axes, using descriptive terms rather than the generic terms, x and y
- Data sources that are reliable and are properly identified and cited

All of them should present data fairly and accurately, a basic principle of academic honesty.[5]

Double-check your presentations to make sure you don't inadvertently mislead the reader. That's easy to do with graphs. If I'm driving fifty miles per hour and you are driving seventy, then a graph where the y-axis begins at forty miles per hour would convey the impression that you were driving three times as fast as I was. That might be misleading . . . or it might not. If the speed limit were forty , then it would accurately show you are driving like a maniac, well over the limit. To show how graphs can manipulate perceptions, here are three presentations of this same speed data:

---

4. Edward Tufte, *The Visual Display of Quantitative Information,* 2nd ed. (Cheshire, CT: Graphics Press, 2001), 9.

5. Charles Lipson, *Doing Honest Work in College: How to Prepare Citations, Avoid Plagiarism, and Achieve Real Academic Success* (Chicago: University of Chicago Press, 2004), chap. 1.

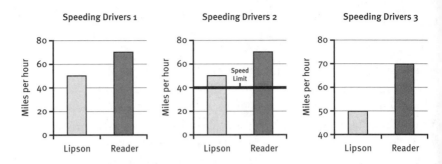

The data is the same, but it produces three distinctive graphs. The one that's best for your presentation depends on the kind of analysis you are conducting.

A key part of the presentation is the scale you use on the *y*-axis (that is, the intervals between the numbers). Sometimes the best interval is a simple arithmetic one, so that the distances between 1, 2, 3, and 4 are equal. At other times, this simple format creates problems. If some magnitude such as the U.S. government budget goes up steadily by 5 percent per year, dollar outlays will increase markedly in later years because of compounding. If you want to focus on the actual dollar increases, these equal intervals are fine. The graph will show dollar outlays expanding more and more rapidly over time. If you want to focus on the steady percentage rise, however, the same intervals are misleading. Use log scales or other appropriate measures to visualize such data accurately. Before you insert a graph in your text, think about questions such as the appropriate intervals for the *x*- and *y*-axes. One size does not fit all.

You should also make careful decisions about what information to add to your charts and graphs and what to leave out. *Don't* make them three-dimensional unless there is a good reason and you hand out those red-and-blue glasses. The third dimension seldom adds anything useful, and it may make the graph harder to read. Even worse, it may actually mislead. Unless the third dimension is equal for all columns, the transformation from two dimensions to three will make the larger columns appear disproportionately bigger.

That sometimes happens on "cute" graphs, like those that show two people or objects. One is twice as tall as the other, and that's supposed to show the quantity is twice as big. It probably shows something entirely different because the figures are three-dimensional and their width and depth are scaled up proportionately. Let's say two suitcases are used to show that one airline carries twice as much luggage as another. The small one is one inch high (as well as one inch deep and one inch wide). The big one is two inches high (and, scaled up proportionately, it is two inches deep and two inches wide). So the bigger one actually has eight times the volume, completely misrepresenting the data on luggage traffic.

To highlight major points on charts and graphs, add labels and text boxes. It may help to add statistical lines, too. A regression line typically adds useful information to a scatter plot. A bar chart is easier to read if there is a simple line indicating the average. Readers can tell which bars rise above the line and which ones fall below. That's why the second graph of the car speeds, with its line indicating the speed limit, is more informative that the first graph, without it. You can also add a text box to graphs, containing statistical summaries, anything from regression coefficients to standard deviations. The graph of widget prices includes a couple of these descriptive boxes.

Tip: When you enter your data in a spreadsheet or statistical package, be sure to include citation information next to data in the spreadsheet itself. It's all too easy to lose track of where the data came from, leaving you with a table or graph without proper citation.

Spreadsheet programs like Excel and Lotus 1-2-3 and sophisticated statistical packages like SPSS and Stata make it easy to transform tables and databases into great-looking charts and graphs.[6] Take advantage of them.

---

6. SPSS and Stata are among the most widely used computer programs for statistical analysis and graphing in the social sciences, natural sciences, and business. They can be found at www.spss.com and www.stata.com.

Tip on graphing from spreadsheets: All spreadsheet programs have simple tools to convert data tables into graphs, with plenty of options about what type of graph to make: line graphs, pie charts, bar charts (either horizontal bars or vertical columns), and so on. Microsoft Excel, for example, has a "chart wizard" to guide you through the process. To access it, click on Excel's "Insert" menu. The finished product can then be inserted into your text. These programs also include tools for curve-fitting and trend lines, everything from linear regressions to moving averages. Of course, statistical packages like Stata and SPSS offer even more powerful tools and more options.

Tip on graphing directly from your word processor: If you don't have a spreadsheet program, you can still make graphs with your word processor. Programs like Microsoft Word have their own simple graph programs. (You can find Word's under the "Insert" menu.) They are adequate for rudimentary graphs but less flexible than graphing with spreadsheets and far inferior to statistical packages.

As useful as these statistical packages are, there are limits to what good software code can do. In the end, *you*—and not your software—have to determine what kind of data analysis is appropriate, how to interpret the results, and what kinds of visual presentations are most accurate and effective. Talk this over with your adviser and, if there are technical issues involved, schedule a meeting with your statistics instructor.

Before you select one type of graph, run the data through several types and compare the different graphs directly. Computer programs make that easy. Give yourself some options and then choose the best.

Let me go through the main choices and their principal uses.

Type of Graph	Best Use	Illustration
Line	Comparisons between data series over time. *Tip:* If there are several data series, such as German and French population, label them on the graph as well as using different style lines for each. Labels on the side are often distracting.	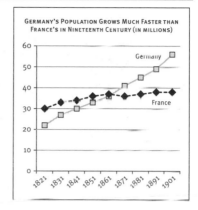
Area	Comparisons between data series over time (similar to line graph but gives stronger visual emphasis to area under line).	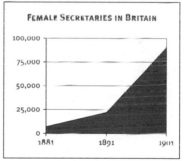 *Source of data:* Peter N. Stearns, *The Industrial Revolution in World History* (Boulder, CO: Westview, 1993), 138. Graph is my own.
Bar chart (vertical column)	Good for comparison of quantities. *Tip:* Be sure to label each column, either on the *x*-axis or on the bar itself. If you make several column graphs with the same categories, keep them in the same order, with the same color scheme. *Tip:* For some charts, it may be useful to add an "average" line.	 *Source of data and graph:* Robert Putnam, *Bowling Alone: The Collapse and Revival of American Community* (New York: Simon & Schuster, 2000), 139.

Type of Graph	Best Use	Illustration
Horizontal bar	A column chart on its side. *Tip:* Better than vertical columns if you need longer descriptive labels for each category. If the top category was "white males over 50," it would fit on the horizontal bar. It would not fit on the *x*-axis of a vertical bar graph.	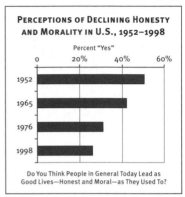 *Source of data and graph:* Robert Putnam, *Bowling Alone: The Collapse and Revival of American Community* (New York: Simon & Schuster, 2000), 139. Based on Putnam's vertical bar chart.
Grouped bars (columns)	Good for comparing same categories in several periods. *Tip:* Label each column clearly. *Tip:* Keep categories in the same order ("fire" on left), and use the same colors ("fire" is always black).	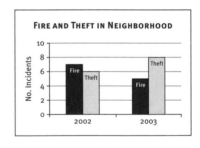
Stacked bars (columns)	Columns, stacked with constituent elements; each column is a data series. In the graph on this page, stacked columns add up to 100 percent. In the following graph, actual dollar amounts are shown. *Tip:* Keep categories in the same order, and mark each one consistently with the same color or pattern. For example, donations by firms are always colored black and placed at the bottom.	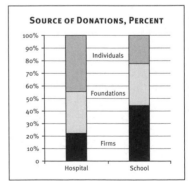

Type of Graph	Best Use	Illustration

Example: The previous graph shows three sources of charitable donations to a hospital and a school. They are percentages that sum to 100 percent for each institution. This graph is based on the same data but shows the dollar amounts given to each.

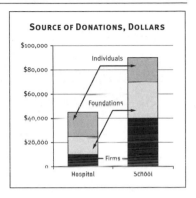

Pie

Percentages of the whole; best for comparing parts to the whole in one data series.

Example: This data might represent all students majoring in the social sciences. The components show their majors as a share of the total. The second chart includes labels for the percentages. Absolute numbers could also be included.

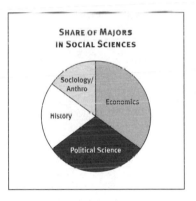

Tip: Pie charts are not good if there are too many categories. Instead of thirteen small slices, use bars.

Tip: Every computer graphics program invites you to turn the pie on its side and make it three-dimensional. Don't. It adds nothing and makes the essential features harder to grasp.

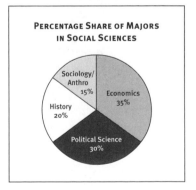

Type of Graph	Best Use	Illustration
XY scatter or scatter plot	Shows individual data points on *x*- and *y*-axes; good if single series is uneven; can be supplemented with line graph (such as a regression line). ***Tip:*** Decide whether it helps the reader to label all the data points, or only the outliers, or perhaps none at all. ***Example:*** For different choices about labeling, see the graphs on the 2000 Palm Beach elections and NIH funding later in this chapter.	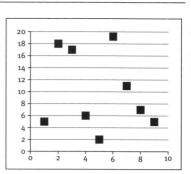
XY scatter with fitted linear regression line	It is often helpful to add a trend line because the eye is not always a reliable guide to the trend. In this case, the trend line is an ordinary-least-squares regression. Likewise, if you are presenting a regression line, consider adding a scatter plot around it. The scatter adds useful information and is easy to grasp. ***Note:*** If the data is nonlinear, be sure to use nonlinear statistical techniques to compute the trend line.	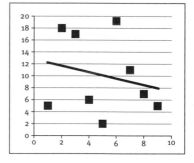

USING GRAPHS TO EXPLAIN

Sometimes, a well-chosen graph can cut to the core of a serious question. That is exactly what Henry Brady and his coauthors found when they investigated another aspect of the 2000 presidential election—the confused voting in Palm Beach County, Florida. In the election, voters in Palm Beach and several other Florida counties used punch cards. The layout of these cards varied from county to county, but all of them required voters to push a metal pin through a hole next to their candidate's name.

In a razor-thin election, these ballots raised two momentous questions. The one that attracted most media attention was how to count ballots when the punches did not go all the way through. There were inevitably questions of interpretation about whether a true vote had been cast and, if so, for whom. A second question received far less attention. Was the Palm Beach ballot so poorly designed that voters, intending to vote for one candidate, actually voted for another? These voters pushed the pin all the way through, so the vote was easy to count. The question is whether they pushed it all the way through for the candidate they actually wanted. Brady and his coauthors decided to study this second question in the days immediately after the election.

There were good reasons to think the voters were befuddled by the ballot. The most obvious one: an extremely conservative candidate, Pat Buchanan, received a very large vote in a liberal county. Many of his votes came from Jewish and black precincts where he had no visible support. Maybe the voters were confused by the ballot. Maybe not.

Two straightforward graphs reveal the basic findings. A scatter plot by Greg Adam and Chris Fastnow shows that Buchanan won a vastly disproportionate share of Palm County's vote, compared to other Florida counties.

OVER-VOTE FOR BUCHANAN IN PALM BEACH COUNTY

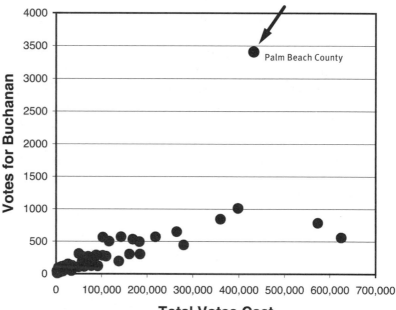

(Notice that only the single outlier is labeled, or needs to be.)

Source: Greg D. Adams and Chris Fastnow, "A Note on Voting Irregularities in Palm Beach, FL," graph in online manuscript, as reproduced by Henry E. Brady et al., "Law and Data: The Butterfly Ballot Episode," *PS Online*, originally published in *PS: Political Science and Politics* 34 (March 2001), 63, fig. 2.

The second graph deals with two different types of votes for each candidate: absentee ballots and Election Day ballots. It shows that almost all Buchanan's "extra" votes came *only* on Election Day in Palm Beach County. He received very few absentee votes. That's important because Palm Beach used different voting procedures for absentee ballots and regular votes. For absentee ballots, it followed the same procedures as other Florida counties. But on Election Day, it used a butterfly ballot (so-called because it folded open like a butterfly). It was the only county to use this particular design.

These differences in ballots form a natural experiment. If Palm Beach had a hidden reservoir of Buchanan support, then it would presumably show up in absentee ballots, as well as on Election Day. If Buchanan received few absentee votes but lots on Election Day, then the strong presumption is that voters were confused by the county's butterfly ballot. A few simple bar graphs tell the tale.

REGULAR VS. ABSENTEE VOTE FOR BUCHANAN IN THREE SOUTH FLORIDA COUNTIES

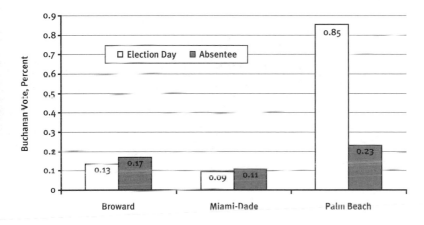

Source of data: Henry E. Brady et al., "Law and Data: The Butterfly Ballot Episode," *PS Online*, originally published in *PS: Political Science and Politics* 34 (March 2001): 59–69. Graph is based on their fig. 3 (p. 65).

Notice that in Broward and Miami-Dade counties, Buchanan received slightly more absentee votes (as a percentage) than he did on Election Day. The dark bars are taller than the adjoining white bars. "But in Palm Beach County," Brady observes, "the people who cast their votes on Election Day were almost four times more likely to vote for Buchanan. This was the smoking gun we had been looking for."[7] That's crystal clear in the tall white column, compared to the short gray one. In this case, then, Brady and his coauthors are using simple bar graphs as powerful explanatory tools.

---

7. Brady and his coauthors' main conclusion: "Palm Beach County was an extraordinary outlier even when compared to the entire nation. Gore supporters and not Bush supporters had mistakenly voted for Buchanan in Palm Beach County. Spoiled ballots came disproportionately from liberal precincts. Almost all of the other analyses posted to the web came to the same conclusions and the dissenters based their complaints on work that had not taken the precautions that we had. Unlike most social science data, these told a very clear and consistent tale." The authors failed legally; their best efforts did not produce a second presidential vote in Palm Beach County. Still, they call their results "the first step in a national civics lesson about the inadequacies of our voting and vote-counting systems." Henry E. Brady et al., "Law and Data: The Butterfly Ballot Episode," *PS Online*, originally published in *PS: Political Science and Politics* 34 (March 2001): 59–69. Titles on the graphs are my own.

Pie charts are almost as common as bar and line graphs. Their special virtue lies in showing how individual parts are related to the whole (with the entire pie representing 100 percent). It is an effective way, for example, to show a city's ethnic mix.

Ethnic Distribution in City, 2004

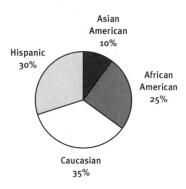

One limitation: Pie charts are confusing if there are more than six or seven categories. It is not an effective way to show the dozen or so nationalities that made up the Austro-Hungarian Empire. Better to use bar graphs, with labels for each nationality.

CHOOSING THE BEST CHART OR GRAPH FOR A SPECIFIC TASK: AN EXAMPLE

If we wanted to show changes in a city's ethnic composition, we could choose between several options: side-by-side pie charts, bar charts, or line graphs. The best way, as I suggested earlier, is simply to experiment and see which works best for your purposes. Let's do that, using the same ethnic data in several charts and graphs.

PIE CHART COMPARISON OF POPULATION CHANGE

Ethnic Distribution in City, 1984

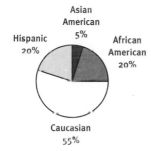

Ethnic Distribution in City, 2004

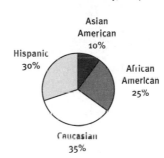

BAR CHART I: COMPARISON OF POPULATION CHANGE (BY ETHNIC GROUPS)
Ethnic Distributions, 1984 and 2004

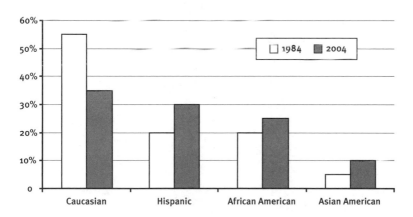

BAR CHART II: COMPARISON OF POPULATION CHANGE (BY YEAR)
Ethnic Distributions, 1984 and 2004

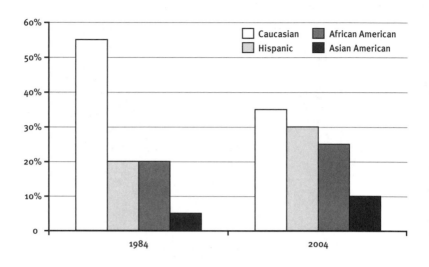

LINE GRAPH COMPARISON OF POPULATION CHANGE
Change in Ethnic Distribution, 1984–2004

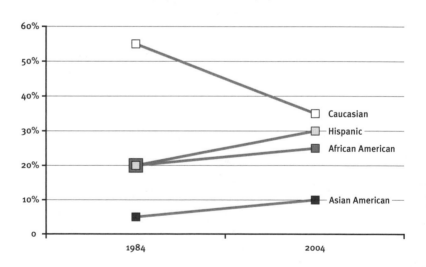

Here's my assessment of the different graphs, all based on the same data. The pie chart works well for a *single* time period but does not work well for two. It is hard to compare the changes for any ethnic group across time. The other three graphs work well, but in different ways. The choice among them would depend on the purpose for which you were using the graph.

The line graph is best at showing the trend. The two bar charts are best at showing static comparisons. The first one, which groups ethnicities in 1984 and 2004 next to each other, is the best way to see changes in each individual group, such as the decline of the city's Caucasian population. The second graph, which groups all ethnicities together in 1984 and then again in 2004, is the best way to see differences in the city's overall makeup. It's easy to compare one ethnic group to all others in 1984 and again in 2004. The line graph is not a good way to make these static comparisons, but it's a great way to see the trends.

So, we can rule out one alternative (the two pie charts) and choose among the other three based on our analytic aims:

- Changes in a particular ethnic group (use bar chart I)
- Changes in the overall composition of the city (use bar chart II)
- Rapidity of each group's increase or decrease (use the line graph)

MANY GRAPHS FROM ONE TABLE AND VICE VERSA

In discussing how to choose graphs, I noted that a single data table can produce quite different-looking graphs. The converse is true, too. Identical graphs can represent very different tables, perhaps misleading or confusing your readers.

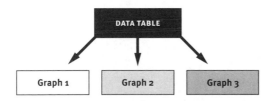

SOLUTION: Choose the most appropriate graph to represent your data without distortion (shown in examples of speeding and city's ethnic mix, where one data set could be represented by several different graphs).

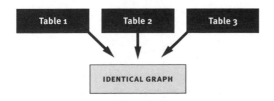

SOLUTION: Add elements to graph to show other characteristics of your data so readers can tell which table it represents.

Linear graphs sometimes give a misleading view of the underlying data because of two basic problems: (a) linear regressions are sensitive to outliers, and (b) the data itself may be nonlinear. F. J. Anscombe showed this with a powerful demonstration. In an article entitled "Graphs in Statistical Analysis," he produced four distinctive tables, each with eleven data points.[8] The demonstration became so well known that the tables are now called Anscombe's Quartet. Although the x,y pairings are different— sometimes strikingly so—each table shares some basic statistical attributes. All four tables are identical in the following ways:

- Mean of the x-values = 9.0
- Mean of the y-values = 7.5
- Least-squared regression line: y = 3 + 0.5x
- Sums of squared errors around the mean = 110.0
- Correlation coefficient = 0.82
- Coefficient of determination = 0.67
- Regression sums of squared errors (variance accounted for by x) = 27.5
- Residual sums of squared errors (about the regression line) = 13.75

Despite these similarities, a mere glance at the scatter points shows dramatic differences in the underlying data. Quartet I is a typical linear scatter. Quartet II is a curve, a complex nonlinear relationship. In quartet III, all the data lies on a straight, sloping line, except for one outlier. In quartet IV, all the data lies on a vertical line (the same x-value), except for one outlier. Yet they produce the same linear regression: y = 3 + 0.5x.

---

8. F. J. Anscombe, "Graphs in Statistical Analysis," *American Statistician* 27 (February 1973): 17–21. Anscombe's work is cited in Tufte, *Visual Display of Quantitative Information*, 13–14.

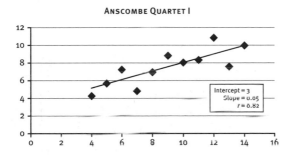

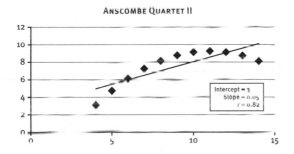

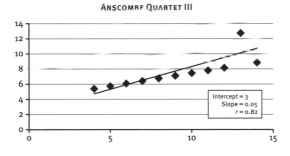

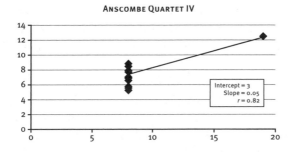

Source: F. J. Anscombe, "Graphs in Statistical Analysis," *American
Statistician* 27 (February 1973): 17–21. I computed these graphs
with Anscombe's "quartet" data. His data points are on page 19.
My graphs are virtually identical to his (pp. 19–20, figs. 1–4).

ANSCOMBE'S QUARTET

	I		II		III		IV
x	y	x	y	x	y	x	y
10	8.04	10	9.14	10	7.46	8	6.58
8	6.95	8	8.14	8	6.77	8	5.76
13	7.58	13	8.74	13	12.74	8	7.71
9	8.81	9	8.77	9	7.11	8	8.84
11	8.33	11	9.26	11	7.81	8	8.47
14	9.96	14	8.10	14	8.84	8	7.04
6	7.24	6	6.13	6	6.08	8	5.25
4	4.26	4	3.10	4	5.39	19	12.50
12	10.84	12	9.13	12	8.15	8	5.56
7	4.82	7	7.26	7	6.42	8	7.91
5	5.68	5	4.74	5	5.73	8	6.89

Same Linear Graph

If you presented only the sloping line—or the equation for it—your readers could not tell which of the four tables you were analyzing. You can help them by including the scatter points. In your thesis, then, you need to decide whether adding data such as scatter points or trend lines will help your readers or merely distract them.

As Anscombe's Quartet shows, outliers are often important. That is true not only in theory but in practice, as countless studies show. When you analyze data, it may prove rewarding to look closely at these outliers instead of drowning them in the data pool.

An excellent example is a statistical study of research grants made by the National Institutes of Health. The NIH is the U.S. government's central agency for medical research grants, and it is run by high-caliber research professionals. We expect NIH grants to be directed at the most serious diseases with the most promising research possibilities. Is that what actually happens?

One potential problem is that different people may have different assessments of what constitutes a "serious disease." Is a disease more serious if it kills 50,000 people a year or if it seriously harms 500,000? What about a disease like smallpox, which hasn't killed anyone in years but poses a catastrophic risk of contagion if it does break out? A second question is whether the granting agency indulges its own tastes for "intriguing problems" or "intellectual puzzles," rather than funding research that has the greatest public impact. Then there's the lurking question of politics. Some diseases have active, mobilized supporters; others don't. There are no city-wide marches for syphilis. None for ulcers, either. Does this affect their share of scientific grants?

That is what Cary Gross, Gerard Anderson, and Neil Powe set out to determine in their article, "The Relation between Funding by the National Institutes of Health and the Burden of Disease."[9] Their dependent variable was one year's NIH funding for specific diseases. Their independent variables were six reasonable measures of the "burden of disease," such as years of life lost and the number of hospital days, figured for each disease. Using these six measures, they calculated expected funding for research on each disease and then compared that with actual funding. Their results showed that funding for twenty-nine diseases is, in their words, "strongly associated with" disease burdens, as the authors measure them.

Still, there were some outliers. As it turns out, sexually transmitted diseases receive more than their expected share of funding, even though nobody's marching for gonorrhea. Breast cancer, diabetes, and dementia such as Alzheimer's also received more than expected. The most generous funding by far went to AIDS research. Several other diseases, such as peptic ulcer, were underfunded.[10]

The authors present this data in elaborate tables, but it is their single graph that has the most impact. It powerfully reveals how most diseases lie close to the regression line (that is, near the expected funding level) and how a few outliers are treated differently. The authors do not try to explain *why* some diseases get different treatment, but their findings set the stage for more research on that. Indeed, until they conducted this research, no one understood that most diseases received roughly the expected funding or that there were some striking outliers. A glance at their graph is enough to see that. What you see is something that no one knew until Gross, Anderson, and Powe conducted their study and graphed the results.

---

9. Cary P. Gross, MD, Gerard F. Anderson, PhD, and Neil R. Powe, "The Relation between Funding by the National Institutes of Health and the Burden of Disease," *New England Journal of Medicine* 340 (June 17, 1999): 1881–87.

10. Relatively underfunded diseases: chronic obstructive pulmonary disease, perinatal conditions, and peptic ulcer. Gross, Anderson, and Powe, "The Relation between Funding."

NIH DISEASE-SPECIFIC RESEARCH FUNDING, 1996

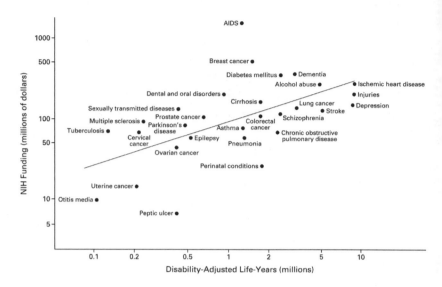

Source of data and graph: Cary P. Gross, MD, Gerard F. Anderson, PhD, and Neil R. Powe, "The Relation between Funding by the National Institutes of Health and the Burden of Disease," *New England Journal of Medicine* 340 (June 17, 1999): 1881–87, fig. 1, http://content.nejm.org/cgi/content/full/340/24/1881 (accessed August 28, 2004).

One more point about the NIH funding graph. Notice the author's decision to label *all* the data points and see how it adds substantive information to the graph. Think how barren the graph would be if the scatter points were not labeled. It would be pointless to label each point on most graphs—too many data points, not much intrinsic interest in any one of them. But, for the NIH study, there are only twenty-nine observations and each represents a major illness the public knows and fears. So labels here add real information, rather than overloading readers.

A FINAL COMMENT ABOUT PRESENTING INFORMATION VISUALLY

Verbal tables, figures, charts, maps, and graphs are powerful tools. They can add information, insights, and persuasive power to your thesis. In the process, they can aid your research and enrich your analysis.

Verbal tables are too often overlooked. Most authors never think of them, and their presentations are weaker for it. That's why you should think carefully about them. Ask yourself whether verbal tables could orient readers or summarize your findings. If the answer is "yes," then use them.

Charts and graphs are almost always the best way to present large data sets. The practical question is which type to use. My advice is to experiment, using the actual data you want to present. Different styles have different strengths. Use your software to produce several alternatives and compare them directly. Then pick the one that best fits your needs—and your readers.'

CHECKLIST: VISUAL PRESENTATIONS

- Cite your information sources for visual presentations.
- Introduce each visual presentation in the preceding text, just as you do with long quotations.
- Title each map, table, figure, picture, chart, or graph.
- Consider adding explanatory captions to visual presentations.
- Highlight points of interest on maps, figures, charts, and graphs.
- Use verbal tables to present your argument and findings succinctly.
- Use charts and graphs to analyze large data sets.
- Label axes on graphs.
- Choose appropriate scales for graphing (such as arithmetic intervals or log scales).
- Compare alternate types of graphs for each presentation, using your actual data.

V

Working
Your Best

13 WORKING EFFICIENTLY

"I'm overwhelmed by all the research I need to do."

"I'm anxious about what I'll be doing next year, and it's affecting my work this year."

"It's so hard to manage my time on a big project like this."

"Applying for a job is taking more time than I ever imagined. It's cutting into my time for courses and the thesis."

Even thesis writers who are trying their best can run into obstacles, sometimes serious ones. Some are intellectual: "I can't find good literature on my topic." Some are emotional: "With all this pressure, my eating problems are back again." Some seem like problems of self-control: "I just can't seem to work steadily on my thesis." Others are beyond your control, either at school or at home: "I have learning disabilities." "My adviser is not much help." "My dad lost his job."

These are difficult issues, and I don't want to sugarcoat them. Fortunately, there are practical approaches that have helped many other students and could help you. In this chapter and the next, I'll share some of these solutions with you. This chapter will concentrate on establishing good work habits, something *every* student needs to do. It's especially important for a major project like your thesis, and it will serve you well for years to come.

The next chapter (14) deals with overcoming specific problems, from stress to procrastination, which affect many students. I'll also briefly discuss issues like alcohol abuse and eating disorders, which affect a few students intensely, and I'll say where help is available.

These two chapters are intertwined. Together, I hope they help you think about and resolve problems that may be affecting your life and impairing your work.

Before discussing specific issues, however, I want to remind you of a couple of things you probably know already. First, your school has resources designed to help. If you don't know the details, ask your academic counselor (not your thesis adviser) or someone in the college dean's office. They know the ins and outs and can offer valuable guidance. For example, they can help set up an appointment with writing tutors, a special service many schools have.

Every school has a learning skills program to help students master better techniques for studying, writing, and managing their time. Each year, they work with thesis students, and, in the process, they have accumulated lots of useful experience. They offer much more than remedial help for students doing poorly. They can help students at all levels, including those who are doing well and want to do better.

Also, every school has a counseling and guidance center to help students cope with emotional issues. Their services are confidential, and the costs are usually covered by student insurance. If the pressure of a thesis, plus a job, and perhaps some problems at home all seem overwhelming, turn to them. That's what they are there for. Please don't think you have to deal with these issues by yourself. Don't think there's nobody you can talk to. There is.

Tip: Your school has valuable resources outside the classroom to help you, including
- Writing tutors and programs
- Study skills center
- Counseling and mental health center

What can you do to work more efficiently? Quite a lot. The answers come in several categories:

- Establishing good work habits
- Keeping a "to do" list
- Balancing competing demands and coping with senior-year issues
- Managing your time

Let's discuss each in turn.

ESTABLISHING GOOD WORK HABITS

Effective study is built on motivation, what one author calls "an intense desire to learn and to achieve," plus your own interest in the subject.[1] To

---

1. Arthur W. Kornhauser, *How to Study: Suggestions for High School and College Students*, revised by Diane M. Enerson, 3rd ed. (Chicago: University of Chicago Press, 1993), 12–13. Kornhauser's brief book is an excellent no-nonsense guide.

work efficiently over the long haul, you need to translate this general desire and broad intellectual curiosity into regular focused work. That means establishing good work habits. Most of all it means working on your project each day, at least a little.

> *Tip:* Try to establish good work habits as part of your thesis project. These habits will serve you well for life.

The single most important habit is to work regularly, not by fits and starts. Don't wait for heavenly inspiration before you start working on your topic or start writing about it. Stendhal, who we now remember for his great novel *The Red and the Black,* said that

> as late as 1806, I was waiting for genius to descend upon me so that I might write. . . . If I had spoken around 1795 of my plan to write, some sensible man would have told me "to write every day for an hour or two." Genius or no genius. That advice would have made me use ten years of my life that I spent stupidly waiting for genius.[2]

The novelist Walker Percy makes a similar point about working regularly, on a predictable schedule:

> You've got to sit down and follow a schedule. Everybody's different, everybody's habits are different. I have to sit down at 9 o'clock in the morning and write for three hours or at least look at the paper for three hours. Some days I don't do *anything*. But unless you do that—punch the time clock—you won't *ever* do anything.[3]

Joan Bolker, a psychologist who has worked with many students (mostly at the doctoral level), urges them to set a target amount of writing rather than a target amount of time, as Percy does. Her experience is that students with severe writing blocks may fritter away the time.[4] Her advice: Try to write a certain number of words each day.

---

2. Quoted in Donald M. Murray, *Shoptalk: Learning to Write with Writers* (Portsmouth, NH: Boynton/Cook Publishers, 1990), 63.

3. Quoted in Murray, *Shoptalk,* 60 (Percy's emphasis).

4. Joan Bolker, *Writing Your Dissertation in Fifteen Minutes a Day: A Guide to Starting, Revising, and Finishing Your Doctoral Thesis* (New York: Henry Holt, 1998).

> *Tip:* Focus on doing some thesis work every day. One goal should be to develop a routine for research and writing on the project. Remember, a thesis is simply too big to pull off in one intense sprint. You need to work at it steadily.

You may want to experiment and see which approach works best for you: a specific amount of time or a specific amount of work and words. Whichever you choose, you should work regularly. *Set a daily target.* That does not require long stretches of writing. Students often begin with a target of one page (250 words), or, alternatively, one hour of writing. Later, they may increase to two or three pages, but seldom more than that on a regular basis. It's a modest amount, something almost everyone can fit into their schedule, especially given the importance of your thesis. Still, if you do it each day and keep at it, the pages pile up. Then your editing skills can take over, and you can shape a polished draft.

> *Tip:* Make a habit of writing regularly on your thesis project—notes, short reports, verbal tables, drafts of paper sections, and so on. Set a daily target amount of work, and show up for work every day. Punch the clock!

Don't wait until you face a crisis deadline. Show up and do the work every day, whether you are feeling inspired or not. Woody Allen, who makes a film every year, once observed that "eighty percent of success is showing up."[5] That's true for academic work, as well.

Establishing a work routine is something you should do at the beginning of your thesis project and carry through to the end. *You* need to establish this routine yourself. No one else will do it for you. After all, there is no class schedule to keep you on track, no set time for exams and term papers. Your daily and monthly schedules are flexible. In fact, your daily thesis schedule is probably more flexible than any you've ever experienced. Since nobody else will establish a routine for you, you have to do it your-

---

5. *Simpson's Contemporary Quotations,* compiled by James B. Simpson (Boston: Houghton Mifflin, 1988), http://www.bartleby.com/63/54/2254.html (accessed August 10, 2004).

self. Your adviser can offer some suggestions, *if you ask,* but you need to take responsibility, just as you do for all aspects of your thesis.

The place to begin is by finding regular places to read and write—quiet ones, close to the sources you need. If you can't say, right now, what those places are, then you probably don't have them. The places that worked well for you last year may not work so well this year because you have much more research and writing to do. Your most pressing task, then, is to find some good study spots ASAP.

If you already have workplaces but are constantly being interrupted there, find new ones, put up a sign on your door, or let friends know that you need to work uninterrupted for the next hour. Turn off diversions like instant messaging and your cell phone. Don't multitask. While you are working on the thesis, concentrate on it.

> *Tip:* Find a quiet place to work regularly, and don't bring your own distractions with you.

Phones are a real problem since we are trained to answer them. When they ring, we salivate like Pavlov's dogs. The solution is to shut off the ringer and turn on the answering machine, or just assume they'll call back. If you ever read interviews with serious writers, they all say exactly the same thing about the phone. They simply refuse to answer it during regular writing hours. Good idea. For thesis writers, the same advice applies to time spent studying your notes and preparing to write, as well as actual writing time. Just let it ring.

Speaking of regular hours, set them up for writing when your project reaches that stage. It doesn't matter whether the hours are morning, afternoon, or night. Do whatever works best for you. Pick the time you are normally most focused and alert. But make it a point to do serious reading, reflection, and writing during that time without distraction, whether you feel inspired or not. Keep it up and work steadily, day after day.

Don't try to cram it all into a few last-minute binge sessions. Even if you reach the finish line after such binges, you'll feel exhausted, and it won't be your best work. You won't have time to step back and reflect on it. You won't have time to do revisions, large or small. As you now know, this editing and revision is essential to doing your best work.

Monitor the success of your work habits and arrangements. If your quiet place turns out to be a noisy place, solve the problem. Ask your friends to turn down the music, buy a white-noise machine, or find another place to work. Any one of these is fine. What's *not* fine is sticking with a bad arrangement. Size up the situation and make some improvements.

As you move forward on the thesis, occasionally reassess your schedule, your workplace, and your habits to see what's working and what's not. Think about these issues and then make the changes you need. If the new arrangements work better, stick with them. If not, try again.

KEEP A "TO DO" LIST—ACTUALLY, KEEP TWO OF THEM

Keep a running "to do" list for your thesis. I've mentioned this before, but it bears repeating. The clearer and more detailed your list is, the better. It should be one of the first files you set up in your computer's thesis folder. Update it near the end of each day, and refer to it as you begin work again the next day.

The goal is to review and update your "to do" list daily. Cross off what you have completed and add whatever you need to handle tomorrow. Doing this review at day's end shouldn't take more than a minute. It will serve as your daily planning session, something you need to do anyway. To make it work, though, you need to do it regularly and then review it as you begin research and writing the next day. Make it a habit. Print it out if you will be working away from the computer. That way you can refer to it during your workday.

Differentiate high-priority items from lesser ones. An item deserves priority if it is important in its own right or if it needs to be completed before you can tackle the next major item in your thesis. Experts say you should handle these high-priority items first thing during the workday. Get them out of the way, even if they are unpleasant (*especially* if they are unpleasant). That way, they won't be hanging over you all day, little clouds of guilt and anxiety.

> *Tip:* Establish a "to do" list for your thesis, prioritize the items on it, and update it daily. Refer to it at the beginning of each new workday. Deal with high-priority items first, even if they're unpleasant.

Keep a second "to do" list solely for nonthesis tasks, everything from paying your bills to buying airline tickets. These tasks have a way of muscling in and demanding your time right this minute. The best way to keep these distractions at bay is to write them down so you can tackle them on *your* schedule, when you have a moment, not when the phone rings or you happen to remember.

I'm not urging you to avoid these tasks. They are important in their own right. But keep these tasks separate so they don't distract you from your research and writing. That way you can pay your electric bill or fill up your car when you need to take a break, not when you happen to think of it. And not when your car runs out of gas on the expressway.

> *Tip:* Establish a second "to do" list for nonthesis items. Keep them separate from your thesis tasks.

BALANCING COMPETING DEMANDS AND COPING WITH SENIOR-YEAR ISSUES

Many items on these "to do" lists are small. Probably none of them are overwhelming, at least by themselves. But there are so many of them, all demanding your time. The problem is one of balancing competing demands, keeping several balls in the air at once. That's even harder as a senior than it was as a sophomore or junior. After all, you not only have courses to take; you also have a thesis to write and plans to make for next year, after you've graduated.

Seniors writing theses face four types of demands that continue through the year:

- Researching and writing the thesis itself
- Keeping up with other course work
- Taking care of normal daily tasks, from shopping to paying bills
- Planning for life after college, which may include applying for jobs or graduate school, taking standardized tests, going for interviews, and more

Two of these—the thesis and postcollege planning—are unique to senior year.

Some of these tasks have important deadlines. Your final exam in economics or chemistry won't wait until you complete the next section of your thesis. Neither will application deadlines for law school or business school. Standardized tests for graduate school—LSATs, GMATs, and GREs—all have fixed dates. So do campus job interviews. You have to adjust your schedule to them. They certainly aren't going to adjust theirs for you. Since your thesis is not due for months, it is tempting to put it off and handle these other pressing matters first.

There are really two big issues here. One is juggling the competing claims on your time. You need to find ways of balancing them—ways that work *for you*. If you have job interviews next week, then you probably should focus on your thesis and course work this week. When tests or job interviews are coming up, let your thesis adviser know and explain that you will be delayed temporarily.

Don't let these delays stretch out. That's the crucial point. One way of preventing that problem is to tell your adviser (and yourself!) exactly when you expect to be back on schedule. If you plan to resume regular thesis writing next Tuesday, say so—to yourself, your friends, and your adviser. Look ahead, anticipate the claims on your time, and do some planning to adjust.

> *Tip:* Balance work on your thesis with other obligations. Working steadily on the thesis and planning ahead will give you flexibility when you need it—time for your job, other courses, and other activities, including some time for fun!

The second big issue is that your future after college hangs over your senior year. That can be exciting, but it can also be nerve-racking. The choices are difficult for three reasons: They cover such a wide array of possibilities; they are novel; and they carry such large consequences.

The range of choices is probably greater than any you have faced before, everything from grad school to volunteer service, from a year traveling abroad to every kind of job imaginable. Some, like going to law school, are long-term career choices. Others, like traveling or volunteering, are meant to last only a year or two. Some choices mean you'll be out of school for the first time since you were five years old.

On top of all that, there's the uncertainty. You may want a particular job or want to go to a particular grad school, but you're not sure if you will get the offer. You may be uncertain about how desirable that job is or whether you really want to move to that city. It's hard to know until you actually do it. You may be unsure if you want to teach, work for a large corporation, or become a lawyer. You haven't done any of them before, and you're uncertain if you'll like your choice or succeed in it. The possibilities are interesting, even exhilarating, but they are also daunting.

Parents and advisers may say, "The choices you make today are important, but they aren't written in stone. You'll make lots of changes along the way." That's right—and it's worth remembering—but it's cold comfort. These are significant choices, some of the biggest you have ever made, and you may well be anxious about them. Understandably so. Are they the right choices for you? Will you get the offer you want? Will your choice prove interesting and rewarding?

My advice is straightforward and familiar. It really helps to talk these issues out. Discuss them with friends and college advisers. If you are close to some teachers, drop in for their office hours and discuss the choices you face. Talk about your values, skills, and aspirations, and how they bear on your decisions. Talk about what's meaningful to you, what you do well, and what you most enjoy doing. Ask for reactions, suggestions.

Talking about these issues can give you useful information and, equally important, it can lessen fears of the unknown. It will certainly help you think about your choices. The more you do that, the more informed your decisions will be.

Most important of all, if you are genuinely troubled or apprehensive, talk with a therapist. These are precisely the issues your college mental health center deals with every day. They can provide support as you sort out your priorities and make choices that work best for you. Their services are confidential, and they're a safe place to talk about all these issues.

> *Tip:* It helps to talk over new issues and uncertainties that accompany senior year. Turn to friends, family, and teachers. If you are deeply anxious or worried, talk with a therapist.

MANAGING YOUR TIME

Your work habits and scheduling are part of a larger issue: managing your time effectively. I will focus here on ordinary issues of time management. In the next chapter, "Overcoming Problems," I will discuss procrastination and writer's block, which are different from day-to-day issues of using time efficiently.

The best way to manage your time, aside from establishing a regular schedule for reading, research, and writing, is to *work on a series of small manageable projects* and to *give each task its own deadline.* Slice your large tasks into bite-size bits. That's a variant on the old joke about how to eat an elephant. "One bite at a time." That's also how to complete a thesis, and there is considerably less gristle.

> *Tip:* The best way to manage any large project, including a thesis, is to
> - Divide it into smaller projects
> - Set deadlines for each project

Take a typical task such as background reading. No matter what your thesis topic, your reading will have several components. Let's say you are studying the 1980 presidential election between incumbent President Jimmy Carter and challenger Ronald Reagan. You probably need to do some research about several aspects of the election: (1) Carter's presidency and his problems in office, (2) Reagan's rise within the Republican Party, (3) major campaign issues, and (4) survey data showing why voters chose as they did. There are four distinct literatures to analyze, and you can tackle each one of them in sequence. By doing that, you've broken up one big task into four more manageable ones. This process works the same way for virtually every topic.

You might decide to summarize each smaller reading project with a one- or two-page paper. Later, you could fold these short papers and other prewriting into your draft thesis. In the process, you have burst through two barriers: breaking down a large topic into its constituent elements and turning your research into writing.

You might present the first couple of reading topics at a meeting with your adviser and then present the remainder at your next meeting. In fact, you can *use these regular meetings as a way to schedule your work* and complete it on time. These meetings can serve as mini-deadlines for small projects.

In fact, that's a great use for meetings with advisers or tutors, or for workshops. They can serve as markers to keep yourself on schedule, moving forward. You can strengthen your commitment to this schedule by telling your adviser exactly what you expect to accomplish by your next session. Be realistic. Don't overpromise. Then do your best to stick to your commitment.

What if you have not finished the task on time? You will be tempted to skip the meeting with your adviser. Don't. *Never skip a scheduled meeting unless you are sick or have an emergency.* If you need to reschedule, always notify the professor. But don't reschedule just to save yourself from embarrassment. We all fall behind occasionally. Come in for a shorter meeting and bring your adviser up-to-date on what you have accomplished so far. Just be brief so you don't waste your time or your adviser's.

> *Tip:* Meet regularly with your adviser. Come with your own agenda and bring written work if possible. If you need to cancel a meeting, notify the adviser.

Regular work overcomes the dreaded problem of inertia. In fact, that's one of its major advantages. We've all experienced it. Students at rest tend to stay at rest. Students in motion tend to stay in motion. (Faculty, too!) That's why it is so important to lay aside distractions and begin work. If you aren't ready to write yet, go over your notes. Organize and amplify them. Synthesize your main points. That's the prewriting process we discussed earlier, and it's valuable in its own right. If you are not at that stage, then read some more and write up your research. Keep working. Keep writing. If you have trouble getting started, then it may help to start with the most enticing items. But get moving so inertia is transformed into momentum, working for you, not against you.

I'll return to these points in the next chapter when I discuss writer's block and procrastination. Although they are more serious problems, the practical approach to solving them is the same: small steps, done on a regular schedule.

CHECKLIST: WORKING EFFICIENTLY

- Establish regular work habits for your project.
- Write frequently—daily if possible—even if it is only a brief note or a commentary on a reading.
- Find a quiet place to read and write without distractions.
- Review your work habits and study locations periodically.
- Keep a separate "to do" list for nonthesis items.
- Meet regularly with your adviser (bring a brief agenda to each meeting).
- Take advantage of your school's learning skills center, writing tutors, and other services.

---

14 OVERCOMING PROBLEMS

"I'm having trouble starting to write."

"My thesis adviser is soooo slow. He takes forever to return my drafts."

"My adviser writes vague comments like 'needs more work.' That's no help at all. What am I supposed to do?"

"My writing never seems any good."

"My mom has been very sick, and she's always on my mind. I'm having trouble concentrating. I not even sure I should stay in school, much less write a thesis."

"This is just too much pressure. I'm having trouble sleeping."

In this chapter I'll focus on problems like these and offer practical solutions, beginning with four issues that confront many students:

- Coping with stress
- Getting enough sleep
- Dealing with serious procrastination
- Overcoming writing blocks

After that, I will consider several issues that touch fewer students but affect them intensely. I briefly discuss substance abuse and eating disorders and urge students with these problems to seek professional help. For students with learning disabilities and attention deficit disorders, I emphasize a few simple steps to make research and writing easier. Finally, I address other personal problems, as well as difficulties that sometimes arise with advisers or family.

A reminder: Your school has a student mental health center, staffed by experienced professionals, to help you deal with important emotional issues. If you face troubling problems, don't hesitate to call them for a confidential appointment. That's what they're there for.

> *Tip:* If personal problems arise or you face emotional issues, you can talk things over privately at your school's mental health center.

MANAGING STRESS

Stress is your mind and body's reaction to the pressures facing you—in this case, the psychological demands of research, writing, and managing a large project by yourself. You cannot get rid of these factors pressing down on you, what psychologists call "stressors." In fact, you may not want to get rid of them entirely. Studies show a little stress can be energizing and motivating. Too much, however, is simply destructive. If the pressures are too great, your main goals should be to

* Reduce them
* Lessen their negative impact
* Learn how to work productively in their shadow

The key is your frame of mind. You can manage stress best if you assume the problems facing you are challenges you can surmount, not billboards that say "You failed" or "Road ahead closed forever." You can cope most effectively if you consider the obstacles temporary, not permanent, and assume they are related to specific tasks, not universal problems that will show up again and again to smack you down.

Tip: Try to see problems as manageable tasks, not permanent obstructions.

Why does this reframing help? Because studies show that optimism—a sense of hopefulness—leads to more productive work. It prepares you to solve problems as they arise. Pessimism does not. Or, to look at the other side of the coin, because mishandled stress can easily morph into a fatalistic, passive attitude that becomes self-perpetuating.

To combat this fatalism, think about what has helped you in the past and turn to it now for reassurance and encouragement. For some, that is religion or inspirational literature. For others, it is friends and community. For still others, it is working with psychotherapists trained in these issues. Therapists not only offer a safe, private place to talk about difficult issues; they can help in other ways. Some specialize in specific problems, everything from procrastination to eating disorders, and have techniques to deal with them. They can also determine whether students could benefit from medications such as antidepressant drugs, which require a prescription and supervision.

One way to reduce pessimism, and the stress associated with it, is to approach your work differently. *Try to make your tasks definite.*[1] Large vague goals can overwhelm anyone. Realistic concrete goals are achievable. They lessen anxiety and relieve the sense of gloom and doom. The idea is to transform looming obstacles into soluble problems, on which you can make headway. This reframing will make a huge difference, both in what you accomplish and how you feel about it.

Another way to improve your outlook is to *give yourself credit for accomplishments* along the way. Ease up on criticizing yourself (or blaming others) for difficulties and failures. Look forward to possibilities, not backward at failures, and try to maintain a sense of hopefulness.

> *Tip:* Problems are more manageable if you pose concrete tasks for yourself and then give yourself credit for success, including partial success at intermediate stages.

When you have successfully completed a task, recognize it and give yourself permission to take a break. You've earned it. That's the whole point: to recognize emotionally that you really have earned it. That may mean a trip to the movies with friends or an evening out, without guilt! You'll return to work refreshed. If you are having trouble completing your work, use these treats as carrots, incentives for finishing the work you need to do. Give yourself smaller rewards for regular weekly accomplishments, larger ones when you have completed major portions of your project.

The idea of rewarding yourself, not putting yourself down, and not assuming every problem is insuperable sounds like the advice of Stuart Smalley, the self-affirmation guru and addiction-recovery expert on *Saturday Night Live*. Stuart (created by Al Franken) struggles with low self-esteem. He belongs to every twelve-step program ever invented. As viewers, we know he'll never conquer his personal demons, but he keeps plugging away at them. His willingness to keep rolling the stone up the mountain is admirable. We know it's a caricature, we laugh, but we sympathize. We pull for him.

---

1. Arthur W. Kornhauser, *How to Study: Suggestions for High School and College Students,* revised by Diane M. Enerson, 3rd ed. (Chicago: University of Chicago Press, 1993), 14.

One of his big goals is to overcome self-blaming and self-hatred. Borrowing from the language of recovery programs, he wants to stop his "Stinkin' Thinkin.'" Stuart's diary reflects the ups and downs. After every one of his New Year's resolutions fails, his entry for January 6 begins, "I am a fraud." Fortunately, his February 7 entry is "I will bounce back," and on February 12 he writes, "Today I can choose to feel good." His memoir has the great self-affirming title *I'm Good Enough, I'm Smart Enough, and Doggone It, People Like Me! Daily Affirmations by Stuart Smalley.*[2] Wonderfully exaggerated, of course, but his approach is exactly right.

Even resilient students are stressed out after a few hours hunched over the computer screen. It doesn't take many hours for physical and emotional tensions to build up. The typing itself can cause repetitive motion injuries. The screen is hard on the eyes. And, of course, you face the additional pressures of trying to fill up that blank screen with intelligent thoughts. You may begin in a relaxed, comfortable posture, but forty-five minutes later, you are bent forward, hands tense at the keyboard, teeth clenched, eyes squinting, like O.J. Simpson in a traffic jam. Not good.

There are a few easy, helpful solutions. You just have to remind yourself to do them. First, when you are working at the computer, take a brief break every ten to fifteen minutes. Stretch your arms, clench and open your fists several times, interlace your fingers and stretch them. These will break the physical tension in your hands, wrists, and arms and lessen the dangers of repetitive motion injuries, which happen after bouts of intense typing.

To ease the strains in your neck, tilt your head very slowly all the way to the right (that is, try to touch your right ear to your right shoulder) while looking straight ahead. Then do it on the left side. Very slowly; it's a stretching motion. To lessen eye strain, look away from the screen and focus on distant objects. Before resuming work, remember to adjust your posture, too. Be sure your keyboard and screen are at the right height and in the right position. Although these are small actions, they will release a lot of the physical strain that has been building up. Every half hour or so, get up and walk around briefly. These short breaks have a remarkably restorative effect. They will make you feel better and improve your work.

---

2. Al Franken, *I'm Good Enough, I'm Smart Enough, and Doggone It, People Like Me! Daily Affirmations by Stuart Smalley* (New York: DTP, 1992).

> *Tip:* During long bouts of work at the computer, take an occasional break and stretch. Every half hour, get up and walk around.

Of all the tips for relaxation, the oddest, easiest, and most useful is to *check your tongue.* That's the offbeat advice of Robert Boice, and despite my initial skepticism (nay, incredulity), he's convinced me. If your tongue is on the roof of your mouth, he says, you are tense. If it's resting on the bottom of your mouth, you are relaxed.[3] If it has a large metal stud in it, you are in hot water with your parents.

Checking your tongue truly works. Try it right now and you'll see. It takes no time. Better yet, relaxing your tongue has real benefits: it relaxes your jaw, neck, and facial muscles. That's why some yoga exercises use it. Odd, I'll grant you, but it works, and that's what counts.

> *Tip:* To relax your head and upper body, try relaxing your tongue!

SLEEP PROBLEMS

"Finish each day before you begin the next," said Ralph Waldo Emerson, "and interpose a solid wall of sleep between the two."[4] Good advice.

Medical professionals use the term "sleep hygiene." That makes me think of hospital orderlies and disinfectants. Actually, it means establishing some comfortable, effective routines before bedtime. That's hard to do at college because class schedules change each day and because some friends are always up late, eager to have you join them.

Why are sleep routines important? Because you need more than a night of tossing and turning. You need the restorative qualities of deep sleep, and you need to get enough of it. You won't get it if your sleep is fragmented, light, or brief. You won't get it if your sleep schedule changes every day to keep up with your classes and social schedule.

---

3. Robert Boice, *How Writers Journey to Comfort and Fluency: A Psychological Adventure* (Westport, CT: Praeger, 1994), 29–30.

4. Quoted in Jon Winokur, ed., *Advice to Writers* (New York: Pantheon Books, 1999), 31.

> *Tip:* Establish sleep routines: regular habits at bedtime and regular times for sleep.

Different people need different amounts of sleep, and most of us can get by with a little less for a few days running. But in the process we build up a sleep deficit, which cumulates and is restored only by an extra amount of deep restorative sleep. It's like overdrawing your bank account. You can't keep it up. Something's gotta give.

> *Tip:* Don't skimp on sleep. You can scrape by with less for a few days, but you'll soon need to make up this sleep deficit.

Some people have more serious, persistent problems such as sleep apnea, in which breathing stops briefly (but frequently), impeding deep sleep. One symptom is constant snoring, although that has many other causes as well. Sufferers feel drowsy much of the time, even though they think they've gotten a full night's sleep. They really haven't. They appear to have been sleeping, but they haven't slept well. They need medical treatment. Fortunately, that treatment has gotten much better in recent years and successful therapies are now available. If you are constantly tired, ask your doctor about it.

More common problems are that students, working hard on their thesis and courses and job applications, go to bed anxious, after too much coffee or too many cigarettes, while somebody in the next room has the stereo turned up to 11, playing music you hate. The effects are predictable.

The country's leading sleep centers all offer the same sensible advice for getting a good night's sleep:

- A quiet, dark room
- A comfortable bed
- No caffeine in the evening
- Exercise, as long as you do it more than a couple of hours before bed
- Easing up on drugs, alcohol, and cigarettes, all of which interfere with deep sleep

Emerson's quote about the need for a solid wall of sleep was followed by his advice not to drink too much. Although alcohol is a sedative, it decreases the quality of sleep and increases the number of times you awaken in the night. If you are taking prescription medicines, ask your doctor if they might be keeping you up.

Naps are fine as long as you are sleeping normally. If you have trouble sleeping, though, you should avoid naps because they prevent the reestablishment of normal deep-sleep patterns. At least that's what experts say. For the same reasons, they recommend going to bed only when you are sleepy. To set your biological clock, try awakening at roughly the same time each morning and try to get some bright sunlight during the day. That allows the body's clock to figure out when it's nighttime and slow down. (Sunlight also reduces seasonal affective disorder, SAD, the mild depression that many suffer during the winter.)

The goal, then, is to minimize a series of problems that can disrupt and fragment your sleep—anything from anxiety to high energy at night. If you do that and still have trouble sleeping, see a doctor for advice.

PROCRASTINATION

While everybody delays some things sometimes, a few people experience more severe problems. They are unable to complete crucial work and find it difficult even to begin essential tasks. Their difficulties go beyond ordinary issues of time management. They need support and sustained treatment from therapists who deal with serious procrastination.

> *Tip:* If procrastination is a serious problem, if it comes up repeatedly or is blocking important goals, see a therapist. Pardon the irony, but don't put it off.

Typically, procrastination problems are rooted in feelings of inadequacy and a poor sense of self-worth. Procrastinators often have little confidence or self-esteem. They may experience genuine fear—a disabling fear of failure, of being judged inadequate. By not completing a project, they avoid being judged on it. They don't even have to judge themselves, at least not on the final product. After all, no one can review the Great American Novel if it's the Great American *Unfinished* Novel. That's true for a thesis, too.

A few students fear success, which carries its own demands. They worry they will have to continue meeting unbearably high standards.

Anger, low frustration tolerance, and self-depreciation can all contribute to the problem. *Perhaps the most important source of procrastination is perfectionism,* a rigid, unrealistic demand that you must get every detail perfect or the entire project is worthless.

Unfortunately, procrastination has a nasty tendency to reinforce itself. Each delay makes the task a little harder to begin, a little harder to even think about finishing. Each delay makes the time pressure a little greater. Predictably, these delays raise your anger at those who make demands and fuel self-loathing for not being able to meet them.

Professional counseling is necessary to get at the underlying sources of this disabling perfectionism and low self-esteem. Fortunately, the behavioral choices to deal with them are less mysterious. That's what I will focus on here.

PRACTICAL WAYS TO OVERCOME PROCRASTINATION

The most important change you can make is to calibrate proper standards for judging your own work. The goal for a senior thesis—for anyone's senior thesis—is not perfectionism or, indeed, any absolute standard of quality. *The right goal is to make your best effort.* Not a perfect effort. Not a twenty-four-hour-a-day effort. Not a senior thesis that matches a doctoral dissertation. Those are unrealistic demands. No one could meet them. No one should try.

You shouldn't try. Don't set impossibly high standards, which guarantee failure and foster a sense of futility. It's fine to set goals a little beyond your current reach and strive for them. That's a worthy ambition, and an attainable one. But don't set such lofty goals that you can never meet them. That will only inhibit your best work and generate self-depreciating (and self-perpetuating) anger.

A better approach is to use the thesis project to learn about the subject and learn about doing research. Then judge the results by whether you have worked intelligently and done your level best. Your best may be better than your roommate's, or worse. Whichever it is, it's still *your best.* That solid effort should be recognized for what it is and rewarded, not ignored or depreciated for what it is not.

So, the first point is to recalibrate your standards and goals. Set them at reasonable levels, measured by your abilities and the time you have available.

Second, give yourself positive recognition for accomplishments, not blame for falling short of perfection.

> *Tip:* Set reasonable standards—not impossible goals—and reward yourself for working hard to meet them. Recognize your achievements. Learn from mistakes, but don't dwell on your shortcomings.

Third, be aware of your own internal dialogue—your mental conversation—as you set standards and try to meet them. Are you trying too hard to please someone with impossibly high standards? Worse yet, have you internalized these unachievable standards and made them your own? Or have you set more healthy, realistic goals that promote your best work? It helps to think about this internal dialogue and ask whether it inhibits your work or encourages it. The best way to make this dialogue more productive is to be aware of it and try self-consciously to make reasonable demands on yourself.

Fourth, recognize that all of us delay more in some areas than others. Business executives who run a tight ship at work may find it impossible to file their taxes by April 15. Every year, they need an extension. Students who can't start writing may do perfectly well in every other area of academic life. The same is true for professors. They may be great teachers and advisers, but have trouble writing. The lesson: Identify which areas are giving you problems and plan to work on those areas.

In fact, just recognizing how selective your procrastination is might suggest some solutions. It encourages you to draw on techniques that work well for you in other areas. And it reassures you that your problems are specific, not global, that they affect some parts of your life, not everything.

> *Tip:* If you procrastinate, monitor your internal dialogue. Try to avoid berating yourself or striving to meet others' unrealistic standards. Recognize that procrastination usually involves some specific areas, not everything. That's not only reassuring; it suggests you might borrow techniques that already work for you in other areas.

Some tips we discussed earlier may help, too. Slicing a big task into manageable small ones is essential. So is a commitment to working each day for a short specific time on a problem area such as writing. Robert Boice calls them "brief, daily sessions."[5] Joan Bolker advocates a similar idea in *Writing Your Dissertation in Fifteen Minutes a Day.*[6] Despite her book's title, she recognizes that no one can actually complete a PhD thesis by writing only fifteen minutes or even thirty minutes a day. But it is equally true that no one will *ever* complete one if they don't start writing at least that much. A half hour or less is such a modest daily commitment that most people, even those with serious writing blocks, can commit to sitting down at the computer for that long. It's a modest concrete promise to yourself to try. That is the essential beginning of a solution.

Another part of the solution is to expect some setbacks along the way. That's true for all of us, whether we suffer from procrastination or not. We all backslide sometimes. The question is what happens *after* these inevitable setbacks. Will they prompt an orgy of self-blame, leading to a downward spiral? Or can you contain the problem and bounce back?

Tip: Everybody has setbacks. Remember that. Learn from mistakes, but don't obsess about past problems. Concentrate on what comes next. Try to resume working with focus and optimism.

Every time I watch a golf tournament, I notice how well the pros handle these setbacks. Even the best players occasionally put a shot into the woods and then hit their recovery shot into a lake. They end up with a horrible score for that hole. Then, they do something that is nearly impossible for us duffers. They tee up at the next hole and play as if nothing had happened. They know that if they fall into a funk, let themselves tense up with self-blame, or press too hard to catch up all at once, they will only compound the problem. They won't have just one bad hole. They'll have a string of them. Their best chance is to limit the disaster to a single hole and resume their normal game.

---

5. Boice, *How Writers Journey*, 30–34.

6. Joan Bolker, *Writing Your Dissertation in Fifteen Minutes a Day: A Guide to Starting, Revising, and Finishing Your Doctoral Thesis* (New York: Henry Holt, 1998).

Frankly, that's the best approach for all of us after a setback, even a serious one. Contain the damage. Look forward. Reestablish a doable plan. Ease up on blaming yourself. And make a reasonable effort (not a superhuman one) to get back on track.

One final point may be helpful. Once you have established some reasonable goals, such as writing a daily one-page research summary, tell a friend or two about it. That will make it real. It will no longer exist solely inside your head; it will be out in the world. Just saying it aloud takes away some of the fear and encourages you to take the commitment seriously.

This commitment also helps in another way: you have now made yourself accountable to someone. Each of us experiences low spots, when our willpower and sense of responsibility may not be enough. That's why we need a friend to exercise with, or a study buddy. Having made ourselves accountable to a friend, we no longer perform for ourselves alone. We are performing for ourselves *plus* someone else we care about. That can really help.

> *Tip:* Tell friends or faculty about your short-term goals, such as completing a thesis section by next Wednesday. It will make you accountable, reduce vague anxieties, and make the task and deadline seem more real.

For some, this sense of accountability is even more important. They can perform better for others than for themselves. Their self-esteem may be low—a serious problem in its own right—but they feel a strong sense of responsibility to others at school, work, or home. For them, making a commitment to others is invaluable. It's a practical answer to a difficult problem.

There are several reasons, then, why it is helpful to talk with friends and advisers about what you intend to accomplish in the near future. It lessens unspoken fears, and it makes the project more tangible. It gives you another chance to think about the project. It offers support while making you accountable. And for some it does more. It substitutes an external sense of responsibility for a weak internal sense.

If you have a strong positive relationship with such a friend, ask her to be a study partner. You don't need to spend hours studying together. Just take a few minutes every day to discuss what you have done and offer each other encouragement about what you intend to do next. The only rule is that your partnership needs to be helpful and supportive, not a litany of complaints and failures.

USING FREEWRITING TO OVERCOME WRITING BLOCKS

Writing blocks are just another form of serious procrastination. The same basic points apply. There is, however, one additional technique that has often proved helpful: *freewriting*.

Students who use this technique are told to write rapidly, without interruption, for ten to fifteen minutes, without trying to stay on topic and without bothering about spelling or grammar. Just keep moving and don't slow down unless your house is on fire. Then call 911 and continue writing. Because self-editing is nearly impossible while writing fast and continuously (and is strongly discouraged, in any case), the process cuts through ingrained habits and sometimes produces striking language and insights.

Freewriting is a low-pressure way to deal with writer's block. There's no room for procrastination if you are told to start typing or handwriting, simply write down whatever ideas pop into your head, and keep doing it without stopping. There's no perfectionism, either, because there are no criteria for judgment.

Some experts urge you to repeat the exercise ("looping"), building on a few ideas you liked during the first round. Before beginning this second round, review your earlier work and highlight what you liked. These ideas or phrases then become the loose focus for the second freewriting exercise. The process can be repeated, picking out what you liked in the previous round and gradually increasing your focus. Parts of the final product may be incorporated in a first draft—or at least spur ideas for it.

Tip: Freewriting is one tested technique to overcome writing blocks.

There is nothing complicated or time-consuming about freewriting, and you can give it a test drive, either to generate ideas or to overcome writing fears. There's nothing to lose. If you suffer writing problems, there's a lot to gain. The only questions are practical ones: Does it yield any ideas worth pursuing? Does it eventually lead to more disciplined, productive writing? Does it produce vigorous language?

A number of writing teachers, led by Peter Elbow, strongly believe it does produce original work. A number of therapists, including Joan Bolker, believe it is the most effective path to overcoming writer's block.[7] If you suffer from writer's block or from a disabling sense of perfectionism and inadequacy about your work, it is well worth trying. Nothing to lose. A lot to gain.

USING PREWRITING TO OVERCOME WRITING BLOCKS

Prewriting, which I've advocated throughout this book, is another good way to tackle writer's block. The reason is simple. Prewriting postpones "real writing" until quite late. Most of the time, you are simply filling in your ideas without writing a structured draft. After you have amplified those ideas and figured out connections among them, you have actually produced most of the text for a draft, even though you never sat down to write a formal first draft. It becomes relatively straightforward to pull together the prewriting into a text and then begin the process of editing and rewriting it.

Prewriting blurs the lines between taking notes, writing an outline, writing a first draft, and even editing some of that text. As you prewrite, you are doing all those things. You are building a draft, block by block, and often editing the prose and finding links among different parts as you go along. Do it steadily as you move through your reading and research.

> *Tip:* Prewriting is another technique to overcome writer's block. Keep amplifying your notes and adding prose paragraphs here and there. Soon, you'll have substantial written work to edit.

One more point about prewriting. Don't wait until you are fully 100 percent prepared to write. That's not the way the process works. It works best if you write down ideas as they arise and then review and edit them from time to time.

---

7. Peter Elbow, *Writing without Teachers,* 2nd ed. (New York: Oxford University Press, 1998); Peter Elbow, *Writing with Power,* 2nd ed. (New York: Oxford University Press, 1998). Joan Bolker shows how this process can be used effectively for doctoral theses. Many of her ideas apply to BA theses, as well. Bolker, *Writing Your Dissertation.*

This idea of *prewriting before you are fully prepared* short-circuits one of the biggest writing blocks: the desire to hold off starting until everything is perfect. It never will be. You are waiting for Godot. He's not just late; he's not coming. Prewriting sidesteps that.

> *Tip:* Begin prewriting a little before you feel completely ready

ALCOHOL, DRUGS, AND EATING DISORDERS

Heavy use of alcohol or drugs is a serious problem, and it requires professional help. It impairs your thinking, blunts your writing, disrupts your sleep, and cuts into your time. Even more important, heavy drinking and drug use are signs of real personal difficulties—and often sources of those difficulties as well. They can threaten everything you care about: your health, your schoolwork, your friendships, and your family. Eating problems such as anorexia and bulimia fall into the same dangerous category. Unfortunately, they won't go away by themselves. Time alone won't cure them.

If these are problems in your life, or if you fear they might be, seek help. Do it sooner rather than later. Make an appointment at your student mental health center, which has the resources to deal with them and considerable experience doing so. There are also some wonderful self-help groups such as Alcoholics Anonymous that provide lifesaving support for participants. They've lasted because they work. Most campuses have chapters, and all cities do.

> *Tip:* If you have drug or alcohol problems or an eating disorder, seek help from professional counselors and support groups.

This help won't start until you ask for it, until *you* determine that you really need it. Even if your well-intentioned friends point out these problems, you won't make progress until you accept the point, deep down. Fortunately, help begins as soon as you recognize there is a serious problem and reach out for assistance. It will be there for you, but you have to take the first step.

LEARNING DISABILITIES AND ATTENTION
DEFICIT DISORDER

Most students with dyslexia, attention deficit disorders (ADD), hyper-activity (ADHD), or other learning difficulties have been diagnosed well before their senior year and have learned strategies to cope. That's how they made it this far, and that's how they will make it through their thesis, too. Students with learning problems *can* complete a thesis. They just need to approach it with self-understanding and a thoughtful plan.

Thesis writing is challenging because it requires students with ADD, ADHD, and learning disabilities (LD) to do what they find especially diffi-cult: long-term planning, sustained work, lots of writing, and even more reading. These are challenges, not permanent roadblocks. They can be overcome or worked around.

If you face these issues, my advice is to do the following:

- Assess how your strengths and weaknesses will affect the thesis project.
- Plan ahead to offset any difficulties.
- Visit your college learning skills center, which has experience with ADD, ADHD, and LD and can provide help tailored to your needs.
- Consider what information you should share with your thesis adviser to enhance your working relationship.

The first two points are essential. You need to evaluate your own strengths and weaknesses and plan your thesis project in ways that accommodate them. The last two points are optional but helpful for many students.

Start by stepping back and asking what impact your learning difficulties might have on your thesis project. Knowing that will give you an opportu-nity to plan ahead, get the support you need, and use the compensatory skills you have already developed. You should identify areas where, based on experience, you expect some difficulties. Then decide how best to ap-proach them. It you have reading problems, for instance, it may be impor-tant to settle on the general topic late in your junior year so you can do some background reading over the summer. That's just one example. The aim is to think about your own learning style and how, given your strengths and weaknesses, you can handle a thesis project most effectively.

Your school's learning center can help in several ways. The staff there will have plenty of experience working with ADD, ADHD, and LD. Aside from offering support and understanding, they can provide concrete assistance in planning a long-term project and keeping it on track. That's important for all students. It is even more important for students with attention deficit or learning disabilities.

Regular meetings with a learning skills adviser can also be very useful. She won't know the details of your subject in sociology, Spanish, or economics, but she will know how to help you plan and execute a large project. She will help you build on your strong points and compensate for your weak ones. And she'll provide one other source of encouragement. She'll remind you that she's worked with many other students who faced similar issues and who managed to complete their own best thesis.

To reap these benefits, you need to take some action. Begin by arranging a get-acquainted meeting at the learning center. After discussing your needs and finding the right counselor there, form a working relationship and return regularly. When should you begin? As soon as you start thinking about writing a thesis. If you are uncertain about whether to write one, a staff member there can help you make an informed decision.

What about your thesis adviser? How much information about learning issues should you share with her? The answers vary, depending upon your needs and your relationship, but the overall goal is clear: You want to *share specific information that will enhance your working relationship.* The clearer your information, the more concrete your requests, the better. You might explain, for instance, that it is very important for you to set deadlines for each part of the thesis and that you would welcome assistance dividing the thesis into smaller, more manageable tasks. You might also ask for special help with the paper's overall structure—something most students need anyway. Simply explain that, based on your experience and learning style, you know this kind of assistance would really make a difference.

You should *not* try to transform your thesis adviser into a learning skills specialist. Your school already has them, and you should make full use of their services. In dealing with your thesis adviser, your aim should be more narrowly focused: to improve your working relationship on the thesis. Share information about yourself and your learning style that you think will improve this working relationship. You may need to remind your adviser occasionally about these issues, about what your learning style is and the specific help you need.

A friend of mine needed to do exactly that when she enrolled in a master's program. She has severe lifelong LD problems, mainly with spelling and grammar, and she knew they would show up in her draft papers. She explained the issue to her adviser, made clear that the problem was not laziness, and said she would have friends check her final drafts to ensure the spelling and grammar were correct. She added that it would not be possible to have friends check every draft this thoroughly but that her final paper would be polished and correct. This clear, straightforward explanation minimized the chance for misunderstandings, contributed to a strong working relationship, and led to a fine thesis.

PROBLEMS WITH ADVISERS

Throughout this book, I have urged you to turn to your adviser for academic guidance and feedback. Most advisers give it willingly, generously, and effectively. Most advisers are helpful and supportive—most, but not all.

Some are slow to return papers or, worse, never bother to read them. Others offer skimpy comments that provide little assistance, even if the comments are positive. What can you do?

Students with poor advisers are in a difficult bind. It is hard (and often impossible) to switch advisers midyear, and it is not easy to ask for better assistance. It's awkward. Professors might consider it an implicit criticism and subtly punish you, or at least you reasonably fear they would. So, it is a difficult situation. But it is not an impossible one.

First, check to see if the problem is temporary. Professors have busy spells, just as students do, and they sometimes fall behind for a few weeks but catch up later. Discreetly ask around and see if this is a temporary problem or a recurrent one. Second, if the problem persists, quietly see if you can change advisers. (Talk with the person in charge of your undergraduate major and explain that you'd like to have a confidential discussion.)

Even if you cannot change advisers—perhaps because it's too late in the year, perhaps because no others are available—there are still some strategies that can help. You can supplement meetings with your adviser by e-mailing specific questions. The more concrete your requests, the better chance you'll have of getting a helpful answer. Communicating like this is often easier than making a request in person. When you do meet with your adviser, arrive with a clear agenda and ask for specific advice. Instead of a general question, ask, "Should I rely more on Professor X's comments on Hemingway or Professor Y's?" You'll get a real response, which might be

"Neither. Rely on Professor Z and compare his work with Professor W." Be concrete. Be specific. You'll get better answers.

Remember, too, that you have other sources for thesis advice. Earlier, I mentioned workshops and tutors. Rely more heavily on them if your adviser is unavailable or unhelpful. Also—and I know this may be difficult—ask other professors for ideas, not about the bad adviser but about the thesis project itself. Raise academic questions you need help on.

Lots of students drop by faculty offices and ask for suggestions about their work. It's not illegal to talk with faculty other than your adviser! I often give advice myself to students who have excellent advisers. They just want to chat about their topic with me. They are usually students who've taken some courses with me, and I'm happy to help them. My students do the same with other professors. Sign up for office hours with professors you have worked with and see which ones are responsive and helpful. Professors are reluctant to read draft papers written for other faculty (it seems too much like interference), but they are glad to discuss topics and ideas. Your school has ample intellectual resources. Seek them out to improve your thesis.

> *Tip:* If your adviser is often unavailable or unhelpful, turn to other sources. See if you can change advisers. Even if you cannot, you can ask other faculty for informal advice on your project. Use e-mail to ask your adviser specific questions, and have clear agendas for each in-person meeting. Also, rely more heavily on thesis workshops.

So far, I have been talking solely about poor academic advising. Far worse is a professor who sexually harasses you. That is simply unacceptable. Tell the person, if you can, that it must stop, and say it firmly. You may also wish to report it to the college official who handles harassment complaints. Your college has confidential procedures for reporting such incidents.

PERSONAL PROBLEMS BEYOND YOUR CONTROL

Every year, some students face unexpected personal difficulties. Your dad may become seriously ill; your mom might lose her job; your roommate may be hospitalized after a car crash; you may get sick yourself. Over the years, I have had students who have faced all these problems.

The big things in life—family, friendship, health—should come first. If it's an emergency and you need to leave campus, it's important to let some key people know. Try to find a reliable contact person on campus, perhaps your academic adviser or someone in the dean of students office. If you have time, you might send a quick e-mail to your thesis adviser, too. You don't need to say a lot, but give your professors and counselors a little information to keep them informed: "My mom is seriously ill and I'm returning to St. Louis to be with her. I'm not sure when I'll be back—that depends on her condition—but I will try to give you an update in a week or so. Meanwhile, I will stay in touch with my school adviser, Joan Herald. Her e-mail is jherald@uxyz.edu." With that information, your adviser will know to call or e-mail Joan Herald (your contact person), who may, in turn, ask your thesis adviser to explain things to other professors in your department. Or she'll call them herself.

Universities can be strong, supportive, and caring communities for students who face difficulties like these. But, first, your advisers and university staff need to know about them. Don't disappear without a trace, leaving everyone to wonder where you are and how you are doing. Your friends, teachers, and advisers will all be worried. They need to know what's up before they can help.

When things calm down a little, talk over the situation with your thesis adviser, your other academic advisers, and perhaps a school therapist. They will help you think about the choices, give you other perspectives on them, and then offer support once you've made your decision.

Depending on the problem, you might decide to postpone your academic schedule, seeking counseling or therapy, or continue in school but lighten your load. That might mean dropping some courses, delaying your thesis, or even dropping it entirely.

Two suggestions: Develop a full list of options available to you, and *postpone any big decisions (if you can) until the turmoil subsides.* You'll make much better decisions that way.

SOME STEPS TO TAKE WHEN YOU FACE PERSONAL CRISES

There is no generic advice about what to do when you face such personal crises. The difficulties and individual situations vary too much. Still, it is important to take several steps.

- Establish a main contact person, usually a college academic adviser or a staff member in the dean of students office.
- Keep your thesis adviser and other faculty informed, either directly or through your contact person.
- Keep your friends informed and talk over your situation with them.
- Seek help from the school's counselors and support staff. That might be your academic counselor, thesis adviser, or therapist, depending on the specific problem.
- Avoid making any major decisions, especially those that are difficult to reverse, until you have a chance to pause and reflect. Postpone these big decisions, if you can, until the immediate pressures have died down.

SUGGESTIONS FOR DEALING WITH PERSONAL CRISES WHILE WRITING A THESIS

- If you have severe difficulty writing
  - Try more prewriting;
  - Experiment with freewriting;
  - See a writing tutor or learning skills counselor.
- If you face serious problems, seek help from therapists and support groups.
- If you have a family crisis or health emergency, remember they take priority over school work.
- If you must leave campus for an emergency, notify a few key people. They can notify others.
- If you face a personal crisis, try to postpone major decisions, if possible. Important choices about your life and academic work are best made after the turmoil has subsided.

VI

Scheduling and Completing Your Thesis

15 THESIS TIME SCHEDULE

Now that we have gone over all the elements of thesis writing, let's talk about how they fit together in a timetable. School schedules vary, of course, and different topics have their own demands, but here is a rough guide for a two-semester thesis. (For a one-semester schedule, see chapter 20.) Use it to talk with your adviser and arrange a personalized schedule that makes sense for your specific project.

TIME SCHEDULE FOR ENTIRE THESIS

	Months 1,2	Months 3, 4, 5, (6)	Final month (6 or 7)
Chapters in this book:	1–4	5–11, 13	Review 11
Reading:	Background reading	Focused research and planning	Fill-in research
Writing:	Proposal and revised proposal	Prewrite middle sections of thesis	Rewrite and polish
	Bibliographic essay	Write and revise middle sections	Refine introduction and conclusion
		Prewrite introduction and conclusion	

Notice that parts of the schedule overlap. In the first month, for example, you should do background reading as you develop your proposal. Later, in months 3 and 4, you should conduct research as you begin prewriting.

Tip: Vital tasks should overlap in your thesis. For example, you should edit the middle sections of the paper as you draft the introduction and conclusion.

This overlap of tasks is deliberate. Prewriting, drafting, and rewriting should be overlapping categories, as earlier chapters make clear. Doing them that way is more productive than trying to outline the whole thesis in advance. (At least that's my view. You are certainly welcome to write detailed outlines if you and your adviser prefer that approach.) Your focused research should lead directly into prewriting and draft writing. As you write, you should continue doing research until the thesis project is nearly complete.

Let's review this schedule.

THESIS SCHEDULE: THE FIRST TWO MONTHS

Begin by reading about your topic as you craft your proposal. Discuss your proposal with your adviser and revise it at least once. That way you will have a solid plan before you begin more targeted research.

After completing your proposal and background reading, write a brief essay summarizing the main points in the literature. Concentrate on major areas where the authors agree and disagree; it will help you understand where your own ideas fit in.

Tip: The first important thesis tasks are to
- Begin general background reading
- Write your proposal; then revise it based on feedback from your adviser
- Summarize background readings in a three- to five-page bibliographic paper

---

TIME SCHEDULE FOR MONTHS 1, 2: THESIS PROPOSAL AND BACKGROUND READING

Reading: Background reading

Writing: Proposal and revised proposal
            Bibliographic essay

THESIS SCHEDULE: THE MIDDLE MONTHS

After doing some general readings and zeroing in on your topic, it's time to begin more focused reading and research. This work should bear directly on your thesis topic, as your proposal defines it. As you move deeper into this phase, you should frame your research plans explicitly and discuss them with your adviser.

Early in this phase, perhaps in month 3, you should develop your own schedule for the remainder of the project. The ones in this chapter can serve as a guide. Revise your schedule as you proceed. Keep an eye on the various deadlines you set. If you miss one, ask yourself if the schedule was too ambitious or if you are simply falling behind.

> *Tip:* Develop your own personalized schedule, share it with your adviser, and update it periodically. Use the schedules in this chapter as a guide, but customize them for your project.

At about the same time (around month 3), write a preliminary version of your thesis statement, that is, the main argument you expect to make in the paper. It should be brief—only two or three sentences. Although you will revise it as you work, an early version is helpful. It will sharpen your thinking, set the stage for discussion, and guide your later work.

> *Tip:* Write a preliminary version of your thesis statement by month 3 or 4, at the latest. The statement should be brief—a few sentences at most—and should be revised as your research builds.

Your reading and research should produce extensive notes. Your next task is to expand on your notes by prewriting, and to organize these materials for inclusion in your paper. You should

- Organize your readings and research materials into four or five major categories
- Extract the main points you wish to emphasize in each category
- Amplify these points with ideas of your own (in writing, of course)
- Line up these sections in a logical order to present your material

It should be clear, then, that prewriting is closely tied to your research. You should do them together since they meld in productive ways.

Once you have formulated your categories and organized your notes, extend them by informal writing. Write sentences and paragraphs whenever ideas crop up. Then file them in the appropriate categories. Check to make sure *each category* is buttressed with solid readings and research materials. Sometimes, at this stage, you'll notice that one such section has almost no references. Now is the time to repair that with a trip to the library. Completing all this reading, research, and prewriting should take three or four months.

> *Tip:* Formulate the main steps of your argument, the path to convincing your readers.
> - These steps will become the sections of your paper. Think of them as the large Roman numerals in an outline.
> - Sort your research and reading notes into these sections.
> - Expand these notes with brief informal writing.
>
> If you (or your adviser) prefer to work from a more detailed outline, write one at this stage. If not, simply begin writing about ideas that might fit into each section.

This prewriting is essential to your thesis. Spend time on it, review your research, and expand your notes with additional comments. Keep jotting down new ideas and filing them in the appropriate section. Keep an active "to do" list to guide your daily research.

Don't postpone this prewriting until you feel 100 percent ready. Don't wait until you have completed all your research. One advantage of prewriting is that it is very flexible. You don't have to write one paragraph after the next. You don't have to write a full draft at this point. You can write short bursts about different aspects of the thesis, areas where you do feel ready. You will learn a lot as you do. Surprising but true.

> *Tip:* Begin prewriting a little before you feel completely ready.

As your prewriting develops, you can begin to assemble whole sections of the thesis. The best way to do this is to gather together your prewriting and research; then use it to write short stand-alone papers for each section. You can actually draft the entire thesis this way if you wish, writing each section independently.

Tip: Turn your prewriting into short papers in two steps.
- Write some sentences and paragraphs expanding on your ideas in each section.
- Use this prewriting and research to write brief stand-alone papers for the different sections.

At this stage, concentrate on the middle sections of your thesis. You'll write the introduction and conclusion a little later.

Once you have these sections in place, you should join them with effective transitions, smoothing out the bumps between them and telling the reader what to expect next. (Specific ideas on how to do this are in chapters 10 and 11.)

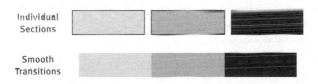

SMOOTHING TRANSITIONS IN MIDDLE SECTIONS OF PAPER

Tip: Create a draft by drawing together these stand-alone sections. If transitions between sections are hard to write, you may have some sections in the wrong spot or need to add new ones.

TIME SCHEDULE FOR MONTHS 3–5
(OR MONTHS 3–6, DEPENDING ON YOUR SCHOOL SCHEDULE):
RESEARCH AND WRITING

Reading: Focused research and planning

Writing: Prewrite middle sections of thesis
Write and revise middle sections
Prewrite the introduction and conclusion

Then, and only then, should you turn to the introductory and concluding sections. They are vital to the project, and you need to polish them carefully. Because you write them last, you have less time to refine them than you do the other sections. That's inevitable. After all, they give an overview of the project, and you can't do that until you have assembled the whole jigsaw puzzle. (A full discussion is in chapter 10.)

> *Tip:* Because you write the introduction and conclusion last, you have less time to polish them. When you finally get to them, you need to edit them more intensively.

Even though you are writing these sections last, you should have a lot of material to work with. Since you have passed the elevator test, you won't mumble about your argument and stumble over its presentation. You can state it openly and confidently in the introduction. You can tell readers why your question matters and how it fits into the literature. You can provide readers with a lucid road map to the rest of the paper since you know how you will proceed, section by section, and since you know why this sequence makes sense. All the work you've done pays off.

As for the conclusion, you should already have extensive prewriting to help you. In addition, you should have notes and ideas from recent talks with your adviser. In fact, your final meetings should concentrate on the concluding section. You want to end your paper on a high note.

As you write the conclusion, remember that it should not merely repeat what you've said before. The goal is to say what your work means and why it matters. The conclusion is the punch line. And like a good punch line, it should be sharp.

> *Tip:* Begin reviewing your major findings with your adviser at least a month before the paper is due. Your conclusions should go beyond a mere summary. They should say what your research really means.

In the time schedule, I suggest taking three or four months to complete all these tasks: conducting research, prewriting, drafting and revising the text, and, finally, crafting the introduction and conclusion. By the end of this stage, you should have assembled a full draft of the paper and smoothed the transitions between sections.

Remember, though, that this is only a general schedule. You should draft a personal one, tailored to your own project. You may not need so much time for research, for instance, if you have already done much of it for a seminar paper. Or your school calendar may give you only three months (not four) to complete this middle stage. Once you've completed this stage, you'll still need a few weeks to polish the final draft and close any holes you find in your research. Be sure to set aside a month at the end for these vital tasks.

THESIS SCHEDULE: THE FINAL MONTH

The final three or four weeks of your thesis project should be devoted to editing and to filling in any lingering gaps in your research.

You will be editing the text at several levels: the wording of sentences and paragraphs, and the architecture of the sections. Does anything need to be moved around, or perhaps shortened or lengthened? Is anything missing or underdeveloped? If so, you may need to do a little fill-in research.

Think about how to make your presentation more effective. Is your thesis statement clear and prominent? Would any additional figures or graphs make your argument more transparent and easier to grasp? What about listing some of your major points as bullet lists to make them stand out? Would it help to explain why your approach is better than a prominent alternative? Would an anecdote or story illustrate a more abstract point or make your opening more engaging?

All these are judgment calls about how to make your presentation more appealing and persuasive. That's exactly what you should be mulling over at this stage. A reminder: As you edit, don't just think about adding text; think about pruning it, as well.

> *Tip:* In the final stages of editing, work to make your presentation more readable and persuasive.

Your adviser will give you feedback on these choices, if you ask. Because you are providing him with polished written work, you should be able to get detailed feedback. As you edit, be sure to tell your adviser what is new and what questions you still have. To get the most useful answers, ask specific questions. The more guidance you can give your professor, the more pointed your inquiries, the better advice you'll receive.

TIME SCHEDULE FOR FINAL MONTH
(MONTH 5 OR 6, DEPENDING ON YOUR SCHOOL SCHEDULE):
EDITING THE TEXT AND FILLING IN GAPS IN RESEARCH

Reading: Fill-in research

Writing: Rewrite and polish

And that's it. Your thesis is complete, polished, done.

16 TIPS AND REMINDERS

Every chapter has offered tips to help you work more productively. In this chapter, I'll draw together some of the most important ones. The most valuable advice I can give is to work steadily (rather than in fits and starts) and to meet with your adviser throughout the project.

- Work steadily on your thesis throughout the year and meet regularly with your adviser to discuss it. There is no substitute for steady work—showing up every day, ready or not, and tackling the task at hand. Frankly, there are few lessons that matter more for the rest of your working life, either.

GETTING ORGANIZED

- Make a computer folder devoted to your thesis. It should include your book notes, prewriting, drafts, and working bibliography. Back it up regularly and store a copy off-site, if possible.
- For all your online research, copy the URLs and put them in your notes. If you expect to return to a Web site often, put it in the "favorites" file of your Web browser.
- Find a quiet place to work, where you can read and write without interruption.
- Keep a "to do" list for your thesis and another one for everything else.

DEPARTMENTAL REQUIREMENTS

- It is your responsibility to know the department's thesis requirements, such as the paper's length and due date. (The right person to ask is a department administrator.)
- Aside from meeting these technical requirements, you should aim for a thesis that roughly matches the length and scope of good articles in your field.

WORKING WITH YOUR ADVISER

- Bring your own agenda and questions to each meeting with your adviser. If you spend a little time planning this agenda, the meetings will be more productive. You will get more out of each session if you
  - Update your adviser on your progress;
  - Raise the most important issues or questions you have;
  - Mention any problems that are stumping you;
  - Explain the next task you intend to work on.
- At the end of each meeting, set a time and a specific task for the next meeting.
- Use brief regular meetings to keep your project on track.
- Don't skip scheduled meetings unless it's essential.
- Try to do some brief informal writing for most meetings. Even very short papers will promote better discussions and prompt new ideas.
  - Bring two copies of any papers to meetings with your adviser.
  - Proofread every paper you hand in, even informal ones.
  - If the papers are short, your adviser can read them at the beginning of your meeting and offer comments right away.
- Besides working closely with your thesis adviser, take advantage of thesis seminars and workshops. They are useful for presenting your work, batting around ideas, and getting feedback.
- Remember that the job of the thesis adviser and seminar leader is to offer guidance. It is your job to plan and write the thesis.

READING AND RESEARCH

- As your first thesis task, compile a reading list and begin general background reading.
- While it is your responsibility to find readings, others can certainly help.
  - Your adviser can suggest initial readings.
  - Reference librarians can often suggest readings, too. A valuable but overlooked resource, they know about new publications, specialized bibliographies, and primary documents. They can show you how to compile a reading list and can help you request materials from other research libraries.
  - Scan the major journals in your field. (Your adviser will know which ones are relevant to your topic.) Look for pertinent

research published in the last few years, as well as review articles comparing new books. Read these articles and use their footnotes to find additional readings.

- As you complete your background reading, write a brief bibliographic essay, discussing the most important books and articles on your topic. Outline the principal issues they raise and the authors' main areas of agreement and disagreement.
- As your topic is gradually refined, your readings should become more focused.
- Maintain a working bibliography, marked up with your notes and ideas. Keep your adviser informed about what you are reading.
- As your bibliography grows, divide it into sections, reflecting the different kinds of readings you are doing. These subdivisions may suggest ways to divide your paper into sections.
- Discuss your research strategy with your adviser. It helps to write down your research strategy as you begin serious inquiry.

THESIS ARGUMENT

- To motivate your thesis, aim for a good question—one that interests you and is manageable.
- Once you have posed a compelling question, focus on two goals.
  ○ Develop a tentative argument or answer to your question. Be succinct. Your argument should be a few sentences at most. Write a preliminary version in the third month of your project. Keep revising it as you write the thesis.
  ○ Lay out a reasonable sequence of steps to explain (or prove) your point. These steps will become the sections in your research files and later in your paper.
- Your thesis should have a thesis. Translation: Your BA paper should have a main argument, clearly expressed.
- To find out if you actually have such an argument, take the elevator test. If you can explain your argument to an intelligent layperson on a short elevator ride, you pass.

SCHEDULING

- During month 3 or 4, write a customized schedule for the remainder of your thesis project. Revise and update it as you continue working.

- It is your responsibility—not your adviser's—to keep the whole project on schedule, moving forward. That's true at every stage of the thesis, beginning in week 1.
- Watch out for missed deadlines. If you miss one, ask yourself what the problem is. Is the schedule unreasonable? Was there an unexpected setback in your work or personal life? Or are you are simply falling behind?

PREWRITING

- The first step in prewriting is to establish the major steps in your argument (similar to capital Roman numerals in a traditional outline).
  - These steps will become the main sections of your paper.
  - To determine these sections and line them up in the proper order, ask yourself, "What are the essential building blocks of my argument?"
- Make a prewriting file, divide it into these sections, and file your notes and ideas in the appropriate sections. These sections will eventually become sections in your paper, perhaps in modified form.
- As your work advances, add new sections, rearrange old ones, and move notes around as needed.
- Add comments and ideas to your notes frequently. Expand them with sentences and paragraphs. Review this material regularly and keep adding to it.
- Whenever you are working intensively on the thesis, carry something to jot down notes. Ideas pop up at odd times, and you should be ready to catch them with a pen and paper or Blackberry.
- Use an "overlapping approach" to prewrite, draft, and edit your thesis.
  - When you have completed most of the research on one section, review your notes and prewriting, then draft a short paper on that aspect of the thesis.
  - Treat it as a stand-alone paper; don't worry about connecting it to other sections at this stage.
  - Edit this stand-alone draft as you work on the rest of the paper. You should research, prewrite, and draft later sections as you edit earlier ones.

○ Later, when you work on the paper as a whole, you can connect these sections and create a unified paper.

THE OVERLAPPING APPROACH:
PREWRITING, DRAFTING, AND EDITING DIFFERENT SECTIONS AT THE SAME TIME

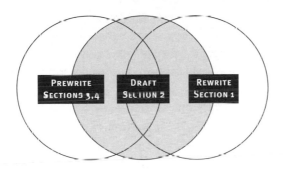

PREWRITE
SECTIONS 3,4

DRAFT
SECTION 2

REWRITE
SECTION 1

WRITING AND EDITING

- When integrating the entire paper, write transitions that tell readers why they are going to the next section.
- If these transitions are difficult to craft, that may signal your next section is actually in the wrong place, or perhaps a section is missing.
- Edit your drafts in red pen so changes will stand out. Then enter these handwritten changes in your computer regularly so you have an up-to-date electronic draft.
- Most of the time, you can simply delete the words you cut. If you think you might want to restore a particular sentence or paragraph, put it in a scrap file. Cut whenever you can, and use the scrap file as a safety net.
- Mark up yesterday's writing as you start work the next day. It's a great time to edit and won't take long. It will also bring you up to speed for the new day's work.
- Periodically print your latest working draft. Mark it up freely with editorial comments. Having a hard copy lying around will encourage you to edit more often.
- Define your most important terms clearly and precisely and do it early in the paper. Then use them consistently as a *core vocabulary*. This is one case where synonyms and variety only cause confusion.
- Keep cutting your text and polishing your language to make it

clearer. Your argument and evidence will become more transparent and understandable.

- Use the active voice to speak directly to your readers.
- Always remember you are writing to communicate.
  - Never talk down to readers. Treat them with courtesy and respect, just as you hope to be treated.
  - For most topics, imagine your readers are fellow seniors or informed laypeople.
  - Even though your thesis has a serious point, your writing should not be stiff.
  - Feel free to include an occasional story or anecdote if it reinforces your point.
  - Choose a writing style you can use comfortably and persuasively. If you prefer an informal style, check with your adviser. And don't go overboard.

INTRODUCTION AND CONCLUSION

- The most important sections of your thesis are the ones you write last—the introduction and conclusion. To make them strong requires a little extra planning and effort.
  - Start discussing your findings with your adviser several weeks before the thesis is due.
  - Work on these sections more intensively. Even though you write them relatively late, you still need to edit them several times. That means you'll just have to work a little harder on these sections.
- Make sure the introduction states your argument crisply in the first couple of pages. Don't keep your readers waiting, and don't dance around your main point. (If you can't state it clearly, you probably don't have one. Go back and work on the elevator test.)
- The conclusion is not a summary or mere repetition of what came before. It should draw together your main findings and explore their significance.

CITATIONS

- Choose one citation style and use it consistently. (Details are in appendix 2, "Footnotes 101.")

- If your paper has a bibliography or reference list, make sure it includes all the works you cited.

COMPLETING YOUR THESIS

- As your thesis moves into its final stages, review your entire schedule-to-completion at each meeting with your adviser. This should only take a minute.
- Leave time for last-minute revisions during the final two weeks.
  - Reread the entire text and use your editorial judgment to revise it.
  - Search for remaining gaps and fill them, even if it requires some last-minute research.
  - If your adviser has time for comments, give him a polished draft at least a week before the final paper is due.

THESIS DEFENSE AND SECOND READERS

- If your department requires you to choose a second faculty reader, ask your adviser for suggestions. Ideally, you want someone who knows the subject well and is amenable to your approach.
- Prepare for a thesis defense by reviewing your answers to three basic questions:
  - What is your main argument or interpretation?
  - How do you support it?
  - How do you respond to the main objections and alternative arguments?

AFTER YOU'RE DONE

- After the thesis is finished, thank your adviser, either in person or with a handwritten note.
- Get a recommendation while your teachers still have a fresh memory of working with you. They can always update it to reflect your subsequent work and studies.

17 FREQUENTLY ASKED QUESTIONS

THESIS TOPICS

Are there thesis topics to avoid?

Yes. Vague, sprawling topics need to be whittled down and made precise, as I discussed earlier. Also, avoid topics about the future. After all, you can't cite a crystal ball or psychic hotline.

Every year or two, a political science major wants to do a thesis on the upcoming presidential election or the future of the European Union. "Where," I ask with a grin, "do you expect to collect the data on this future event?" Long silence. "How will you evaluate the alternative predictions and show that you are right and they are wrong?" Eerie silence.

As interesting as it would be to know the future, it's just too speculative for a thesis topic. If you are interested in an emerging issue, the best approach is to look at recent events and trends you *can* research. Then, in the concluding section, turn to future possibilities. That captures your interests and makes good use of your conclusion, all within a sturdy thesis framework.

> *Tip:* Avoid thesis topics that deal mainly with the future. There is no way to research them.

Beside topics about the future, are there any other topics to avoid?

Yes, avoid topics that are primarily normative evaluations—where the main question is "Should?"—*unless* you intend to delve deeply into the criteria for evaluation and the arguments pro and con.

Normative arguments are obviously fine in philosophy, theology, and some subfields in other disciplines, such as political philosophy. They can also be part of an empirically based argument, as long as the questions are well framed. You might ask, for example, "Should the death penalty be abolished?" As it stands, that could be a thesis topic in philosophy. If you are writing in sociology or criminal justice, however, the topic only works if it is part of a solid empirical study covering the police, courts, and prison system. In these subjects, the primary question should be a researchable one, such as, "Are minorities more likely to receive the death penalty?" or "How common are serious errors in the original trial?" Once you have analyzed those empirical questions, you can raise the hard normative issues.

> *Tip:* If you wish to study a normative topic—where the main question is "should"—then you *must* concentrate on the criteria for evaluation, the arguments for and against, and the ethical or philosophical underpinnings of your own argument.

Just remember: when you raise normative questions, your answers need to be supported with philosophical reasoning or data (or both) and should respond intelligently to the best counterarguments. Otherwise, it's just flimsy opinion.

THESIS LENGTH

How many pages should the thesis be?
Standards vary widely, and the most important advice is to *check with your department about the rules* and ask your thesis adviser about his preferences. Do that early and keep it in the back of your mind, but don't think much about it until you are well into drafting the paper. Until then, you should simply aim to write a thesis that is about as long as a good journal article in your field. (As you start drafting, you might want to double-check my suggestion with your adviser.)

Articles—and theses—tend to be longer in fields such as history and anthropology, which require a fair amount of description alongside the analysis. Articles are shorter in fields like economics that rely on mathematical models and quantitative analysis. Fields like political science and sociology lie somewhere in the middle. In international relations, for example, most journals ask for articles than run about fourteen thousand words, including footnotes, which is between fifty and sixty pages (assuming 250 words/page). That is a common range for senior theses in international relations, as well.

In reviewing different schools' standards for length, I am struck by (a) how widely they vary, across universities and across departments; (b) how broad the permissible range is within single departments; and (c) how many departments don't have any clear standard at all, or don't bother to say whether their standard paper is supposed to be single-spaced or double-spaced. Just comparing history departments in major research universities: one says a thesis should be forty pages, while another says sixty pages is the minimum and implies it should be longer. Big difference.

The lesson I draw from this is that you *must* check with your department and thesis adviser and make sure you are clear about the requirements and the expectations.

> *Tip:* A thesis is generally as long as a good article in your field. Still, you *must* check on your department's requirements.

FAQS ABOUT THE THREE MAIN REFERENCE STYLES

What are the main reference styles?
There are three main styles: MLA, APA, and Chicago. MLA originated with the Modern Language Association and is now widely used in the humanities. APA originated with the American Psychological Association and is now widely used in the social sciences and some natural sciences. Chicago style is used across the social sciences and humanities. It originated with the *Chicago Manual of Style,* now in its fifteenth edition.

What are the differences between the styles?
APA and MLA both use short parenthetical citations in the text itself. A reference list with full publishing information appears at the end of the article, paper, or book.

Chicago uses footnotes (at the bottom of each page) or endnotes (at the end of the article). These notes contain the same information; the only difference is their location. Beyond that, there are two variants of Chicago style. One uses complete notes, giving all the information about each item in its first note. In that case, no bibliography is necessary. In the other variant, each item is cited only in abbreviated form. Full information about it appears in a bibliography.

WHAT SHOULD I CITE?

Do I need to cite everything I use in the paper?
Pretty much. Cite anything you rely on for data or authoritative opinions. Cite both quotes and paraphrases. Cite personal communications such as e-mails, interviews, or conversations with professors if you rely on them

for your paper. If you rely heavily on any single source, make that clear, either with multiple citations or with somewhat fewer citations plus a clear statement that you are relying on a particular source for a particular topic.

There is one exception. Don't cite sources for well-known facts.

How many citations does a paper have, anyway?
It varies and there is no exact number, but a couple per page is common in well researched papers. More is fine. If there are no citations for several pages in a row, something's probably wrong. Mostly likely, you just forgot to include them. You need to go back and fix the problem.

WHAT GOES IN A CITATION?

What about citing a work I found in someone else's footnotes? Do I need to cite the place where I discovered the work?
This issue comes up all the time because it's one of the most important ways we learn about other works and other ideas. Reading a book by E. L. Jones, for example, you find an interesting citation to Adam Smith. As it turns out, you are more interested in Smith's point than in Jones's commentary, so you decide to cite Smith. That's fine—you can certainly cite Smith—but how should you handle it?

There's a choice. One way is to follow the paper trail from Jones's note to Adam Smith's text, read the relevant part, and simply cite it, with no reference at all to Jones. That's completely legitimate for books like Smith's that are well known in their field. You are likely to come across such works in your normal research, and you don't need to cite Jones as the guide who sent you there. To do that honestly, though, you have to go to the Smith reading and examine the relevant parts.

The rule is simple: *Cite only texts you have actually used and would have found in the normal course of your research,* not obscure texts used by someone else or works you know about only secondhand. You don't have to read several hundred pages of Adam Smith. You do have to read the relevant pages in Smith—the ones you cite. Remember the basic principle: *When you say you did the work yourself, you actually did it.*

Alternatively, if you don't have time to read Smith yourself (or if the work is written in a language you cannot read), you can cite the text this way: "Smith, *Wealth of Nations,* 123, as discussed in Jones, *The European Miracle.*" Normally, you don't need to cite the page in Jones, but you can if you wish. An in-text citation would look different but accomplish the same thing: (Smith 123, qtd. in Jones).

This alternative is completely honest, too. You are referencing Smith's point but saying you found it in Jones. This follows another, equally important principle: *When you rely on someone else's work, you cite it.* In this case, you are relying on Jones, not Smith himself, as your source for Smith's point.

Follow the same rule if Jones leads you to a work that is unusual or obscure *to you*, a work you discovered only because Jones did the detailed research, found it, and told you about it. This alternative is completely honest, too.

The specific rules here are less important than the basic concepts:

- Cite only texts you found in the normal course of your research and have actually used.
- Cite all your sources openly and honestly.

Follow these and you'll do just fine.

> *Tip:* If you find a work because another scholar mentions it, there are two ways to cite it.
> - You can cite the work indirectly, saying that it is referenced by another scholar.
> - You can cite the work directly, without mentioning the other scholar, *but only if*
>   ○ You actually go to the work and read the relevant part, *and*
>   ○ You would probably have found the work anyway during your research (that is, it is not an obscure work that you found only because of the other scholar's efforts).

BIBLIOGRAPHY OR REFERENCE LIST

Do I need to have a bibliography?
Yes, for all styles *except* complete Chicago footnotes. (The details are explained in appendix 2.) By the way, MLA calls this list "Works Cited"; APA calls it a "Reference List."

Should my bibliography (or reference list) include the general background reading I did?

The answer depends on how much you relied on a particular reading and which reference style you use. MLA and APA include only the works you have actually cited. Chicago-style bibliographies are more flexible and can include works you haven't cited in a note.

My advice is this: If a work was really useful to you, then check to make sure you have acknowledged that debt somewhere with a citation. After you've cited it once, the work will appear in your bibliography, regardless of which style you use. If a particular background reading wasn't important in your research, don't worry about citing it.

Does the bibliography raise any questions about my work?

Yes, readers will scan your bibliography to see what kinds of sources you used and whether they are the best ones. There are five problems to watch out for:

- Old, out-of-date works
- Bias in the overall bibliography
- Omission of major works in your subject
- Reliance on poor or weak sources
- Excessive reliance on one or two sources

These are not really problems with the bibliography, as such. They are problems with the text that become apparent by looking at the bibliography.

> *Tip:* A quick scan of your bibliography will show whether your references are the best up-to-date works and whether they cover all sides of an issue. If they fall short, that's not a problem with the bibliography. That's a problem with your paper.

The remedy for all these problems is the same. You need to read a variety of major works in your subject and indicate that with citations. Make sure your sources are considered solid, reliable, and up-to-date. If an issue has contemporary significance, it is especially important that you check for current sources (and be cautious about relying heavily on older ones). If an issue is controversial, you should include sources from all sides. Your professors and teaching assistants can really help here. They know the literature and should be valuable guides.

CITING QUOTATIONS

I am using a quotation that contains a second quote within it. How do I handle the citation?
Let's say your paper includes the following sentence:

> According to David M. Kennedy, Roosevelt began his new presidency "by reassuring his countrymen that 'this great nation will endure as it has endured, will revive and will prosper. . . . The only thing we have to fear . . . is fear itself.'"

Of course, you'll cite Kennedy, but do you need to cite *his* source for the Roosevelt quote? No. It's not required. In some cases, however, your readers will benefit from a little extra information about the quote within a quote. You can easily do that in your footnote or endnote:

> [99]Kennedy, *Freedom from Fear,* 134. The Roosevelt quote comes from his 1933 inaugural address.

I am quoting from some Spanish and French books and doing the translations myself. How should I handle the citations?
Just include the words "my translation" immediately after the quote or in the citation. You don't need to do this each time. After the first quotation, you can tell your readers that you are translating all quotes yourself. Then cite the foreign-language text you are using.

You might want to include quotes in both the original and translation. That's fine. Either the translation or the original can come first. If the English translation follows, place it in parentheses. If the foreign-language original follows, place it in brackets.

CITING ELECTRONIC MATERIALS

I am citing lots of Web items, how do I do that?
There are plenty of examples in appendix 2, "Footnotes 101." Besides items under "Web sites" and "Weblogs [or blogs]," there are examples of online journal articles, newspaper articles, and many more.

Does citing Web sources raise questions about my work?

Only if the sources themselves are lousy. There is absolutely nothing wrong with citing solid sources that happen to be posted online. If you read an electronic version of the *New York Times,* that's just as good as picking up a paper, and you won't have to wipe off ink smudges. If you cite a journal article from JSTOR or an electronic database, that's fine and is increasingly common. No problem.

But problems can arise with other citations because there is so much junk online. You have to guard against it. Unlike scholarly journals and academic books, there is no peer review for most online sites and therefore no screening for quality. So screen it yourself and be wary. Just because it is published online does not mean it is worth the electrons it agitates.

> *Tip:* Some online sources are reliable and have been reviewed by competent specialists, but many have not. Double-check your electronic sources to make sure they are solid and trustworthy.

Do I need to include the URL in my citations?

Yes. Include the URL (the uniform resource locator), which is the item's Web address. Most citation styles also require that you include the date you accessed the site.

If you are returning to a Web site often, add it to your browser's "favorites" list. If you already have lots of items there, create a special thesis folder.

> *Tip on returning to useful Web sites:* If sites are particularly useful for your thesis, add them to your browser's "favorites" list. To keep them organized, it usually helps to create a new category (or folder) named for the thesis and drop the new URLs into it. Having a special folder will prevent sites from getting lost in your long list of favorites.

The URL I'm citing is long and needs to go on two lines. How do I handle the line break?

Here's the technical answer. If the URL takes up more than one line, break *after* a

- slash
- double slash

break *before* a

- period
- comma
- question mark
- tilde (~)
- ampersand (&)
- hyphen
- underline
- number sign

Here are some examples:

Full URL	http://www.charleslipson.com/index.htm
Break after slash	http://www.charleslipson.com/ index.htm
Break before other punctuation	http://www.charleslipson .com/index.htm

These "break rules" apply to all citation styles.

There's a rationale for these rules. If periods, commas, or hyphens came at the end of a line, they might be mistaken for punctuation marks. By contrast, when they come at the beginning of a line, they are clearly part of the URL. To avoid confusion, don't add hyphens to break long words in the URL.

You can produce such breaks in two ways. One is to insert a line break by pressing the shift-enter keys simultaneously, at least on Windows-based systems. Alternatively, you can insert a space in the URL so your word-processing program automatically wraps the URL onto two lines. (Without such a space, the word processor would force the entire URL on one line.)

Even though you are technically allowed to break URLs before periods, commas, and hyphens, I avoid such breaks because these punctuation marks are easy to overlook and confuse readers. Instead, I try to break only after a slash or double slash, and then only when I am printing the final version of the paper. When I'm sending it electronically, I try to avoid breaks altogether. That way, the recipient will have "live" hyperlinks to click on.

Tips on citing Web pages: As you take notes, write down the
- URL for the Web site or Web page
- Name or description of the page or site
- Date you accessed it

Writing the name or description of a Web site is useful because If the URL changes (as they sometimes do), you still can find it by searching.

As for the access date, some citation styles, such as APA and MI A, require it. Others, such as the *Chicago Manual of Style,* make it optional. They tell you to include it only when it's relevant, such as for time-sensitive data.

18 WHAT TO DO WHEN YOU'RE ALL DONE

Done! It's a great feeling!

Take a few days off to relax and celebrate—you've earned it—and then take care of a couple of important items: thanking your adviser and getting a recommendation for your files.

First, thank your adviser, as well as the tutors and workshop leaders who helped you. A brief handwritten thank-you note is best, and I know, from personal experience, that they will appreciate it. You'll feel good about it, too. If you had a supportive relationship with your adviser, you should also drop by to say thanks in person. Later, you might want to send an e-mail with your new e-mail address. Students I worked with send me occasional updates, reporting a new job, marriage, kids, or other events in their lives, and I enjoy responding. Don't think you are intruding on your professor with an occasional letter like that. It's great to hear from students. It's one of the joys of teaching.

> *Tip:* Be sure to thank your adviser and others who helped you.

Second, now is the best time to get a new letter of recommendation or to have an existing one updated. Your thesis adds lots of positive information about you. It lets employers and graduate schools know you can manage a major independent project—one that requires extensive planning, research, and writing. That's very important news about your training and abilities.

> *Tip:* Get recommendations from your adviser and other faculty *now,* while their memories of working with you are fresh.

Your thesis adviser is not the only person to ask. Check with other faculty who may want to update their letters to include comments about your senior year and your successful thesis. Make sure you have a copy of the thesis to give them. The best time to do it is now, before senior year ends, while everybody is still around campus and your experience with them is still recent.

It's important to get a recommendation now *even if you are not quite sure what you will use it for.* A couple of years from now, you might decide to return for graduate study or apply for a different job. When you do, your professors can easily revise their recommendations, tailoring them for law school or a business promotion, adding information about your recent activities. Revisions are easy. What's hard—and here again I speak from experience—is for a professor to write a new recommendation from scratch for a student who has been gone for several years. It is much better to get a recommendation when the experience is fresh so it can include details about your abilities, achievements, and personal qualities.

My suggestions here apply to all faculty recommendations, whether or not the professor worked with you on the thesis.

Naturally, the best letters come from teachers who know you well and in whose courses you did your best work. Think about faculty who supervised papers, led seminars, and met with you for discussions during office hours. They know you and can say good things about you.

For most purposes, it is *much* better to get two very good recommendations than to get two very good ones and one mediocre one. It is worthwhile, then, to ask potential recommendation writers if they could please review your materials and let you know if they will be able to write a positive recommendation. You might add, "If you don't know me well enough to write a strong recommendation, or if you don't have time, I will understand and appreciate your telling me."

I know it's awkward to ask if a faculty member feels comfortable writing a good recommendation. That's one reason you asked if the faculty member "has time to write." It provides a graceful excuse for someone who cannot be helpful, for whatever reason. Take my word, you don't want them writing for you. That's why you should make it easy for them to say no, rather than urge them to write a lukewarm recommendation.

> *Tip:* Ask for recommendations in a way that allows faculty to turn you down if they are less than enthusiastic. That way you will get only strong, positive recommendations.

Of course, most faculty who have worked with you really do want to help. You need to give them the tools to do the job right. Do that by assembling an information packet that explains your achievements, academic and otherwise. It should include these items:

- Cover sheet with your name, address, phone, and e-mail
- Purpose of recommendation: job, grad school, law school, business school, or whatever
- List of grades and courses by academic year, including course title and professor (you should compile this list yourself; you can add an official transcript if you wish)
- Grade point average, both overall and in your major
- Candid explanation of the strong and weak points in your record
- Research papers and exams; if they are strong, include copies in the packet
- Your written statement, if one was required for a job or graduate school
- Extracurricular activities
- Work history
- Statement about your immediate postcollege plans such as a job
- Special skills such as mathematics, languages, extensive travel or study abroad, and any other skills that might be relevant
- Scores on GREs or LSATs with percentile ranking
- Date when recommendations are due
- Central location to send the confidential file, either at your school or a professional service such as www.interfolio.com

The more pertinent information you include in the packet, the better. Take this explanation about grades: "My sophomore grades were a bit low because my mother was very sick and I visited her several times. My grades picked up again junior year and are a better reflection of my academic abilities." Or you may wish to explain that you worked long hours at a work-study job or were bogged down in first-year Mandarin. A good recommendation letter can help explain weak points in your record, but only if the recommender knows about them.

The recommendation can also underscore positive information that might be overlooked by employers or admissions committees. You might tell the recommendation writer that "I received an A in this course mainly because of my research paper on nuclear deterrence." If your grades got better over time, or if you did particularly well on longer papers, highlight that. Concrete information like this can lead to a stronger recommendation, one that is filled with telling details.

Include copies of important papers you wrote. If the professor wrote something nice about the paper, include a copy of that, whether it's a note on the paper itself or an e-mail. I sometimes include these positive comments by other faculty as direct quotes in my recommendations. You might even include copies of some final exams if they are relevant. When professors have all this writing available, they can say something meaningful about your academic abilities.

Give the professor copies so you don't need to retrieve them (and let the professor know that). Also, let her know if you worked closely with a particular teaching assistant. That TA might be able to provide her with details about your class performance. (Generally speaking, it's better for a faculty member rather than a teaching assistant to write your recommendation, but there may be some exceptions. In any event, a TA who knows you can speak with the professor who is writing your recommendation.)

If you wrote a personal statement when you applied for jobs or graduate school, enclose that, too. It provides useful information for recommendations, too.

Be sure to include a list of your activities outside class. Were you involved in athletics, charity work, student government, tutoring kids, or other activities? These allow the recommender to give a fuller picture of your abilities and interests. Also, mention your job and the number of hours you work. If you made excellent grades while working, say, ten hours a week and doing extensive extracurricular activities, that makes your record even more impressive. Likewise, if your summer jobs or travel are relevant to your recommendation, mention them.

If you have skills in mathematics, languages, computers, or other areas that should be included in the recommendation, list them. If you are not a native English speaker, the recommendation writer may wish to note that you speak, read, and write English fluently, and that you are proficient in other languages as well. Make that clear in the information you provide.

Finally, list any honors you won and any offices you held in college. Let others brag for you.

Tip: Give recommendation writers a packet of written materials so they can write a well-rounded letter for you. Include grades, papers, and statements of future plans. Say whether the recommendation is for a job, law school, business school, or something else.

Explain where you want the recommendation sent and whether they need to meet any urgent deadlines. Most faculty members will try to accommodate you. In return, it helps if you ask them to send out only one or two letters. Most faculty do not have secretaries, so it's difficult and time-consuming to send out twelve separate recommendations. Worse, they may not get it done on time. Far better for you to set up a central file, either at your university or at a commercial service such as www.interfolio.com. I have used Interfolio often for student recommendations and found it quick and easy to upload letters there. It certainly simplifies life for students. For law schools, you can set up a file at the Law School Admission Council, www.lsac.org, which will forward them to any law schools you request. The addresses for these organizations are listed below.

> *Tip:* Don't ask your recommenders to send too many recommendation letters. It's better (for you and for them) if you set up your file at a central location such as www.interfolio.com.

Now that you have assembled all this information, put it in a manila envelope, put your name on the outside, and hand a copy to each faculty member who is writing a recommendation.

I know it seems like a lot of material, but, believe me, it will ensure you get detailed letters that highlight your strengths and achievements. The more you explain to your recommendation writer, the better the resulting letter will be.

Once the recommenders have written their letters, it's thoughtful to send a note thanking them, just as you did after the thesis. A brief note is fine—handwritten if you're still on campus, by e-mail if you're not. Here is a real one:

> Dear Professor XXX,
> I'm very grateful you took the time to write a recommendation letter for me. Your letter is an essential part of my next career steps, and I really appreciate your thoughtfulness.
> With thanks,
> Joan YYY

Your note should express similar thoughts in your own words.

Now you *really* are all done, You've completed a major independent project and, I hope, learned a lot in the process. It's a real achievement. Congratulations!

CHECKLIST: AFTER COMPLETING THE THESIS

- Thank your adviser, either in person or with a brief handwritten note.
- Thank tutors, workshop leaders, and others who helped you.
- Ask for written recommendations for your files before you leave school.
  - Assemble a packet for recommendation writers.
  - Include a list of courses, activities, and skills, plus copies of major papers.
  - State the purpose of the recommendation (for law school? a job?).

CENTRAL LOCATIONS FOR LETTERS OF RECOMMENDATION

All schools	www.interfolio.com Excellent site. Used by many universities for student credentials, including letters of recommendation. Individuals can set up their own files for nominal cost. Confidential letters are uploaded to the student's file by the recommendation writer.	Interfolio, Inc. PO Box 19127 Washington, DC 20036 Phone: 877-77-FOLIO E-mail: help@interfolio.com
Law school	www.lsac.org Recommenders must use official form filled out by applicant and available online; recommendation letters must be mailed in.	Law School Admissions Council 661 Penn St. PO Box 8508 Newtown, PA 18940-8508 Phone: 215-968-1001
Medical school	www.aamc.org/students/amcas/ start.htm	Association of American Medical Colleges (AAMC) 2450 N Street NW Washington, DC 20037-1123 Phone: 202-828-0400 E-mail: amcas@aamc.org

VII

Dealing with Special Requirements

19 THESIS DEFENSE AND SECOND READERS: QUESTIONS AND ANSWERS

Some departments—but not all—require a thesis defense, where you present the final paper to several faculty and answer their questions. I'll discuss what this defense is like and how you can prepare for it effectively.

Other departments omit the defense but do require a second faculty member to read and approve your paper. Rules differ considerably here. Some departments assign these "second readers" after you've turned in the paper. Others let you choose your own reader, either after you've completed the paper or in its final stages. If you are allowed to choose, you'll certainly have questions about how to do it. I'll answer those below.

If you are unsure what your department rules are, whether it requires a thesis defense or second reader, simply ask your adviser or a departmental administrator.

THESIS DEFENSE

My department requires a thesis defense. What's that like? How do I prepare?

It's a nightmare, terrible beyond your worst imaginings.

Just kidding. What's the worst that could happen? You might be asked to do one more revision. That's no fun, but it's not like being sent to San Quentin.

How can you avoid that (the revisions, I mean)? Three ways. First, get your adviser's evaluation *before* the defense. Give her your final draft in time for a discussion and revisions before you circulate the draft to the other committee members.

Second, if you have any choice about who will serve on the examining committee, ask your adviser. If she thinks the sky is blue, you don't want to be examined by someone who thinks it has always been pink. I call that a "taffy pull," in which the examiners pull in different directions and you are the taffy. Also, you don't want to ask someone who has never figured out that a BA thesis is really not the same as a PhD dissertation. You can avoid all these problems by talking with your adviser before making your choices.

Third, and most important of all, think about the questions the committee will ask so you can work out your answers in advance. That's not as hard as it sounds. By now, you should know your thesis argument and research well. The committee will ask you three things about them:

- What is your main argument or interpretation? (That's the elevator test.)
- How do you support it?
- How do you respond to the main objections or alternative arguments?

Usually, the exam opens by letting you explain your thesis briefly. You'll probably have five to ten minutes for the presentation. (Ask your adviser how long you'll have.) Your emphasis should be on the first two questions: What is your argument, and what evidence can you present to support it? The committee will then follow up with some questions about those points and pose a few hypothetical objections. "You say the sky is blue, but don't some authors think it is pink?"

Your answer should be grounded in your research and writing: "Yes, authors X, Y, and Z do argue it is pink, but they are a distinct minority. In my thesis, I show that the sky only appears pink to them because they are wearing sunglasses."

I've been to a lot of thesis defenses at every academic level, and they are all devoted to these three questions. That means you can prepare for them.

One more thing: The committee is not seeking to fail you. This is less an exam than a conversation about your work. The committee wants you to succeed, based on good answers to these three questions.

How should I prepare for a thesis defense?

Read your completed thesis and think about your answers to the three big questions: What's your argument? How do you support it? What's your response to the alternatives? In the defense itself, relax as best you can, listen to their specific questions, and present your answers with confidence. Party afterward.

SECOND READERS

What about finding a second reader?

There's a lot of variety here. Some departments don't require a second reader; others do. Of those that do, some allow the student to select the reader, usually in the final months of the thesis project. Other departments (like mine) select the second reader themselves after the paper has been completed.

Whatever the selection method, the purpose of these additional readers is the same. They offer a second independent view of the final paper. (Sometimes a third reader is brought in if the first two disagree. That's usually because one thinks it deserves honors and one doesn't.)

If you are allowed to choose a second reader, use the same criteria you would use for choosing a defense committee. Ideally, you want someone who

- Knows the subject matter you've studied;
- Knows you, at least a little;
- Is open-minded and gets along intellectually with your adviser. (That does not mean they need to agree, only that they are tolerant of each other's views.)

Ask your adviser for suggestions, just as you would in selecting a thesis defense committee.

20 A ONE-SEMESTER THESIS

What if you have only one semester to write your thesis, not the two we've assumed throughout the book? How does that change the recommendations I've made? How does it affect the time schedules, offered in many chapters and summarized in chapter 15?

First, some reassurance: You *can* complete a thesis in one semester, if necessary. To do it, though, you must focus considerably more attention on the project and get off to a quicker start. In the next few pages, I'll explain some ways to do that.

These suggestions complement the rest of the book. *All* the earlier chapters are relevant to a one-semester thesis. There's no difference in how you refine your topic, conduct your research, do your prewriting, edit the text, or anything else. The only difference is that you face a tighter schedule.

Your most pressing goals are to line up a thesis adviser and settle on a topic. With less than four months to complete the thesis, you need to line up an adviser at the very beginning of the semester or, if possible, before it begins. The earlier, the better.

Once you've picked an adviser, you can move to stage 2: settling on your thesis topic so you can begin focused work. If you want to explore alternative topics and do extensive background readings, you should probably do that before the thesis semester. That's an inherent limitation of a one-semester thesis, unfortunately. You simply don't have a lot of time to wander and explore during the semester itself. You need to spend your limited time doing actual thesis research and writing, not fishing for a topic.

What you should *not* shortchange, however, is the thesis proposal. It launches you in the right direction and guides your subsequent work. It's even worthwhile to revise the proposal, just as I suggest for a two-semester project.

The most useful suggestions are those that give you more time to research and write. Here are four proven strategies:

- Meet with your adviser each week, even if it's just a short session.
- Build on earlier seminar papers.

- Do not take courses requiring longer papers this semester.
- Take a special reading course with your adviser (or a thesis seminar).

I'll review these strategies briefly and explain how each one can help.

First, whether your thesis takes one semester or two, you should meet with your adviser regularly. For a one-semester project, frequent meetings are essential. You need immediate feedback on what you have done already and what you plan to do in the week ahead. If you need to make a mid-course correction, why waste an extra week before finding out? You're on a tight schedule and don't have that week to fritter away. Getting this feedback doesn't require long meetings. Ten or fifteen minutes is probably enough, sometimes more than enough. But it does require meetings almost every week.

Second, you can jump-start your thesis by beginning with a seminar paper you've written. (Again, that's true whether the thesis project lasts one semester or two.) It's a great idea to build on work you enjoyed and did well. You've already completed some of the background reading and explored some of the issues, so you're well on your way. That's a tremendous asset when you face a tight schedule.

If you start from prior work, however, you *must* tell your adviser. That's a basic rule of academic honesty. It applies at every university. You cannot use work from other courses, even though you did it yourself, without telling faculty in the subsequent course.

It won't be a problem, believe me. In fact, your adviser will probably be delighted you have a strong base to build on. Go beyond mere disclosure. Ask your adviser to read the earlier paper; you should add a cover sheet explaining how you intend to modify and extend it. The discussion based on this paper can become the foundation for your thesis project.

Third, pay careful attention to course scheduling this semester. Avoid courses that have major exams or papers due at the same time as your thesis. Otherwise, you'll find yourself squeezed hard during the final weeks, just when you should be revising your thesis. Of course, you can't always avoid conflicts, but you should try to minimize them. That means planning your academic schedule.

As you plan, you might foresee some tight corners ahead. If you expect a crunch during week 12, for example, you might avert it by writing a class paper before it's due or taking an early final. No fun, I'll grant you, but maybe better than the alternative.

The same considerations apply to your nonacademic obligations, such as your job schedule. If you let your boss know several weeks in advance, you have a much better chance of working around the problem.

Fourth, consider taking a reading course with your adviser, rather than another standard lecture or seminar. A reading course is a tutorial, where you read a list of books and discuss them with the professor. Usually, you make up the reading list yourself, with advice from the faculty member. In this case, your reading list is the working bibliography for your thesis. Your initial list will cover essential background readings, along with a clear statement that you intend to add more publications as your research advances. If the course requires any writing, you can review some of those books or produce short papers related to your thesis.

Most schools permit reading courses if you can find a willing professor. Ask a departmental administrator if your school allows such courses and if they count toward your major. Quietly ask around to find out if your adviser ever teaches them. If the answer is yes, then discuss it directly with your adviser. He's probably willing to sign on once he knows *why* you are doing it and *what readings* you plan. Think about those before asking.

The advantage of such a reading course is that it allows you to concentrate on your thesis. The disadvantage is that it replaces some other course you might want to take. That's a trade-off you need to consider.

If you can't do an individual reading course, a thesis seminar is almost as good. It, too, lets you focus on your research and writing. And while it doesn't provide one-on-one mentoring, it does offer some compensating advantages: a chance to present your ideas publicly and get feedback from the seminar leader and fellow students.

Don't take *both* a thesis seminar and a reading course during the same semester. That's overkill. They cover the same issues. You'd miss a chance to take other courses or do something else.

Now, let's turn to the thesis time schedule. The first stages—formulating your topic—should take about a month or six weeks, a little shorter than a two-semester thesis. As I said earlier, you need to zero in on your topic quickly. The bulk of the semester will then be spent doing focused research, prewriting, and drafting the middle sections of the paper. These sections are the substantive core of the thesis. During the last three or four weeks, you should draw together these middle sections, write an introduction and conclusion, and begin editing and polishing the entire paper.

Be sure to start discussing your conclusions with your adviser before the deadline looms. Otherwise you'll have no chance to think over your findings and test them out with your adviser. That weakens your thesis precisely where it should be strongest: the argument and findings. They are the heart of your project; contemplate them with care.

This schedule is swifter than a two-semester paper, but the sequence of reading, research, and writing is exactly the same.

TIME SCHEDULE FOR ONE-SEMESTER THESIS

	First 4 weeks	Middle 6–7 weeks	Last 3 weeks
Chapters in this book:	1–4	5–11, 13	Review 11
Reading:	Background reading	Focused research and planning	Fill-in research
Writing:	Proposal and revised proposal	Prewrite middle sections of thesis	Finish introduction and conclusion
	Bibliographic essay	Write and revise middle sections	
		Prewrite introduction and conclusion	Edit/rewrite entire paper

VIII

Citing Your Sources and Getting More Advice

APPENDIX 1
BEST SOURCES FOR MORE HELP

There are great resources about most topics covered in this book. If you want to find out more about one of them, here are some of the best books I've found.

WRITING

There are three outstanding resources on writing, all of them brief.

Strunk, William, Jr., and E. B. White. *The Elements of Style*. 4th ed. New York: Longman, 2000.

▸ The classic book on writing, emphasizing brevity and clarity.

Trimble, John. *Writing with Style: Conversations on the Art of Writing*. 2nd ed. Upper Saddle River, NJ: Prentice Hall, 2000.

Zinsser, William. *On Writing Well*. 6th ed. New York: HarperCollins, 1998.

▸ Zinsser's *Writing to Learn* (New York: Harper & Row, 1988) is also filled with good advice.

For a more advanced treatment, grounded in academic research:

Williams, Joseph. *Style: Toward Clarity and Grace*. Chicago: University of Chicago Press, 1990.

For helpful ideas directed at academic writers:

Becker, Howard. *Writing for the Social Sciences: How to Start and Finish Your Thesis, Book, or Article*. Chicago: University of Chicago Press, 1986.

McCloskey, Deirdre N. *Economical Writing*. 2nd ed. Long Grove, IL: Waveland Press, 2000.

▸ A little gem, directed at writers in the social sciences but useful for everyone.

EDITING

Since editing is essential to good writing, nearly all books on writing treat it extensively. You may also wish to consult a couple of specialized texts:

Murray, Donald M. *The Craft of Revision*. Fort Worth, TX: Holt, Rinehart, and Winston, 1991.

▸ Concentrates on the large issues of editing, particularly the paper's structure.

Ross-Larson, Bruce. *Edit Yourself: A Manual for Everyone Who Works with Words*. New York: W. W. Norton, 1996.

▸ Focuses on line-by-line changes.

BEST PRACTICAL GUIDES TO CURRENT ENGLISH USAGE

Garner, Bryan A. *Garner's Modern American Usage.* New York: Oxford University Press, 2003.

Goldstein, Norm, ed. *The Associated Press Stylebook and Briefing on Media Law.* Cambridge, MA: Perseus, 2002.

BEST SOURCE FOR SYNONYMS AND WORD SELECTION

Kipfer, Barbara Ann. *Roget's International Thesaurus Indexed Edition.* 6th ed. New York: HarperCollins, 2001.

▸ Best, first-rate, splendid, tip-top [colloquial], a bit of all right [English] . . . All word-processing programs now have a built-in thesaurus. They are convenient and increasingly wide-ranging, but none has the depth of *Roget's* in print.

> *Tip:* Turn to a thesaurus to find new words and avoid dull repetition. But remember, it's no substitute for your own editorial judgment. Whenever you choose a synonym, try it out in the sentence you are writing and listen for subtle variations in tone and meaning.

WRITING PROCESS: HOW TO WORK BETTER WHILE WRITING

Boice, Robert. *How Writers Journey to Comfort and Fluency: A Psychological Adventure.* Westport, CT: Praeger, 1994.

▸ This is a hard book to find, but it's worth the effort. Boice is an experienced teacher who shares his techniques for helping writers who are blocked or who find writing a painful process. Also see Boice's *Procrastination and Blocking: A Novel, Practical Approach* (Westport, CT: Greenwood, 1996).

Bolker, Joan. *Writing Your Dissertation in Fifteen Minutes a Day: A Guide to Starting, Revising, and Finishing Your Doctoral Thesis.* New York: Henry Holt, 1998.

▸ Another experienced guide. Although Bolker's book focuses on doctoral students, her advice is useful for BA and MA thesis writers, too.

RESEARCH

Booth, Wayne C., Gregory G. Colomb, and Joseph M. Williams. *The Craft of Research.* 2nd ed. Chicago: University of Chicago Press, 2003.

▸ Best general guide.

Research in the social sciences:

Elster, Jon. *Nuts and Bolts for the Social Sciences.* Cambridge: Cambridge University Press, 1989.

Gerring, John. *Social Science Methodology: A Criterial Framework.* Cambridge: Cambridge University Press, 2001.

King, Gary, Robert O. Keohane, and Sidney Verba. *Designing Social Inquiry: Scientific Inference in Qualitative Research.* Princeton, NJ: Princeton University Press, 1994.

Research in the humanities:

Altick, Richard Daniel, and John Fenstermaker. *The Art of Literary Research.* 4th ed. New York: W. W. Norton, 1993.

➤ Although the title refers only to literary research, the suggestions are broadly useful across the humanities.

Qualitative research:

Taylor, Steven J., and Robert Bogdan. *Introduction to Qualitative Research Methods: A Guidebook and Resource.* 3rd ed. New York: John Wiley, 1998.

Case studies:

Hamel, Jacques, with Stéphane Dufour and Moninic Fortin. *Case Study Methods.* Newbury Park, CA: Sage, 1993.

Orum, Anthony M., Joe R. Feagin, and Gideon Sjoberg. "The Nature of the Case Study." In *A Case for the Case Study,* ed. Joe R. Feagin, Anthony M. Orum, and Gideon Sjoberg. Chapel Hill: University of North Carolina Press, 1991, pp. 1–26.

RESEARCH AND WRITING IN SPECIALIZED FIELDS

Art:

Barnet, Sylvan. *A Short Guide to Writing about Art.* 7th ed. New York: Longman, 2003.

Economics:

Thomson, William. *A Guide for the Young Economist.* Cambridge, MA: MIT Press, 2001, pp. 1–70.

➤ Intended for graduate students or advanced undergraduates; also useful for students doing advanced empirical work in other social sciences.

Film:

Corrigan, Timothy. *A Short Guide to Writing about Film.* 5th ed. New York: Pearson Longman, 2004.

History:

Howell, Martha C., and Walter Prevenier. *From Reliable Sources: An Introduction to Historical Methods.* Ithaca, NY: Cornell University Press, 2001.

Marius, Richard, and Melvin E. Page. *A Short Guide to Writing about History.* 4th ed. New York: Longman, 2001.

Norton, Mary Beth, ed. *The American Historical Association's Guide to Historical Literature,* assoc. ed. Pamela Gerardi. 3rd ed. New York: Oxford University Press, 1995.

Storey, William Kelleher. *Writing History: A Guide for Students.* New York: Oxford University Press, 1999, pp. 25–57.

Literary analysis:

Barnet, Sylvan, and William E. Cain. *A Short Guide to Writing about Literature.* 9th ed. New York: Longman, 2003.

Harner, James L. *Literary Research Guide: An Annotated Listing of Reference Sources in English Literary Studies.* 4th ed. New York: Modern Language Association of America, 2002.

Müller, Gilbert H., and John A. Williams. *Ways In: Approaches to Reading and Writing about Literature.* New York: McGraw-Hill, 1994.

Music:

Bellman, Jonathan. *A Short Guide to Writing about Music.* 9th ed. New York: Longman, 2000.

Philosophy:

Feinberg, Joel. *Doing Philosophy: A Guide to the Writing of Philosophy Papers.* Belmont, CA: Wadsworth/Thomson Learning, 2002, pp. 81–118.

Seech, Zachary. *Writing Philosophy Papers.* 3rd ed. Belmont, CA: Wadsworth, 2000, pp. 1–28, 61–70.

Psychology:

Rosnow, Ralph L., and Mimi Rosnow. *Writing Papers in Psychology: A Student Guide to Research Reports, Essays, Proposals, Posters, and Brief Reports.* Belmont, CA: Thomson/Wadsworth, 2003.

Sternberg, R. J. *The Psychologist's Companion: A Guide to Scientific Writing for Students and Researchers.* 4th ed. Cambridge: Cambridge University Press, 1993.

TYPES OF ARGUMENTS

Weston, Anthony. *A Rulebook for Arguments.* 2nd ed. Indianapolis, IN: Hackett, 1992.

GRAPHS AND CHARTS

Cleveland, William S. *Visualizing Data.* Summit, NJ: Hobart, 1993.

▶ Assumes a sophisticated understanding of statistics.

Tufte, Edward. *The Visual Display of Quantitative Information.* 2nd ed. Cheshire, CT: Graphics Press, 2001.

▶ Tufte's focus is on displaying quantitative information in ways that are clear, undistorted, and tied to the narrative. He has written several books on the topic; this is the best one to start with.

REFERENCES, FOOTNOTES/ENDNOTES, AND QUESTIONS OF ACADEMIC STYLE

Quick guide to references: appendix 2, "Footnotes 101."
Guide to citations in every format:
Lipson, Charles. *Doing Honest Work in College: How to Prepare Citations, Avoid Plagiarism, and Achieve Real Academic Success.* Chicago: University of Chicago Press, 2004.

▸ Covers Chicago-style citations, MLA, and APA, plus many other formats, each in a separate chapter with examples of how to cite books, articles, Web pages, and so forth. There is also an extensive list of frequently asked questions about citations, along with practical answers.

Comprehensive guide to academic style plus Chicago-style notes:
The Chicago Manual of Style: The Essential Guide for Writers, Editors, and Publishers. 15th ed. Chicago: University of Chicago Press, 2003.

MLA citation style:
Gibaldi, Joseph. *MLA Handbook for Writers of Research Papers.* 6th ed. New York: Modern Language Association of America, 2003.
Gibaldi, Joseph. *MLA Style Manual and Guide to Scholarly Publishing.* 2nd ed. New York: Modern Language Association of America, 1998, pp. 149–254.

APA citation style:
Publication Manual of the American Psychological Association. 5th ed. Washington, DC: American Psychological Association, 2001.

GRAMMAR AND PUNCTUATION

The Chicago Manual of Style: The Essential Guide for Writers, Editors, and Publishers. 15th ed. Chicago: University of Chicago Press, 2003, pp. 145–275.

▸ *The Chicago Manual of Style* has chapters on grammar and punctuation that will answer almost any question.

Strunk, William, Jr., and E. B. White. *The Elements of Style.* 4th ed. New York: Longman, 2000, sec. 1.

▸ The first section of Strunk and White is a brief list of grammatical "do's and don'ts" with examples and comments. It's worth reading, even though you already know where to put a comma.

PLAGIARISM

Lipson, Charles. *Doing Honest Work in College: How to Prepare Citations, Avoid Plagiarism, and Achieve Real Academic Success.* Chicago: University of Chicago Press, 2004, chap. 3.

▸ Includes examples of how to paraphrase, when to cite, and more.

OVERCOMING PROBLEMS

For general issues about working and writing effectively, including procrastination and writer's block, Robert Boice and Joan Bolker, listed above, under "Writing Process," are excellent.

PROCRASTINATION

Burka, Jane B., and Lenora M. Yuen. *Procrastination: Why You Do It, What to Do about It.* Reading, MA: Addison-Wesley, 1983.

Fiore, Neil. *The NOW Habit: A Strategic Program for Overcoming Procrastination and Enjoying Guilt-Free Play.* New York: Jeremy P. Tarcher/Putnam, 1989.

WRITER'S BLOCK

Hjortshoj, Keith. *Understanding Writing Blocks.* New York: Oxford University Press, 2001.

Plus books by Robert Boice.

STUDY SKILLS

Armstrong, William H. *Study Is Hard Work.* 2nd ed. Boston: David R. Godine, 1995.
► An old-fashioned teacher's lucid advice.

Kornhauser, Arthur W. *How to Study: Suggestions for High School and College Students,* revised by Diane M. Enerson. 3rd ed. Chicago: University of Chicago Press, 1993.
► Brief no-nonsense guide.

SLEEP PROBLEMS

Dement, William C. *The Promise of Sleep: A Pioneer in Sleep Medicine Explores the Vital Connection between Health, Happiness, and a Good Night's Sleep.* New York: Delacorte, 1999.

APPENDIX 2

FOOTNOTES 101

There are three major citation styles:

- Chicago (or Turabian), used in many fields
- MLA, used in the humanities
- APA, used in social sciences, education, engineering, business, and business

I will cover each one, providing clear directions and plenty of examples so you won't have any trouble writing correct citations. That way, you can concentrate on your paper, not on the type of citation you're using. I'll cover each style separately, so you can turn directly to the one you need.

I will focus on the items you are likely to cite in each style. Using this information, you'll be able to cite books, articles, government documents, musical performances, Web sites, and much more—almost anything you might use in your thesis. If you need additional examples, go to the official manuals for each citation styles (listed later in this appendix). They are available in your library.

All three citation styles have the same basic goals:

- To identify and credit the sources you use
- To give readers specific information so they can go to these sources themselves, if they wish

Fortunately, the different styles include a lot of the same information. That means you can write down the same things as you take notes, without worrying about what kind of citations you will ultimately use. You should write down that information as soon as you start taking notes on a new book or article. If you photocopy an article, write all the reference information on the first page. If you do it first, you won't forget. You'll need it later for citations.

Chicago notes are either complete citations or shortened versions plus a complete description in the bibliography or in a previous note. Their name comes from their original source, *The Chicago Manual of Style*, published by the University of Chicago Press. This format is sometimes called "Turabian" after a popular book based on that style, Kate Turabian's *A Manual for Writers of Term Papers, Theses, and Dissertations.*[1]

If you use complete-citation notes, you might not need a bibliography at all since the first note for each item includes all the necessary data. If you use the shortened form, though, you definitely need a bibliography since the notes skip vital information.

Whether you use complete-citation notes or the shortened version, you can place them either at the bottom of each page or the end of the document. Footnotes and endnotes are identical, except for their placement. Footnotes appear on the same page as the citation in the text. Endnotes are bunched together at the end of the paper, article, chapter, or book. Word processors give you an easy choice between the two.

MLA and APA citation styles were developed to provide alternative ways of referencing materials. They use in-text citations such as (Stewart 154) or (Stewart, 2004) with full information provided only in a reference list at the end.[2] Because these in-text citations are brief, a reference list is needed to provide full information about each publication. I'll describe each style in detail and provide lots of examples, just as I will for Chicago citations.

In case you are wondering about the initials: APA stands for the American Psychological Association, MLA for the Modern Language Association. Both styles have been adopted well beyond their original fields.

Your department, school, or adviser may prefer one style, or even require it, or they might leave it up to you. Check on that as soon as you begin handing in papers with citations. Why not do it consistently from the beginning?

---

1. Kate Turabian, *A Manual for Writers of Term Papers, Theses, and Dissertations*, 6th ed. (Chicago: University of Chicago Press, 1996); *The Chicago Manual of Style*, 15th ed. (Chicago: University of Chicago Press, 2003).

2. Reference lists are similar to bibliographies, but there are some technical differences. To avoid a needless proliferation of citation styles, I include only the most common ones in each academic field. That means I leave out others, such as Turabian's shortened citations.

Tip: Check with your department and adviser early to find out what style citations they prefer. Then use that style consistently.

Speaking of consistency . . . it's an important aspect of footnoting. Stick with the same abbreviations and capitalizations, and don't mix styles within a paper.

HANGING INDENTS

One final point about shared bibliographic style. Most bibliographies and reference lists—Chicago, MLA, APA, and some others—use a special style known as "hanging indents." This applies only to the bibliographies and reference lists, not to footnotes or endnotes. It is the opposite of regular paragraph indention, where the first line is indented and the rest are regular length. In a hanging indent, the first line of each citation is regular length and the rest are indented. For example:

Rothenberg, Gunther E. "Maurice of Nassau, Gustavus Adolphus, Raimondo Montecuccoli, and the 'Military Revolution' of the Seventeenth Century." In *Makers of Modern Strategy from Machiavelli to the Nuclear Age,* edited by Peter Paret, 32–63. Princeton, NJ: Princeton University Press, 1986.
Spooner, Frank C. *Risks at Sea: Amsterdam Insurance and Maritime Europe, 1766–1780.* Cambridge: Cambridge University Press, 1983.

There's a good reason for this unusual format. Hanging indents are designed to make it easy to skim down the list of references and see the authors' names. To remind you to use this format, I'll use it myself when I illustrate references.

To make the authors' names stand out further, most bibliographies list their last names first. If an author's name is repeated, however, the styles differ. APA repeats the full name for each citation. MLA uses three hyphens, followed by a period. Chicago uses three em dashes (that is, long dashes), followed by a period.[3]

---

3. Because em dashes are longer than hyphens, they show up differently on-screen and in print. The em dashes show up as a solid line, the hyphens as separate dashes. Three em dashes: ———. Three hyphens: ---. Frankly, you don't need to worry about this for your papers. Use the preferred one if you can, but either is fine.

> Lipson, Charles. *Barbecue, Cole Slaw, and Extra Hot Sauce.* Midnight, MS: Hushpuppy, 2004.
>
> ———. *More Gumbo, Please.* Thibodeaux, LA: Andouille Press, 2005.

You can arrange hanging indents easily on your word processor. Go to the format feature and, within it, to the section on paragraphs. Choose hanging indentation instead of regular or none.

Now that we've covered these general aspects of citation, let's turn to the specific style you will use in your thesis. I have organized the references so they are most convenient for you, putting all the documentation for each style in its own section: Chicago, followed by MLA, then APA.

CHICAGO MANUAL OF STYLE CITATION SYSTEM

Chicago citations are based on the authoritative *Chicago Manual of Style.* The manual, now in its fifteenth edition, is the bible for references and academic style. A briefer version, covering most aspects of student papers, is Kate Turabian's *A Manual for Writers of Term Papers, Theses, and Dissertations.* This section, however, should cover all you need to document your sources, even if they're unusual.

Full Notes, Short Notes, and Bibliography

Chicago-style notes come in two flavors, and I include both in this section.[4]

1. A complete first note + short follow-up notes.
   The first note for any item is a full one, giving complete information about the book, article, or other document. Subsequent entries for that item are brief. There is no need for a bibliography since all the information is covered in the first note.
2. Short notes only + bibliography.
   All notes are brief. Full information about the sources appears only in the bibliography.

---

4. *The Chicago Manual of Style* and Turabian also describe another style, the author-date system. These citations appear in parentheses in the text, listing the author and the date of publication. For example: (Larmore 2004). Full citations appear in a reference list at the end. For simplicity, I have omitted this style since it is similar to APA, also discussed in this appendix.

This means there are three ways to cite individual items. All of them are illustrated in this appendix.

A. Full first notes
B. Short notes
C. Bibliographic entries

The first flavor combines A + B; the second combines B + C.

This section covers everything from edited books to reference works, from sheet music to online databases, and lots of things in between. To make it easy to find what you need, I've listed them here alphabetically, together with the pages they are on. At the end of this section, I answer some question about using this style.

INDEX OF CHICAGO CITATIONS IN THIS APPENDIX

CHICAGO MANUAL OF STYLE: NOTES AND BIBLIOGRAPHY

Book, one author	Full first note	[99] Charles Lipson, *Reliable Partners: How Democracies Have Made a Separate Peace* (Princeton, NJ: Princeton University Press, 2003), 22–23.

> ➤ This is note number 99 and refers to pages 22–23.
> ➤ Footnotes and endnotes do not have hanging indents. Only the bibliography does.

	Short note	[99] Lipson, *Reliable Partners,* 22–23.

> ➤ Shorten titles to four words or less, if possible.

	Bibliography	Lipson, Charles. *Reliable Partners: How Democracies Have Made a Separate Peace.* Princeton, NJ: Princeton University Press, 2003.

Books, several by same author	First note	[99] Gerhard L. Weinberg, *Germany, Hitler, and World War II: Essays in Modern German and World History* (Cambridge: Cambridge University Press, 1995). [100] Gerhard L. Weinberg, *A World at Arms: A Global History of World War II* (Cambridge: Cambridge University Press, 1994).
	Short note	[99] Weinberg, *Germany, Hitler, and World War II.* [100] Weinberg, *World at Arms.*
	Bibliography	Weinberg, Gerhard L. *Germany, Hitler, and World War II: Essays in Modern German and World History.* Cambridge: Cambridge University Press, 1995. ———. *A World at Arms: A Global History of World War II.* Cambridge: Cambridge University Press, 1994.

> ► The repetition of the author's name uses three em dashes (which are simply long dashes), followed by a period. You can find em dashes by digging around in Microsoft Word. Go to "Insert," then "Symbols," then "Special Characters." After you do it once, you can simply copy and paste it. If, for some reason, you can't find the em dash, just use three hyphens.
> ► List works for each author alphabetically, by title.

Book, multiple authors	First note	⁹⁹ Dan Reiter and Allan C. Stam, *Democracies at War* (Princeton, NJ: Princeton University Press, 2002), 15–26.
	Short note	⁹⁹ Reiter and Stam, *Democracies at War,* 15–26. ► Titles with four words or less are not shortened.
	Bibliography	Reiter, Dan, and Allan C. Stam. *Democracies at War.* Princeton, NJ: Princeton University Press, 2002. ► List up to ten coauthors in the bibliography. If there are more, list the first seven, followed by "et al."
Book, multiple editions	First note	⁹⁹ William Strunk Jr. and E. B. White, *The Elements of Style,* 4th ed. (New York: Longman, 2000), 12.
	Short note	⁹⁹ Strunk and White, *Elements of Style,* 12. ► To keep the note short, the title doesn't include the initial article (~~The~~ *Elements of Style*) or the edition number.
	Bibliography	Strunk, William, Jr., and E. B. White. *The Elements of Style.* 4th ed. New York: Longman, 2000.
Book, edited	First note	⁹⁹ Francis Robinson, ed., *Cambridge Illustrated History of the Islamic World* (Cambridge: Cambridge University Press, 1996).

Book, edited (*continued*)		[99] David Taras, Frits Pannekoek, and Maria Bakardjieva, eds., *How Canadians Communicate* (Calgary, AB: University of Calgary Press, 2003).
		▶ Use standard two-letter abbreviations for Canadian provinces.
	Short note	[99] Robinson, *History of Islamic World.*
		▶ Choose the most relevant words when shortening the title. Also, drop the abbreviation for editor.
		[99] Taras, Pannekoek, and Bakardjieva, *How Canadians Communicate.*
	Bibliography	Robinson, Francis, ed. *Cambridge Illustrated History of the Islamic World.* Cambridge: Cambridge University Press, 1996.
		Taras, David, Frits Pannekoek, and Maria Bakardjieva, eds. *How Canadians Communicate.* Calgary, AB: University of Calgary Press, 2003.
Book, anonymous or no author	First note	[99] Anonymous, *Through Our Enemies' Eyes: Osama Bin Laden, Radical Islam, and the Future of America* (Washington, DC: Brassey's, 2003).
		[99] *Golden Verses of the Pythagoreans* (Whitefish, MT: Kessinger, 2003).
	Short note	[99] Anonymous, *Through Our Enemies' Eyes.*
		[99] *Golden Verses of Pythagoreans.*
	Bibliography	Anonymous, *Through Our Enemies' Eyes: Osama Bin Laden, Radical Islam, and the Future of America.* Washington, DC: Brassey's, 2003.
		Golden Verses of the Pythagoreans. Whitefish, MT: Kessinger, 2003.
		▶ If a book lists "anonymous" as the author, then that name should be included. If no author is listed, then you may list "anonymous" or simply begin with the title.

Book, online	First note	[99] Charles Dickens, *Great Expectations* (1860–61; Project Gutenberg, 1998), etext 1400, http://www.gutenberg.net/etext98/grexp10.txt. ▸ The etext number is helpful but not essential.
	Short note	[99] Dickens, *Great Expectations.*
	Bibliography	Dickens, Charles. *Great Expectations* (1860–61; Project Gutenberg, 1998). Etext 1400. http://www.gutenberg.net/etext98/grexp10.txt.

Multivolume work	First note	[99] Otto Pflanze, *Bismarck and the Development of Germany,* 3 vols. (Princeton, NJ: Princeton University Press, 1963–90), 1:153.
	Short note	[99] Pflanze, *Bismarck,* 1:153.
	Bibliography	Pflanze, Otto. *Bismarck and the Development of Germany.* 3 vols. Princeton, NJ: Princeton University Press, 1963–90.

Single volume in multivolume work	First note	[99] Otto Pflanze, *Bismarck and the Development of Germany,* vol. 3, *The Period of Fortification, 1880–1898* (Princeton, NJ: Princeton University Press, 1990), 237. [99] Akira Iriye, *The Globalizing of America,* Cambridge History of American Foreign Relations, edited by Warren I. Cohen, vol. 3 (Cambridge: Cambridge University Press, 1993), 124. ▸ Pflanze wrote all three volumes. Iriye wrote only the third volume in a series edited by Cohen.
	Short note	[99] Pflanze, *Bismarck,* 3:237. [99] Iriye, *Globalizing of America,* 124.
	Bibliography	Pflanze, Otto. *Bismarck and the Development of Germany.* Vol. 3, *The Period of Fortification, 1880–1898.* Princeton, NJ: Princeton University Press, 1990.

Single volume in multivolume work (*continued*)		Iriye, Akira. *The Globalizing of America.* Cambridge History of American Foreign Relations, edited by Warren I. Cohen, vol. 3. Cambridge: Cambridge University Press, 1993.
Reprint of earlier edition	First note	[99] Jacques Barzun, *Simple and Direct: A Rhetoric for Writers,* rev. ed. (1985; repr., Chicago: University of Chicago Press, 1994), 27. [99] Adam Smith, *An Inquiry into the Nature and Causes of the Wealth of Nations* (1776), ed. Edwin Cannan (Chicago: University of Chicago Press, 1976). ▸ The year 1776 appears immediately after the title because that's when Smith's original work appeared. The editor, Edwin Cannan, worked only on its modern publication. The Barzun volume, by contrast, is simply a reprint so the original year appears as part of the publication information.
	Short note	[99] Barzun, *Simple and Direct,* 27. [99] Smith, *Wealth of Nations,* vol. I, bk. IV, chap. II: 477. ▸ This modern edition of Smith is actually a single volume, but it retains the volume numbering of the 1776 original. You could simply cite the page number, but the full citation helps readers with other editions.
	Bibliography	Barzun, Jacques. *Simple and Direct: A Rhetoric for Writers.* 1985. Chicago: University of Chicago Press, 1994. Smith, Adam. *An Inquiry into the Nature and Causes of the Wealth of Nations.* 1776. Ed. Edwin Cannan. Chicago: University of Chicago Press, 1976.
Translated volume	First note	[99] Max Weber, *The Protestant Ethic and the Spirit of Capitalism* (1904–5), trans. Talcott Parsons (New York: Charles Scribner's Sons, 1958), 176–77.

[99] Alexis de Tocqueville, *Democracy in America* (1835), ed. J. P. Mayer, trans. George Lawrence (New York: HarperCollins, 2000).

► Translator and editor are listed in the order in which they appear on the book's title page.

[99] Seamus Heaney, trans., *Beowulf: A New Verse Translation* (New York: Farrar, Straus and Giroux, 2000).

► For *Beowulf,* the translator's name appears before the book title because Heaney's is the only name on the title page. (The poem is anonymous.) The same treatment would be given to an editor or compiler whose name appeared alone on the title page.

Short note

[99] Weber, *Protestant Ethic,* 176–77.
[99] Tocqueville, *Democracy in America.*
[99] *Beowulf.*

► Or

[99] Heaney, trans., *Beowulf.*

Bibliography

Weber, Max. *The Protestant Ethic and the Spirit of Capitalism.* 1904–5. Trans. Talcott Parsons. New York: Charles Scribner's Sons, 1958.

Tocqueville, Alexis de. *Democracy in America.* 1835. Ed. J. P. Mayer. Trans. George Lawrence. New York: HarperCollins, 2000.

Heaney, Seamus, trans. *Beowulf: A New Verse Translation.* New York: Farrar, Straus and Giroux, 2000.

Chapter in edited book

First note

[99] Robert Keohane, "The Demand for International Regimes," in *International Regimes,* ed. Stephen Krasner, 55–67 (Ithaca, NY: Cornell University Press, 1983).

Short note

[99] Keohane, "Demand for International Regimes," 56–67.

Bibliography

Keohane, Robert. "The Demand for International Regimes." In *International Regimes,* edited by Stephen Krasner, 56–67. Ithaca, NY: Cornell University Press, 1983.

Journal article	First note	[99] Charles Lipson, "Why Are Some International Agreements Informal?" *International Organization* 45 (Autumn 1991): 495–538.
	Short note	[99] Lipson, "International Agreements," 495–538.
	Bibliography	Lipson, Charles. "Why Are Some International Agreements Informal?" *International Organization* 45 (Autumn 1991): 495–538.
Journal article, multiple authors	First note	[99] William G. Thomas III and Edward L. Ayers, "An Overview: The Differences Slavery Made; A Close Analysis of Two American Communities," *American Historical Review* 108 (December 2003): 1299–307.
	Short note	[99] Thomas and Ayers, "Differences Slavery Made," 1299–307.
	Bibliography	Thomas, William G., III, and Edward L. Ayers. "An Overview: The Differences Slavery Made; A Close Analysis of Two American Communities." *American Historical Review* 108 (December 2003): 1299–307.
Journal article, online	First note	[99] Christopher Small, "Why Doesn't the Whole World Love Chamber Music?" *American Music* 19:3 (Autumn 2001): 340–59. http://links.jstor.org/sici?sici=0734-4392%28200123%2919%3A3%3C340%3AWDTWWL%3E2.0.CO%3B2-J (accessed March 15, 2004).
	Short note	[99] Small, "Chamber Music," 340–59.
	Bibliography	Small, Christopher. "Why Doesn't the Whole World Love Chamber Music?" *American Music* 19:3 (Autumn 2001): 340–59. http://links.jstor.org/sici?sici=0734-4392%28200123%2919%3A3%3C340%3AWDTWWL%3E2.0.CO%3B2-J (accessed March 15, 2004).

Newspaper or magazine article, no author	First note	[99] "Report of 9/11 Panel Cites Lapses by C.I.A. and F.B.I.," *New York Times,* July 23, 2003 (national edition), 1.
		► This refers to page 1.
		► If the article has a byline and you wish to include the reporter's name, you certainly can: David Johnston, "Report of 9/11 Panel . . . ."
		► Short articles in newsweeklies like *Time* are treated the same as newspaper articles. Longer articles with bylines are treated like journal articles.
	Short note	[99] "Report of 9/11 Panel," *New York Times,* 1.
		► Since newspapers are usually omitted from the bibliography, use a full citation for the first reference.
	Bibliography	► Newspapers articles are left out of bibliographies, but you can include an especially important article:
		"Report of 9/11 Panel Cites Lapses by C.I.A. and F.B.I." *New York Times,* July 23, 2003, national edition, 1.
Newspaper or magazine article, with author	First note	[99] Jason Horowitz, "Vatican Official Is Killed by Gunmen in Burundi," *New York Times,* December 30, 2003 (national edition), A9.
	Short note	[99] Horowitz, "Vatican Official Is Killed," A9.
	Bibliography	► Newspaper and magazine articles are rarely included in bibliographies.
Newspaper or magazine article, online	First note	[99] Karl Vick, "Iranians Flee Quake-Devastated City," *Washington Post,* December 31, 2003, A01, http://www.washingtonpost.com/wp-dyn/ articles/A42890-2003Dec30.html (accessed March 14, 2004).
	Short note	[99] Vick, "Iranians Flee Quake-Devastated City."
	Bibliography	► Rarely included.

Review	First note	[99] H. Allen Orr, "What's Not in Your Genes," review of *Nature via Nurture: Genes, Experience, and What Makes Us Human,* by Matt Ridley, *New York Review of Books* 50 (August 14, 2003): 38–40. [99] Zdravko Planinc, review of *Eros and Polis: Desire and Community in Greek Political Theory,* by Paul W. Ludwig, *Perspectives on Politics* 1 (December 2003): 764–65.
	Short note	[99] Orr, "What's Not in Your Genes." [99] Planinc, review of *Eros and Polis.*
	Bibliography	Orr, H. Allen. "What's Not in Your Genes." Review of *Nature via Nurture: Genes, Experience, and What Makes Us Human,* by Matt Ridley. *New York Review of Books* 50 (August 14, 2003): 38–40. Planinc, Zdravko. Review of *Eros and Polis: Desire and Community in Greek Political Theory,* by Paul W. Ludwig. *Perspectives on Politics* 1 (December 2003): 764–65.
Unpublished paper, thesis, or dissertation	First note	[99] Janice Bially-Mattern, "Ordering International Politics: Identity, Crisis, and Representational Force" (paper presented at the Program on International Politics, Economics, and Security, University of Chicago, February 5, 2004), 1–25. [99] Nicole Childs, "The Impact of Hurricane Floyd on the Children of Eastern North Carolina" (master's thesis, Eastern Carolina University, 2002), 24. [99] Soon-Yong Choi, "Optimal Quality Choices: Product Selection in Cable Television Services" (PhD diss., University of Texas, Austin, 1996).
	Short note	[99] Bially-Mattern, "Ordering International Politics." [99] Childs, "Impact of Hurricane Floyd." [99] Choi, "Optimal Quality Choices."
	Bibliography	Bially-Mattern, Janice. "Ordering International Politics: Identity, Crisis, and Representational Force." Paper presented at

the Program on International Politics, Economics, and Security, University of Chicago, February 5, 2004.

Childs, Nicole. "The Impact of Hurricane Floyd on the Children of Eastern North Carolina." Master's thesis, Eastern Carolina University, 2002.

Choi, Soon-Yong. "Optimal Quality Choices: Product Selection in Cable Television Services." PhD diss., University of Texas, Austin, 1996.

Preprint	First note	[99] Richard Taylor, "On the Meromorphic Continuation of Degree Two L-Functions," preprint, http://abel.math.harvard.edu/~rtaylor/ (accessed January 5, 2004).
	Short note	[99] Taylor, "Meromorphic Continuation."
	Bibliography	Taylor, Richard. "On the Meromorphic Continuation of Degree Two L-Functions," preprint. http://abel.math.harvard.edu/~rtaylor/ (accessed January 5, 2004).
Microfilm, microfiche	First note	[99] Martin Luther King Jr., *FBI File*, ed. David J. Garrow (Frederick, MD: University Publications of America, 1984), microform, 16 reels. [99] Alice Irving Abbott, *Circumstantial Evidence* (New York: W. B. Smith, 1882), in *American Fiction, 1774–1910* (Woodbridge, CT: Gale/Primary Source Microfilm, 1998), reel A-1.
	Short note	[99] King, *FBI File*, 11:23–24. [99] Abbott, *Circumstantial Evidence*, 73.
	Bibliography	King, Martin Luther, Jr., *FBI File*. Ed. David J. Garrow. Frederick, MD: University Publications of America, 1984. Microform. 16 reels. Abbott, Alice Irving. *Circumstantial Evidence*. New York: W. B. Smith, 1882. In *American Fiction, 1774–1910*. Reel A-1. Woodbridge, CT: Gale/Primary Source Microfilm, 1998.

Microfilm, microfiche (*continued*)		▸ You can omit any mention of microfilm or microfiche if it simply preserves a source in its original form. Just cite the work as if it were the published version. So, to cite the Abbott book: Abbott, Alice Irving. *Circumstantial Evidence.* New York: W. B. Smith, 1882.

Archival materials and manuscript collections, hard copies and online	First note	[99] Isaac Franklin to R. C. Ballard, February 28, 1831. Series 1.1, folder 1, Rice Ballard Papers, Southern Historical Collection, Wilson Library, University of North Carolina, Chapel Hill.
		▸ Here is the order of items within the citation:
		  1. Author and brief description of the item
		  2. Date, if possible
		  3. Identification number for item or manuscript
		  4. Title of the series or collection
		  5. Library (or depository) and its location; for well-known libraries and archives, the location may be omitted.
		[99] Mary Swift Lamson, "An Account of the Beginning of the B.Y.W.C.A.," MS, [n.d.], and accompanying letter, 1891. Series I, I-A-2, Boston YWCA Papers, Schlesinger Library, Radcliffe Institute for Advanced Study, Harvard University.
		▸ "MS" = manuscript = papers (plural: "MSS")
		[99] Sigismundo Taraval, Journal recounting Indian uprisings in Baja California [handwritten ms.], ¶ 23, 1734–1737. Edward E. Ayer Manuscript Collection No. 1240, Newberry Library, Chicago, IL.
		▸ This journal has numbered paragraphs. Page numbers, paragraphs, or other identifiers aid readers.
		[99] Horatio Nelson Taft, Diary, February 20, 1862, p. 149 (vol. 1, January 1, 1861–April 11, 1862). Manuscript Division, Library of Congress, http://memory.loc.gov/ammem/tafthtml/tafthome.html (accessed May 30, 2004).
		[99] Henrietta Szold to Rose Jacobs, February 3, 1932. Reel 1, book 1, Rose Jacobs–Alice L.

Seligsberg Collection, Judaica Microforms,
Brandeis Library, Waltham, MA.

▶ Abbreviations: Because the collection's name
and location are often repeated, they may be
abbreviated after the first use:

⁹⁹ Henrietta Szold to Rose Jacobs, March 9,
1936. A/125/112, Central Zionist Archives,
Jerusalem (hereafter cited as CZA).
¹⁰⁰ Szold to Eva Stern, July 27, 1936. A/125/912,
CZA.

Short note

⁹⁹ Isaac Franklin to R. C. Ballard, February 28,
1831. Series 1.1, folder 1, Rice Ballard Papers.

▶ Short-form citation varies for archival items.
The main concerns are readers' convenience
and the proximity of full information in
nearby notes.

⁹⁹ Mary Swift Lamson, "Beginning of the
B.Y.W.C.A.," MS, [1891]. Boston YWCA Papers,
Schlesinger Library.

⁹⁹ Sigismundo Taraval, Journal recounting
Indian uprisings in Baja California. Edward E.
Ayer Manuscript Collection, Newberry Library.

▶ Or

⁹⁹ Taraval, Journal. Ayer MS Collection,
Newberry Library.

⁹⁹ Horatio Nelson Taft, Diary, February 20, 1862,
149.

⁹⁹ Henrietta Szold to Rose Jacobs, February 3,
1932. Reel 1, book 1, Rose Jacobs–Alice L.
Seligsberg Collection.

¹⁰⁰ Szold to Jacobs, March 9, 1936. A/125/112,
CZA.

¹⁰¹ Szold to Eva Stern, July 27, 1936. A/125/912,
CZA.

Bibliography

Rice Ballard Papers. Southern Historical
Collection. Wilson Library. University of
North Carolina, Chapel Hill.

▶ In footnotes and endnotes, the specific archival
item is usually listed first because it is the most
important element in the note. For example:
Isaac Franklin to R. C. Ballard, February 28,

| Archival materials and manuscript collections, hardcopies and online (*continued*) | | 1831. In bibliographies, however, the collection itself is usually listed first because it is more important. Individual items are not mentioned in the bibliography *unless* only one item is cited from a particular collection.

Boston YWCA Papers. Schlesinger Library. Radcliffe Institute for Advanced Study, Harvard University.

➤ Or

Lamson, Mary Swift. "An Account of the Beginning of the B.Y.W.C.A." MS, [n.d.], and accompanying letter. 1891. Boston YWCA Papers. Schlesinger Library. Radcliffe Institute for Advanced Study, Harvard University.

➤ If Lamson's account is the only item cited from these papers, then it would be listed in the bibliography.

Ayer, Edward E., Manuscript Collection. Newberry Library. Chicago, IL.

Taft, Horatio Nelson. Diary. Vol. 1, January 1, 1861–April 11, 1862. Manuscript Division, Library of Congress, http://memory.loc.gov/ammem/tafthtml/tafthome.html (accessed May 30, 2004).

Rose Jacobs–Alice L. Seligsberg Collection. Judaica Microforms. Brandeis Library. Waltham, MA.

Central Zionist Archives, Jerusalem. |
| Encyclopedia, hard copy and online | First note | [99] *Encyclopaedia Britannica,* 15th ed., s.vv. "Balkans: History," "World War I."

➤ s.v. (*sub verbo*) means "under the word." Plural: s.vv.

➤ You must include the edition but, according to the *Chicago Manual of Style,* you can omit the publisher, location, and page numbers for well-known references like *Encyclopaedia Britannica.*

[99] *Encyclopaedia Britannica Online,* s.v. "Balkans," http://search.eb.com/eb/article?eu=119645 (accessed January 2, 2004). |

⁹⁹ George Graham, "Behaviorism," in *Stanford Encyclopedia of Philosophy,* http://plato
.stanford.edu/entries/behaviorism/ (accessed January 3, 2004).

▸ Or

⁹⁹ *Stanford Encyclopedia of Philosophy,* "Behaviorism" (by George Graham), in http:// plato.stanford.edu/entries/behaviorism/ (accessed January 3, 2004).

Short note   ⁹⁹ *Encyclopaedia Britannica,* s.v. "World War I."
⁹⁹ Graham, "Behaviorism."

▸ Or

⁹⁹ *Stanford Encyclopedia,* "Behaviorism."

Bibliography   *Encyclopaedia Britannica.* 15th ed. s.vv.
"Balkans: History." "World War I."
Encyclopaedia Britannica Online. s.v.
"Balkans." http://search.eb.com/eb/
article?eu=119645 (accessed January 2,
2004).
Graham, George. "Behaviorism," in *Stanford
Encyclopedia of Philosophy.* http://plato
.stanford.edu/entries/behaviorism/
(accessed January 3, 2004).

▸ Or

Stanford Encyclopedia of Philosophy.
"Behaviorism" (by George Graham). http://
plato.stanford.edu/entries/behaviorism/
(accessed January 3, 2004).

Reference book, hard copy and online   First note   ⁹⁹ *Reference Guide to World Literature,* 3rd ed.,
2 vols., ed. Sara Pendergast and Tom
Pendergast (Detroit: St. James Press/Thomson-
Gale, 2003).
⁹⁹ *Reference Guide to World Literature,* 3rd ed.,
ed. Sara Pendergast and Tom Pendergast,
e-book (Detroit: St. James Press, 2003).
⁹⁹ Edmund Cusick, "The Snow Queen, story by
Hans Christian Andersen," in *Reference Guide
to World Literature,* 3rd ed., 2 vols., ed. Sara
Pendergast and Tom Pendergast (Detroit: St.
James Press/Thomson-Gale, 2003), 2:1511–12.

Reference book, hard copy and online (*continued*)		[99] "Great Britain: Queen's Speech Opens Parliament," November 26, 2003, *FirstSearch,* Facts On File database, accession no. 2003302680.
	Short note	[99] *Reference Guide to World Literature.* [99] Cusick, "Snow Queen," II:1511–12. [99] "Great Britain: Queen's Speech."
	Bibliography	*Reference Guide to World Literature.* 3rd ed. 2 vols. Ed. Sara Pendergast and Tom Pendergast. Detroit: St. James Press/Thomson-Gale, 2003. *Reference Guide to World Literature.* 3rd ed. Ed. Sara Pendergast and Tom Pendergast. E-book. Detroit: St. James Press, 2003. Cusick, Edmund. "The Snow Queen, story by Hans Christian Andersen." In *Reference Guide to World Literature.* 3rd ed. 2 vols. Ed. Sara Pendergast and Tom Pendergast, 2:1511–12. Detroit: St. James Press/Thomson-Gale, 2003. "Great Britain: Queen's Speech Opens Parliament." November 26, 2003. *FirstSearch.* Facts On File database. Accession no. 2003302680.
Dictionary, hard copy, online, or CD-ROM	First note	[99] *Merriam-Webster's Collegiate Dictionary,* 11th ed., s.v. "chronology." ▸ You must include the edition but can omit the publisher, location, and page numbers for well-known references like *Merriam-Webster's.* [99] *Compact Edition of the Oxford English Dictionary,* s.vv. "class, *n.,*" "state, *n.*" ▸ The words "class" and "state" can be either nouns or verbs, and this reference is to the nouns. [99] Dictionary.com, s.v. "status," http://dictionary.reference.com/search?q=status (accessed February 2, 2004). [99] *American Heritage Dictionary of the English Language,* 4th ed., CD-ROM.

	Short note	[99] *Merriam-Webster's,* s.v. "chronology." [99] *Compact O.E.D.,* s.vv. "class, *n.,*" "state, *n.*" [99] Dictionary.com, s.v. "status." [99] *American Heritage Dictionary of the English Language* on CD-ROM.
	Bibliography	► Standard dictionaries are not normally listed in bibliographies, but you may wish to include more specialized reference works: *Middle English Dictionary, W.2,* ed. Robert E. Lewis. Ann Arbor: University of Michigan Press, 1999. *Medieval English Dictionary* online. s.v. "boidekin." http://ets.umdl.umich .edu/cgi/m/mec/med-idx?type=id&id =MED5390.
Bible	First note	[99] Genesis 1:1, 1:3–5, 2:4. [99] Genesis 1:1, 1:3–5, 2:4 (New Revised Standard Version). ► Books of the Bible can be abbreviated: Gen. 1:1. ► Abbreviations for the next four books are Exod., Lev., Num., and Deut. Abbreviations for other books are easily found with a Web search for "abbreviations + Bible."
	Short note	[99] Genesis 1:1, 1:3–5, 2:4.
	Bibliography	► Biblical references are not normally included in the bibliography, but you may wish to include a particular version or translation: *Tanakh: The Holy Scriptures: The New JPS Translation according to the Traditional Hebrew Text.* Philadelphia: Jewish Publication Society, 1985. ► Thou shalt omit the Divine Author's name.
Speech, academic talk, or course lecture	First note	[99] Henry S. Bienen, "State of the University Speech" (Northwestern University, Evanston, IL, March 6, 2003). [99] Theda Skocpol, "Voice and Inequality: The Transformation of American Civic Democracy" (Presidential address, American Political

| Speech, academic talk, or course lecture (*continued*) | | Science Association convention, Philadelphia, PA, August 28, 2003).
[99] Gary Sick, lecture on U.S. policy toward Iraq (course on U.S. Foreign Policy Making in the Persian Gulf, Columbia University, New York, March 14, 2004). |
| | | ▶ The title of Professor Sick's talk is not in quotes because it is a regular course lecture and does not have a specific title. I have given a description, but you could simply call it a lecture and omit the description. For example: Gary Sick, lecture (course on U.S. Foreign . . .). |
| | Short note | [99] Bienen, "State of the University Speech."
▶ Or, to differentiate it from Bienen's 2002 talk:
[99] Bienen, "State of the University Speech," 2003.
[99] Skocpol, "Voice and Inequality."
[99] Sick, lecture on U.S. policy toward Iraq. |
| | Bibliography | Bienen, Henry S. "State of the University Speech." Northwestern University, Evanston, IL, March 6, 2003.
Skocpol, Theda. "Voice and Inequality: The Transformation of American Civic Democracy," Presidential address, American Political Science Association convention, Philadelphia, PA, August 28, 2003.
Sick, Gary. Lecture on U.S. policy toward Iraq. Course on U.S. Foreign Policy Making in the Persian Gulf, Columbia University, New York, March 14, 2004. |
| Interview, personal, telephone, or in print | First note | [99] V. S. Naipaul, personal interview, January 14, 2004.
[99] Tony Blair, telephone interview, February 16, 2004.
[99] Gloria Macapagal Arroyo, "A Time for Prayer," interview by Michael Schuman, *Time,* July 28, 2003, http://www.time.com/time/nation/article/0,8599,471205,00.html. |
| | Short note | [99] Naipaul, personal interview. |

⁹⁹ Blair, telephone interview.
⁹⁹ Arroyo, "Time for Prayer."

Bibliography	Naipaul, V. S. Personal interview. January 14, 2004.
	Blair, Tony. Telephone interview. February 16, 2004.
	Arroyo, Gloria Macapagal. "A Time for Prayer." Interview by Michael Schuman. *Time,* July 28, 2003. http://www.time.com/time/ nation/article/0,8599,471205,00.html.

Poem	First note	⁹⁹ Elizabeth Bishop, "The Fish," *The Complete Poems, 1927–1979* (New York: Noonday Press/Farrar, Straus and Giroux, 1983), 42–44.
	Short note	⁹⁹ Bishop, "The Fish," 42–44.
	Bibliography	Bishop, Elizabeth. "The Fish." *The Complete Poems, 1927–1979,* 42–44. New York: Noonday Press/Farrar, Straus and Giroux, 1983.

Play	First note	⁹⁹ Shakespeare, *Romeo and Juliet,* 2.1.1–9. ▸ Refers to act 2, scene 1, lines 1–9. ▸ If you wish to cite a specific edition, then: ⁹⁹ Shakespeare, *Romeo and Juliet,* ed. Brian Gibbons (London: Methuen, 1980).
	Short note	⁹⁹ Shakespeare, *Romeo and Juliet,* 2.1.1–9.
	Bibliography	Shakespeare, *Romeo and Juliet.* Ed. Brian Gibbons. London: Methuen, 1980.

Performance of play or dance	First note	⁹⁹ *Kiss,* choreography Susan Marshall, music Arvo Pärt, perf. Cheryl Mann, Tobin Del Cuore, Hubbard Street Dance Chicago, Chicago, March 12, 2004. ⁹⁹ *Topdog/Underdog,* by Suzan Lori-Parks, dir. Amy Morton, perf. K. Todd Freeman, David Rainey, Steppenwolf Theater, Chicago, November 2, 2003. ▸ If you are concentrating on one person or one position such as director, put that person's

Performance of play or dance (*continued*)		name first. For example, if you are concentrating on David Rainey's acting: [99] David Rainey, perf., *Topdog/Underdog,* by Suzan Lori-Parks, dir. Amy Morton . . . .
	Short note	[99] *Kiss.* [99] *Topdog/Underdog.*
	Bibliography	*Kiss.* Choreography Susan Marshall. Music Arvo Pärt. Perf. Cheryl Mann, Tobin Del Cuore. Hubbard Street Dance Chicago, Chicago. March 12, 2004. *Topdog/Underdog.* By Suzan Lori-Parks. Dir. Amy Morton. Perf. K. Todd Freeman, David Rainey. Steppenwolf Theater, Chicago. November 2, 2003. ▶ Or, if you are concentrating on Rainey's acting: Rainey, David, perf. *Topdog/Underdog.* By Suzan Lori-Parks. Dir. Amy Morton . . . .
Television program	First note	[99] *Seinfeld,* "The Soup Nazi," episode 116, November 2, 1995. ▶ Or, a fuller citation: [99] *Seinfeld,* "The Soup Nazi," episode 116, dir. Andy Ackerman, writer Spike Feresten, perf. Jerry Seinfeld, Jason Alexander, Julia Louis-Dreyfus, Michael Richards, Alexandra Wentworth, Larry Thomas, NBC, November 2, 1995.
	Short note	[99] *Seinfeld,* "Soup Nazi."
	Bibliography	*Seinfeld,* "The Soup Nazi." Episode 116. Dir. Andy Ackerman. Writer Spike Feresten. Perf. Jerry Seinfeld, Jason Alexander, Julia Louis-Dreyfus, Michael Richards, Alexandra Wentworth, Larry Thomas. NBC, November 2, 1995.
Film	First note	[99] *Godfather II.* DVD, dir. Francis Ford Coppola (1974; Los Angeles: Paramount Home Video, 2003).

> ► If you wish to cite individual scenes, which are accessible on DVDs, treat them like chapters in books. "Murder of Fredo," *Godfather II* . . . .

Short note ⁹⁹ *Godfather II.*

Bibliography *Godfather II.* DVD. Dir. Francis Ford Coppola. Perf. Al Pacino, Robert De Niro, Robert Duvall, Diane Keaton. Screenplay by Francis Ford Coppola and Mario Puzo based on novel by Mario Puzo. 1974; Paramount Home Video, 2003.

> ► Title, director, studio, and year of release are all required. So is the year the video recording was released, if that's what you are citing.
> ► Optional: the actors, producers, screenwriters, editors, cinematographers, and other information. You can include what you need for your paper, in order of their importance to your analysis. Their names appear between the title and the distributor.

Artwork, original

First note ⁹⁹ Jacopo Robusti Tintoretto, *The Birth of John the Baptist,* 1550s, Hermitage, St. Petersburg.
> ► The year of the painting is optional.

Short note ⁹⁹ Tintoretto, *Birth of John the Baptist.*

Bibliography Tintoretto, Jacopo Robusti. *The Birth of John the Baptist.* 1550s. Hermitage, St. Petersburg.

Artwork, reproduction

First note ⁹⁹ Jacopo Robusti Tintoretto, *The Birth of John the Baptist,* 1550s, in Tom Nichols, *Tintoretto: Tradition and Identity* (London: Reaktion Books, 1999), 47.

Short note ⁹⁹ Tintoretto, *The Birth of John the Baptist.*

Bibliography Tintoretto, Jacopo Robusti. *The Birth of John the Baptist.* 1550s. In Tom Nichols, *Tintoretto: Tradition and Identity,* 47. London: Reaktion Books, 1999.

Artwork, online	First note	[99] Jacopo Robusti Tintoretto, *The Birth of John the Baptist,* 1550s, Hermitage, St. Petersburg, http://www.hermitage.ru/html_En/index.html (accessed February 1, 2004). [99] Jacopo Robusti Tintoretto, *The Birth of John the Baptist* (detail), 1550s, Hermitage, St. Petersburg. http://cgfa.floridaimaging.com/t/p-tintore1.htm (accessed January 6, 2004).
	Short note	[99] Tintoretto, *The Birth of John the Baptist.*
	Bibliography	Tintoretto, Jacopo Robusti. *The Birth of John the Baptist.* 1550s. Hermitage, St. Petersburg. http://www.hermitage.ru/html_En/index .html (accessed February 1, 2004). Tintoretto, Jacopo Robusti. *The Birth of John the Baptist* (detail). 1550s. Hermitage, St. Petersburg. http://cgfa.floridaimaging .com/t/p-tintore1.htm (accessed January 6, 2004).
Photograph	First note	[99] Ansel Adams, *Monolith, the Face of Half Dome, Yosemite National Park,* 1927, Art Institute, Chicago.
	Short note	[99] Adams, *Monolith.*
	Bibliography	Adams, Ansel. *Monolith, the Face of Half Dome, Yosemite National Park.* 1927. Art Institute, Chicago.
Figures: map, chart, graph, or table	First note	▸ Citation for a map, chart, graph, or table normally appears as a credit below the item rather than as a footnote or endnote. *Source:* Daryl G. Press, "The Myth of Air Power in the Persian Gulf War and the Future of Warfare," *International Security* 26 (Fall 2001): 17, fig. 2. *Source:* http://www.usatoday.com/news/vote2000/cbc/map.htm (accessed August 30, 2004). *Source:* Topographic Maps (California), National Geographic Society, 2004, http://mapmachine

		.nationalgeographic.com/mapmachine/ viewandcustomize.html?task=getMap &themeId=113&size=s&state=zoomBox (accessed August 30, 2004).
	Short citation	*Source:* Press, "Myth of Air Power," 17, fig. 2.
	Bibliography	Press, Daryl G. "The Myth of Air Power in the Persian Gulf War and the Future of Warfare." *International Security* 26 (Fall 2001): 5–44. Electoral Vote Map [2000]. http://www .usatoday.com/news/vote2000/cbc/map .htm (accessed August 30, 2004). Topographic Maps (California). National Geographic Society. 2004. http:// mapmachine.nationalgeographic.com/ mapmachine/viewandcustomize.html ?task=getMap&themeId=113&size=s&state =zoomBox (accessed August 30, 2004).
Musical recording	First note	[99] Robert Johnson. "Cross Road Blues," 1937, *Robert Johnson: King of the Delta Blues Singers* (Columbia Records 1654, 1961). [99] Samuel Barber, "Cello Sonata, for cello and piano, Op. 6," in *Barber: Adagio for Strings, Violin Concerto, Orchestral and Chamber Works,* disc 2, St. Louis Symphony, Leonard Slatkin, cond.; Alan Stepansky, cello; Israela Margalit, piano (EMI Classics 74287, 2001).
	Short note	[99] Johnson, "Cross Road Blues." [99] Barber, "Cello Sonata, Op. 6."
	Bibliography	Johnson, Robert. "Cross Road Blues." *Robert Johnson: King of the Delta Blues Singers.* Columbia Records 1654, 1961. Barber, Samuel. "Cello Sonata, for cello and piano, Op. 6." *Barber: Adagio for Strings, Violin Concerto, Orchestral and Chamber Works.* Disc 2, St. Louis Symphony. Leonard Slatkin, cond.; Alan Stepansky, cello; Israela Margalit, piano. EMI Classics 74287, 2001.

Sheet music	First note	[99] Johann Sebastian Bach, "Toccata and Fugue in D Minor," 1708, BWV 565, arr. Ferruccio Benvenuto Busoni for solo piano (New York: G. Schirmer, LB1629, 1942).
	Short note	[99] Bach, "Toccata and Fugue in D Minor."
	Bibliography	Bach, Johann Sebastian. "Toccata and Fugue in D Minor." 1708. BWV 565. Arr. Ferruccio Benvenuto Busoni for solo piano. New York: G. Schirmer LB1629, 1942. ▶ This piece was written in 1708 and has the standard Bach classification BWV 565. This particular arrangement was published by G. Schirmer in 1942 and has their catalog number LB1629.
Liner notes	First note	[99] Steven Reich, liner notes for *Different Trains* (Elektra/Nonesuch 9 79176-2, 1988).
	Short note	[99] Reich, liner notes. ▶ Or [99] Reich, liner notes, *Different Trains*.
	Bibliography	Reich, Steven. Liner notes for *Different Trains*. Elektra/Nonesuch 9 79176-2, 1988.
Government document, hard copy and online	First note	[99] Senate Committee on Armed Services, *Hearings on S. 758, A Bill to Promote the National Security by Providing for a National Defense Establishment,* 80th Cong., 1st sess., 1947, S. Rep. 239, 13. ▶ "S. Rep. 239, 13" refers to report number 239, page 13. [99] Environmental Protection Agency (EPA), *Final Rule, Air Pollution Control: Prevention of Significant Deterioration; Approval and Promulgation of Implementation Plans, Federal Register* 68, no. 247 (December 24, 2003): 74483–91. [99] United States, Department of State. "China—25th Anniversary of Diplomatic Relations," press statement, December 31, 2003, http://

www.state.gov/r/pa/prs/ps/2003/27632.htm (accessed March 15, 2004).

Short note   [99] Senate, *Hearings on S. 758,* 13.
[99] EPA, *Final Rule, Air Pollution Control.*
[99] State Department, "China—25th Anniversary."

Bibliography   U.S. Congress. Senate. Committee on Armed Services. *Hearings on S. 758, Bill to Promote the National Security by Providing for a National Defense Establishment.* 80th Cong., 1st sess., 1947. S. Rep. 239.
Environmental Protection Agency. *Final Rule, Air Pollution Control: Prevention of Significant Deterioration; Approval and Promulgation of Implementation Plans. Federal Register* 68, no. 247 (December 24, 2003): 74483–91.
United States, Department of State. "China— 25th Anniversary of Diplomatic Relations," press statement, December 31, 2003. http:// www.state.gov/r/pa/prs/ps/2003/27632 .htm.

Software   First note   [99] *Stata 8* (for Linux 64) (College Station, TX: Stata, 2003).
[99] *Dreamweaver MX 2004* (San Francisco: Macromedia, 2003).

Short note   [99] *Stata 8* (for Linux 64).
[99] *Dreamweaver MX 2004.*

Bibliography   *Stata 8* (for Linux 64). College Station, TX: Stata, 2003.
Dreamweaver MX 2004. San Francisco: Macromedia, 2003.

Database   First note   [99] *Corpus Scriptorum Latinorum* database of Latin literature, http://www.forumromanum .org/literature/index.html.
▸ For a specific item within this database:

Database (*continued*)	[99] Gaius Julius Caesar, *Commentarii de bello civili,* ed. A. G. Peskett (Loeb Classical Library; London: W. Heinemann, 1914), in *Corpus Scriptorum Latinorum* database of Latin literature, http://www.thelatinlibrary.com/caes.html. [99] *Intellectual Property Treaties, InterAm Database* (Tucson, AZ: National Law Center for Inter-American Free Trade), http://www.natlaw.com/database.htm (accessed January 10, 2004). ▶ For a specific item within this database: [99] "Chile-U.S. Free Trade Agreement (June 6, 2003)," in *Intellectual Property Treaties, InterAm Database* (Tucson, AZ: National Law Center for Inter-American Free Trade), http://www.natlaw.com/treaties/chileusfta.htm (accessed January 12, 2004).
Short note	[99] *Corpus Scriptorum Latinorum.* [99] *Intellectual Property Treaties, InterAm Database.* [99] "Chile-U.S. Free Trade Agreement."
Bibliography	*Corpus Scriptorum Latinorum.* Database of Latin literature. http://www.forumromanum.org/literature/index.html. Caesar, Gaius Julius. *Commentarii de bello civili,* ed. A. G. Peskett. Loeb Classical Library. London: W. Heinemann, 1914. In *Corpus Scriptorum Latinorum* database of Latin literature. http://www.thelatinlibrary.com/caes.html. *Intellectual Property Treaties, InterAm Database.* Tucson, AZ: National Law Center for Inter-American Free Trade. http://www.natlaw.com/database.htm (accessed January 10, 2004). ▶ For a specific item within the database: "Chile-U.S. Free Trade Agreement (June 6, 2003)." In *Intellectual Property Treaties, InterAm Database.* Tucson, AZ: National Law Center for Inter-American Free Trade. http://

www.natlaw.com/treaties/chileusfta.htm
(accessed January 12, 2004).

Web site, entire	First note	[99] Digital History Web site, ed. Steven Mintz, http://www.digitalhistory.uh.edu/index.cfm?. [99] Internet Public Library (IPL), http://www.ipl.org/. [99] Yale University, History Department home page, http://www.yale.edu/history/. ▸ You may omit "home page" if it is obvious.
	Short note	[99] Digital History Web site. [99] Internet Public Library. [99] Yale History Department home page.
	Bibliography	Digital History Web site. Ed. Steven Mintz. http://www.digitalhistory.uh.edu/index.cfm?. Internet Public Library (IPL). http://www.ipl.org/. Yale University. History Department home page. http://www.yale.edu/history/.
Web page	First note	[99] Charles Lipson, "Scholarly Tools Online to Study World Politics," http://www.charleslipson.com/scholarly-links.htm.
	Short note	[99] Lipson, "Scholarly Tools."
	Bibliography	Lipson, Charles. "Scholarly Tools Online to Study World Politics." http://www.charleslipson.com/scholarly-links.htm. ▸ Include the title or description of the Web page if available. That way, if the link changes, it may still be possible to find the page through a search.
Weblog entries and comments	First note	[99] Daniel Drezner, "Blogger Weirdness," *Daniel W. Drezner* Weblog, entry posted December 30, 2003, http://www.danieldrezner.com/blog/ (accessed March 14, 2004). [99] Tyler Cowen, "Trial by Jury," *Volokh Conspiracy* Weblog, entry posted December 30,

Weblog entries and comments (*continued*)

2003, http://volokh.com/ (accessed January 6, 2004).

[99] Kiwi (Janice Walker), "Citing Weblogs," *Kairosnews: A Weblog for Discussing Rhetoric, Technology, and Pedagogy,* comment posted December 13, 2003, http://kairosnews.org/node/view/3542 (accessed December 28, 2003).

[99] Josh Chafetz, untitled Weblog entry, *OxBlog* Weblog, posted 12:06 p.m., December 27, 2003, http://oxblog.blogspot.com/ (accessed December 31, 2003).

Short note

[99] Drezner, "Blogger Weirdness."
[99] Cowen, "Trial by Jury."
[99] Kiwi (Janice Walker), "Citing Weblogs."
[99] Chafetz, untitled Weblog entry, December 27, 2003.

Bibliography

Drezner, Daniel. "Blogger Weirdness." *Daniel W. Drezner* Weblog. Entry posted December 30, 2003. http://www.danieldrezner.com/blog/ (accessed March 14, 2004).

Cowen, Tyler. "Trial by Jury." *Volokh Conspiracy* Weblog. Entry posted December 24, 2003. http://volokh.com/ (accessed January 6, 2004).

Kiwi (Janice Walker). "Citing Weblogs." *Kairosnews: A Weblog for Discussing Rhetoric, Technology, and Pedagogy.* Weblog comment posted December 13, 2003, to http://kairosnews.org/node/view/3542 (accessed December 28, 2003).

Chafetz, Josh. [Untitled Weblog entry.] *OxBlog.* Entry posted 12:06 p.m., December 27, 2003. http://oxblog.blogspot.com/ (accessed December 31, 2003).

▶ Chafetz's posting had no title and is one of several he posted the same day to this group blog. Listing the time identifies it.

CHICAGO: CITATIONS TO TABLES AND NOTES

Citation	Refers to
106	page 106
106n	only note appearing on page 106
107 n. 32	note number 32 on page 107, a page with several notes
89, table 6.2	table 6.2, which appears on page 89; similar for graphs and figures

CHICAGO: COMMON ABBREVIATIONS IN CITATIONS

and others	et al.	editor	ed.	page	p.
appendix	app.	especially	esp.	pages	pp.
book	bk.	figure	fig.	part	pt.
chapter	chap.	note	n.	pseudonym	pseud.
compare	cf.	notes	nn.	translator	trans.
document	doc.	number	no.	versus	vs.
edition	ed.	opus	op.	volume	vol.

Note: All abbreviations are lowercase, followed by a period. Most form their plurals by adding "s." The exceptions are note (n. → nn.), opus (op. → opp.), page (p. → pp.), and translator (same abbreviation).

In citing poetry, do not use abbreviations for "line" or "lines" since a lowercase "l" is easily confused with the number one.

FAQS ABOUT CHICAGO-STYLE CITATIONS

Why do you put the state after some publishers and not after others?
The Chicago Manual of Style recommends using state names for all but the largest, best-known cities. To avoid confusion, they use Cambridge, MA, for Harvard and MIT presses, but they use just Cambridge for Cambridge University Press in the ancient English university town. Also, you can drop the state name if it is already included in the publisher's title, such as Ann Arbor: University of Michigan Press.

What if a book is forthcoming?
Use "forthcoming" just as you would use the year. Here's a bibliographic entry:

Godot, Shlomo. *Still Waiting.* London: Verso, forthcoming.

What if the date or place of publication is missing?
Same idea as "forthcoming." Where you would normally put the date or place, use "n.d." (no date) or "n.p." (no place). For example: (Montreal, QC: McGill-Queen's University Press, n.d.).

What if the author is anonymous or not listed?
Usually, you omit the anonymous author and begin with the title.

If an author is technically anonymous but is actually known, put the name in brackets, as in [Johnson, Samuel] or [Madison, James] and list it wherever the author's name falls.

One book I cite has a title that ends with a question mark. Do I still put periods or commas after it?
No.

Are notes single-spaced or double-spaced? What about the bibliography?
Space your footnotes and endnotes the same way you do your text.

As for your bibliography, I think it is easiest to read if you single space within entries and put a double space between the entries. But check your department's requirements. They may require double spacing for everything.

I'm reading Mark Twain. Do I cite Twain or Samuel Clemens?
When pseudonyms are well known such as Mark Twain or Mother Teresa, you can use them alone, without explanation, if you wish.

If you want to include both the pseudonym and the given name, the rule is simple. Put the better-known name first, followed by the lesser-known one in brackets. It doesn't matter if the "real" name is the lesser-known one.

> George Eliot [Mary Ann Evans]
> Isak Dinesen [Karen Christence Dinesen, Baroness Blixen-Finecke]
> Le Corbusier [Charles-Edouard Jeanneret]
> Benjamin Disraeli [Lord Beaconsfield]
> Lord Palmerston [Henry John Temple]
> Krusty the Clown [Herschel S. Krustofski]

If you wish to include the pseudonym in a bibliographic entry, it reads:

> Aleichem, Sholom [Solomon Rabinovitz]. *Fiddler on the Roof* . . . .

MLA CITATION SYSTEM

The Modern Language Association (MLA) has developed a citation style that is widely used in the humanities. Instead of footnotes or endnotes, it uses in-text citations such as (Strier 125). Full information about each item appears in the bibliography, which MLA calls "Works Cited." Like other bibliographies, it contains three essential nuggets of information about each item: the author, title, and publication data. To illustrate, let's use a book by Fouad Ajami. The full entry in the Works Cited is

> Ajami, Fouad. The Dream Palace of the Arabs: A Generation's Odyssey. New York: Pantheon, 1998.

Titles are underlined rather than italicized.

In-text citations are brief and simple. To cite the entire book, just insert (Ajami) at the end of the sentence, or (Ajami 12) to refer to page 12. If your paper happens to cite several books by Ajami, be sure your reader knows which one you are referring to. If that's not clear in the sentence, then include a very brief title: (Ajami, Dream 12).

MLA citations can be even briefer—and they should be, whenever possible. They can omit the author and the title as long as it's clear which work is being cited. For example:

> As Ajami notes, these are long-standing problems in Arab intellectual life (14–33).

You can omit the in-text reference entirely if the author and title are clear and you are not citing specific pages. For instance:

> Gibbon's Decline and Fall of the Roman Empire established new standards of documentary evidence for historians.

In this case, there's nothing to put in an in-text reference that isn't already in the sentence. So, given MLA's consistent emphasis on brevity, you simply skip the reference. You still include Gibbon in your Works Cited.

Because in-text references are so brief, you can string several together in one parenthesis: (Bevington 17; Bloom 75; Vendler 51). The authors' names are separated by semicolons.

If Ajami's book were a three-volume work, then the citation to volume 3, page 17, would be (Ajami 3: 17). If you need to differentiate this work from others by the same author, then include the title: (Ajami, <u>Dream</u> 3: 17). If you wanted to cite the volume but not a specific page, then use (Ajami, vol. 3) or (Ajami, <u>Dream,</u> vol. 3). Why include "vol." here? So readers won't think you are citing page 3 of a one-volume work.

If several authors have the same last name, simply add their first initials to differentiate them: (C. Brontë, <u>Jane Eyre</u>), (E. Brontë, <u>Wuthering Heights</u>). Of course, full information about the authors and their works appears at the end, in the Works Cited.

Books like *Jane Eyre* appear in countless editions, and your readers may wish to look up passages in theirs. To make that easier, the MLA recommends that you add some information after the normal page citation. You might say, for example, that the passage appears in chapter 1. For poems, you would note the verse and lines.

Let's say that you quoted a passage from the first chapter of *Jane Eyre,* which appeared on page 7 in the edition you are using. Insert a semicolon after the page and add the chapter number, using a lowercase abbreviation for chapter: (E. Brontë, <u>Wuthering Heights</u> 7; ch. 1). For plays, the act, scene, and lines are separated by periods (<u>Romeo and Juliet</u> 1.3.12–15).

When you refer to online documents, there are often no pages to cite. As a substitute, include a section or paragraph number, if there is one. Just put a comma after the author's name, then list the section or paragraph: (Padgett, sec. 9.7) or (Snidal, pars. 12–18). If there's no numbering system, just list the author. Don't cite your printout because those pages vary from person to person, printer to printer.[5]

In-text citations normally appear at the end of sentences and are followed by the punctuation for the sentence itself. To illustrate:

> A full discussion of these citation issues appears in the <u>MLA Handbook</u> (Gibaldi).

In this style, you can still use regular footnotes or endnotes for limited purposes. They can *only* be used for commentary, however, not for citations. If you need to cite some materials within the note itself, use in-text citations there, just as you would in the text.

---

5. These recommendations follow the MLA's own recommendation. MLA, "Frequently Asked Questions about MLA Style," http://www.mla.org/publications/style/style_faq/style_faq7.

For brevity—a paramount virtue of the MLA system—the names of publishers are also compressed: Princeton University Press becomes Princeton UP, the University of Chicago Press becomes U of Chicago P. For the same reason, most month names are abbreviated.

MLA throws brevity overboard, however, when referencing electronic information. If the works were originally printed, the Works Cited include all the print information, plus some extra information about the online versions, including Web sites, sponsoring organizations, access dates, and URLs. Of all citation styles, only MLA requires listing the sponsoring organization. This leads to redundancy. You are supposed to write: Encyclopaedia Britannica Online. 2004. Encyclopaedia Britannica . . . . Or CBSNews.com. 5 Jan. 2004. CBS . . . . The underlined titles are the works cited; the repeated name is the sponsoring organization. Actually, we'll see the name a third time in the URL, <http://www.cbs.com>. This seems like overkill to me, at least when the sponsoring organization is evident. But that's the current MLA style.

If an item is exclusively online, like a Web page or Weblog, the citation includes the author, the title of the Web page or site, the date it was created (or updated), plus information about the Web site, sponsoring organization, the date it was accessed, and the URL. It makes for a long list.

I have provided detailed information and examples in a table below. Because MLA style is often used in the humanities, where citations to plays, poems, paintings, and films are common, I include all of them. If you want still more examples or less common items, consult two useful books published by the MLA:

- Joseph Gibaldi, *MLA Style Manual and Guide to Scholarly Publishing,* 2nd ed. (New York: Modern Language Association of America, 1998), 149–254.
- Joseph Gibaldi, *MLA Handbook for Writers of Research Papers,* 6th ed. (New York: Modern Language Association of America, 2003).

They should be available in your library's reference section.

To make it easy to find the MLA citations you need, I've listed them here alphabetically, along with the pages where they are described.

INDEX OF MLA CITATIONS IN THIS APPENDIX

MLA: WORKS CITED AND IN-TEXT NOTES

Book, one author	Works Cited	Lipson, Charles. <u>Reliable Partners: How Democracies Have Made a Separate Peace</u>. Princeton: Princeton UP, 2003. Reed, Christopher A. <u>Gutenberg in Shanghai: Chinese Print Capitalism, 1876–1937</u>. Vancouver: U British Columbia P, 2004. ▸ MLA style omits the publisher's state or province.
	In-text	(Lipson, <u>Reliable</u> 22–23) or (Lipson 22–23) or (22–23) ▸ Refers to pages 22–23. (Reed, <u>Gutenberg</u> 136) or (Reed 136) or (136)
Books, several by same author	Works Cited	Weinberg, Gerhard L. <u>Germany, Hitler, and World War II: Essays in Modern German and World History</u>. Cambridge: Cambridge UP, 1995. ---. <u>A World at Arms: A Global History of World War II</u>. Cambridge: Cambridge UP, 1994. ▸ The repetition of the author's name uses three hyphens, followed by a period.
	In-text	(Weinberg, <u>Germany</u> 34; Weinberg, <u>World</u> 456)
Book, multiple authors	Works Cited	Binder, Guyora, and Robert Weisberg. <u>Literary Criticisms of Law</u>. Princeton: Princeton UP, 2000. ▸ If four or more authors: Binder, Guyora, et al.
	In-text	(Binder and Weisberg, <u>Literary Criticisms</u> 15–26) or (Binder and Weisberg 15–26)
Book, multiple editions	Works Cited	Strunk, William, Jr., and E. B. White. <u>The Elements of Style</u>. 4th ed. New York: Longman, 2000. ▸ If this were a multivolume work, then the volume number would come after the edition: 4th ed. Vol. 2.
	In-text	(Strunk and White, <u>Elements</u> 12) or (Strunk and White 12)

Book, edited	Works Cited	Robinson, Francis, ed. <u>Cambridge Illustrated History of the Islamic World.</u> Cambridge: Cambridge UP, 1996. Gallagher, Kathleen, and David Booth, eds. <u>How Theatre Educates: Convergences and Counterpoints with Artists, Scholars, and Advocates.</u> Toronto: U Toronto P, 2003.
	In-text	(Robinson) (Gallagher and Booth)

Book, online	Works Cited	Dickens, Charles. <u>Great Expectations.</u> 1860–61. <u>Project Gutenberg Archive.</u> Etext 1400. 14 Jan. 2004 ‹http://www.gutenberg.net/etext98/grexp10.txt›. ▸ The date when you access the online content (in this case, 14 Jan. 2004) comes immediately before the URL. Notice that the day comes before the month; that's standard with MLA. There is no punctuation between this date and the URL.[6]
	In-text	(Dickens) ▸ Since this electronic version does not have pagination, cite the chapter numbers. (Dickens, ch. 2)

Multivolume work	Works Cited	Pflanze, Otto. <u>Bismarck and the Development of Germany.</u> 3 vols. Princeton: Princeton UP, 1963–90.
	In-text	(Pflanze) or (Pflanze 3: 21) ▸ This refers to volume 3, page 21. (Pflanze, vol. 3) ▸ When a volume is referenced without a specific page, then use "vol." so the volume won't be confused for a page number.

---

6. This follows the MLA's most recent recommendation: http://www.mla.org/publications/style/style_faq/style_faq4.

Single volume in multivolume work	Works Cited	Pflanze, Otto. <u>The Period of Fortification, 1880–1898</u>. Princeton: Princeton UP, 1990. Vol. 3 of <u>Bismarck and the Development of Germany</u>. 3 vols. 1963–90.
		Iriye, Akira. <u>The Globalizing of America</u>. Cambridge: Cambridge University Press, 1993. Vol. 3 of <u>Cambridge History of American Foreign Relations,</u> ed. Warren I. Cohen, 4 vols. 1993.
	In-text	(Pflanze)
		(Iriye)

Reprint of earlier edition	Works Cited	Barzun, Jacques. <u>Simple and Direct: A Rhetoric for Writers</u>. 1985. Chicago: U of Chicago P, 1994.
		Smith, Adam. <u>An Inquiry into the Nature and Causes of the Wealth of Nations</u>. 1776. Ed. Edwin Cannan. Chicago: U of Chicago P, 1976.
	In-text	(Barzun, <u>Simple</u>) or (Barzun)
		(Smith, <u>Wealth of Nations</u>) or (Smith)

Translated volume	Works Cited	Weber, Max. <u>The Protestant Ethic and the Spirit of Capitalism</u>. 1904–5. Trans. Talcott Parsons. New York: Charles Scribner's Sons, 1958.
		Tocqueville, Alexis de. <u>Democracy in America</u>. Ed. J. P. Mayer. Trans. George Lawrence. New York: HarperCollins, 2000.
		► Editor and translator are listed in the order in which they appear on the book's title page.
		<u>Beowulf: A New Verse Translation</u>. Trans. Seamus Heaney. New York: Farrar, Straus and Giroux, 2000.
		► *Beowulf* is an anonymous poem. The translator's name normally comes after the title. But there is an exception. If you wish to comment on the translator's work, then place the translator's name first. For example:

Translated volume (*continued*)		Seamus Heaney, trans. <u>Beowulf: A New Verse Translation.</u> New York: Farrar, Straus and Giroux, 2000.
		Parsons, Talcott, trans. <u>The Protestant Ethic and the Spirit of Capitalism,</u> by Max Weber. 1904–5. New York: Charles Scribner's Sons, 1958.
	In-text	(Weber, <u>Protestant Ethic</u>) or (Weber)
		(Tocqueville, <u>Democracy in America</u>) or (Tocqueville)
		(Heaney, <u>Beowulf</u>) or (<u>Beowulf</u>)
		(Parsons)
Chapter in edited book	Works Cited	Keohane, Robert. "The Demand for International Regimes." In <u>International Regimes,</u> ed. Stephen Krasner. Ithaca: Cornell UP, 1983. 56–67.
	In-text	(Keohane 56–67)
Journal article	Works Cited	Kleppinger, Stanley V. "On the Influence of Jazz Rhythm in the Music of Aaron Copland." <u>American Music</u> 21.1 (Spring 2003): 74–111.
		▸ Refers to volume 21, number 1.
		▸ The issue number is optional if it is clear how to find the article (perhaps because you have already included the month or because the pages run continuously through the year). But if each issue begins with page 1 and you include only the year, then you need to add the issue number or month to show where the article appears: <u>American Music</u> 21.1 (2003): 74–111.
	In-text	(Kleppinger) or (Kleppinger 74–82) or (Kleppinger, "Aaron Copland" 74–82)
		▸ The title may be needed to differentiate this article from others by the same author.
Journal article, multiple authors	Works Cited	Koremenos, Barbara, Charles Lipson, and Duncan Snidal. "The Rational Design of International Institutions." <u>International Organization</u> 55 (Autumn 2001): 761–99.

> ▸ If there are four or more authors: Koremenos, Barbara, et al.

In-text | (Koremenos, Lipson, and Snidal 761–99)

Journal article, online	Works Cited	Small, Christopher. "Why Doesn't the Whole World Love Chamber Music?" American Music 19.3 (Autumn 2001): 340–59. JSTOR 15 Mar. 2004 ‹http://www.jstor.org/search›.
		▸ This is a normal print journal, available online from multiple sources, with the same pagination as the print version. Here I list it through JSTOR. The URL is quite long, so MLA recommends listing only the search page.
		North, Dan. "Magic and Illusion in Early Cinema." Studies in French Cinema 1.2 (2001): 70–79. EBSCOhost Research Database 6 Jan. 2004 ‹http://search.epnet .com›.
	In-text	(Small) or (Small 341–43) or (Small, "Chamber Music" 341–43)
		(North) or (North 70–79) or (North, "Magic" 70–79)

Newspaper or magazine article, no author	Works Cited	"Report of 9/11 Panel Cites Lapses by C.I.A. and F.B.I." New York Times 23 July 2003: 1.
		▸ This refers to page 1.
	In-text	("Report of 9/11 Panel" 1)

Newspaper or magazine article, with author	Works Cited	Bruni, Frank. "Pope Pleads for End to Terrorism and War." New York Times 26 Dec. 2003, national ed.: A21.
		▸ It's always fine to include the headline and reporter's name. The MLA says you can omit them, though, if they do not add to the point you are making in the text.
	In-text	(Bruni A21)

Newspaper or magazine article, online	Works Cited	"European Unity: The History of an Idea." <u>The Economist</u> 30 Dec. 2003. 6 Jan. 2004 ‹http://www.economist.com/world/europe/displayStory.cfm?story_id=2313040›. ▸ The first date refers to the article, the second to the day it was accessed. ▸ For magazines and newspapers, there is no need to reference the sponsoring organization. Salamon, Julie. "Collaborating on the Future at the Modern." <u>New York Times</u> 26 Dec. 2003. 2 Jan. 2004 ‹http://www.nytimes.com/2003/12/26/arts/design/26CURA.html›.
	In-text	("European Unity") (Salamon) or (Salamon, "Collaborating") if you cite more than one article by this author.
Review	Works Cited	Orr, H. Allen. "What's Not in Your Genes." Rev. of <u>Nature via Nurture: Genes, Experience, and What Makes Us Human,</u> by Matt Ridley. <u>New York Review of Books</u> 50 (14 Aug. 2003): 38–40.
	In-text	(Orr) or (Orr, "Genes")
Unpublished paper, thesis, or dissertation	Works Cited	Nishi, Takayushi. "The Humiliating Gift: Negative Reactions to International Help." Paper presented at the Program on International Politics, Economics, and Security, U Chicago. 4 Mar. 2004. Besser-Jones, Lorraine. "The Moral Commitment to Public Reason." MA thesis. Claremont Graduate School, 1997. Pérez-Torres, Rafael. "Screen Play and Inscription: Narrative Strategies in Four Post-1960s Novels." Diss. Stanford, 1989.
	In-text	(Nishi 1–35) (Besser-Jones) (Pérez-Torres)

Microfilm, microfiche	Works Cited	Abbott, Alice Irving. <u>Circumstantial Evidence.</u> New York: W. B. Smith, 1882. In <u>American Fiction, 1774–1910.</u> Reel A-1. Woodbridge: Gale/Primary Source Microfilm, 1998. King, Martin Luther, Jr., <u>FBI file</u> [microform]. Ed. David J. Garrow. 16 reels. Frederick: U Publications of Am, 1984.
	In-text	(Abbott) To cite page 13 on reel A-1, use (Abbott A-1: 13) (King) To cite reel 2, page 12, use (King 2: 12)
Archival materials and manuscript collections, hard copies and online	Works Cited	Franklin, Isaac. Letter to R. C. Ballard. 28 February 1831. Series 1.1, folder 1. Rice Ballard Papers. Southern Historical Collection. Wilson Lib. U of North Carolina, Chapel Hill. Lamson, Mary Swift. <u>An Account of the Beginning of the B.Y.W.C.A.</u> Ms. Boston YWCA Papers. Schlesinger Library. Radcliffe Institute, Harvard University. Cambridge, MA. 1891. ▶ Manuscript is abbreviated ms. Typescript is ts. Spell out "notebook" and "unpublished essay." Szold, Henrietta. Letter to Rose Jacobs. 3 February 1932. Reel 1, book 1. Rose Jacobs–Alice L. Seligsberg Collection. Judaica Microforms. Brandeis Library. Waltham, MA. Szold, Henrietta. Letter to Rose Jacobs. 9 March 1936. A/125/112. Central Zionist Archives, Jerusalem. Taraval, Sigismundo. <u>Journal Recounting Indian Uprisings in Baja California.</u> Handwritten ms. 1734–1737. Edward E. Ayer Manuscript Collection No. 1240, Newberry Library. Chicago, IL. Taft, Horatio Nelson. Diary. Vol. 1, January 1, 1861–April 11, 1862. Manuscript Division, Library of Congress. 30 May 2004 ‹http://memory.loc.gov/cgi-bin/ampage?collId=mtaft&fileName=mtaft1/mtaftmtaft1.db&recNum=148›.

Archival materials and manuscript collections, hard copies and online (*continued*)	In-text	(Franklin) or (Franklin to Ballard) or (Franklin to Ballard, 28 Feb. 1831) (Lamson) or (Lamson 2) (Szold) or (Szold to Jacobs) or (Szold to Jacobs, 3 Feb. 1932) (Szold) or (Szold to Jacobs) or (Szold to Jacobs, 9 Mar. 1936) (Taraval) or (Taraval ¶ 23) ▸ This manuscript uses paragraph numbers, not pages. (Taft) or (Taft 149).
Encyclopedia, hard copy and online	Works Cited	"African Arts." <u>Encyclopaedia Britannica.</u> 15th ed. 1987. 13: 134–80. ▸ Alphabetize by the first significant word in title. ▸ Volume and page numbers are optional. ▸ Edition and year are required, but you can omit the city and publisher for well-known encyclopedias, dictionaries, and other references. "Art, African." <u>Encyclopaedia Britannica Online.</u> 2004. Encyclopaedia Britannica. 5 Jan. 2004 ‹http://search.eb.com/eb/article?eu=119483›. ▸ Why does the name, *Encyclopaedia Britannica,* appear twice? Because it is both the publication and the "sponsoring organization," and MLA rules currently require that you list both. Chanda, Jacqueline. "African Art and Architecture," <u>Microsoft Encarta Online Encyclopedia.</u> 2004. Microsoft Corporation. 7 Jan. 2004 ‹http://encarta.msn.com/encyclopedia_761574805/African_Art.html›.
	In-text	("African Arts" 13: 137) (Chanda)
Reference book, hard copy and online	Works Cited	Pendergast, Sara, and Tom Pendergast, eds. <u>Reference Guide to World Literature.</u> 3rd ed. 2 vols. Detroit: St. James Press/Thomson-Gale, 2003.

Cannon, John, ed. Oxford Companion to British
History. New York: Oxford University Press,
2002. ‹http://www.oxfordreference
.com/views/BOOK_SEARCH.html?book
=t110&subject=s11›.
Cicioni, Mirna, "The periodic table (Il sistema
periodico), prose by Primo Levi, 1975."
Reference Guide to World Literature. Ed.
Sara Pendergast and Tom Pendergast. 3rd
ed. 2 vols. Detroit: St. James
Press/Thomson-Gale, 2003. 2: 1447.
"Polytheism." The New Dictionary of Cultural
Literacy. Ed. E. D. Hirsch Jr., Joseph F. Kett,
and James Trefil. 3rd ed. Boston: Houghton
Mifflin, 2002. 2 Feb. 2004 ‹http://www
.bartleby.com/59/5/polytheism.html›.
➤ This is a hard-copy book that is also available
online.
"Napoleon I." The Biographical Dictionary.
2004. S-9 Technologies. 5 Jan. 2004 ‹http://
www.s9.com/biography/search.html›

In-text | (Pendergast and Pendergast)
(Cannon)
(Cicioni 2: 1447)
("Polytheism")
("Napoleon I")

Dictionary, hard copy, online, and CD-ROM | Works Cited | "Historiography." Merriam-Webster's
Collegiate Dictionary. 11th ed. 2003.
➤ You can omit the publisher information.
"Protest, *v.*" Compact Edition of the Oxford
English Dictionary. 1971 ed. 2: 2335.
➤ The word "protest" is both a noun and a verb,
and I am citing the verb here.
"Pluck, *n.*" Def. 1. Oxford English Dictionary.
Ed. J. A. Simpson and E. S. C. Weiner. 2nd
ed. Oxford: Clarendon Press, 1989. Oxford
University Press. 5 Jan. 2004 ‹http://
dictionary.oed.com/cgi/entry/00181836›.
➤ There are two separate entries for the noun
pluck, and I am citing the first, hence *n.* Def. 1.
The second is for an obscure fish.

Dictionary, hard copy, online, and CD-ROM (*continued*)		"Balustrade." <u>Microsoft Encarta Online Dictionary.</u> 2004. Microsoft. 5 Jan. 2004 ‹http://encarta.msn.com/dictionary_/balustrade.html›. "Citation." <u>American Heritage Dictionary of the English Language.</u> 4th ed. CD-ROM. Boston: Houghton Mifflin, 2000.
	In-text	("Protest" 2: 2335) (<u>Compact OED</u> 2: 2335) ("Citation") or (<u>American Heritage Dictionary</u>)
Bible	Works Cited	<u>Tanakh: The Holy Scriptures: The New JPS Translation according to the Traditional Hebrew Text.</u> Philadelphia: Jewish Publication Society, 1985.
		➤ The Bible does *not* usually appear in Works Cited, although you can include it if you wish to cite a particular version or translation.
	In-text	Genesis 1.1, 1.3–5, 2.4.
		➤ Books may be abbreviated, such as Gen. 1.1, 1.3–5, 2.4.
		➤ Abbreviations for the next four books are Ex., Lev., Num., and Deut. Abbreviations for other books are easily found with a Web search for "abbreviations + Bible."
Speech, academic talk, or course lecture	Works Cited	Ferrell, Will. "Class Day Speech." Speech at Harvard. Cambridge, MA. 4 June 2003. Kamhi, Michelle. "Rescuing Art from 'Visual Culture.'" Speech to annual convention of the National Art Education Association. Minneapolis, MN. 7 Apr. 2003. Doniger, Wendy. Course lecture. University of Chicago. Chicago, IL. 12 Mar. 2004.
		➤ Or, using a more descriptive name for an untitled lecture:
		Doniger, Wendy. Course lecture on evil in Hindu mythology. University of Chicago. Chicago, IL. 12 Mar. 2004.

	In-text	(Ferrell)
		(Kamhi)
		(Doniger)

Interview, personal, telephone, or in print	Works Cited	King, Coretta Scott. Personal interview. 14 Jan. 2004. Wiesel, Elie. Telephone Interview. 16 Feb. 2004. Arroyo, Gloria Macapagal. "A Time for Prayer." Interview with Michael Schuman. Time. 28 July 2003. 13 Jan. 2004 ‹http://www.time.com/time/nation/article/0,8599,471205,00.html›.
	In-text	(King)

Poem	Works Cited	Bishop, Elizabeth. "The Fish." The Complete Poems, 1927–1979. New York: Noonday Press/Farrar, Straus and Giroux, 1983. 42–44. Lowell, Robert. "For the Union Dead." The Top 500 Poems. Ed. William Harmon. New York: Columbia University Press, 1992. 1061–63.
	In-text	(Bishop 42–44) or (Bishop, "The Fish" 42–44) or ("The Fish" 42–44) or (42–44) ▸ For poems such as "The Fish," you can note the verse and lines separated by periods or state (lines 10–12). (Lowell 1061–63) or (Lowell, "Union Dead" 1061–63)

Play	Works Cited	Shakespeare, Romeo and Juliet. ▸ If you wish to cite a specific edition, then: Shakespeare, Romeo and Juliet. Ed. Brian Gibbons. London: Methuen, 1980.
	In-text	(Shakespeare, Romeo and Juliet 1.3.12–15) or (Romeo and Juliet 1.3.12–15) or (1.3.12–15) if the play's name is clear in the text. ▸ This refers to act 1, scene 3, lines 12–15 (separated by periods).

Performance of play or dance	Works Cited	<u>Kiss.</u> Chor. Susan Marshall. Music Arvo Pärt. Perf. Cheryl Mann, Tobin Del Cuore. Hubbard Street Dance Chicago. Joan W. and Irving B. Harris Theater for Music and Dance, Chicago. Mar. 12, 2004.

<u>Topdog/Underdog.</u> By Suzan Lori-Parks. Dir. Amy Morton. Perf. K. Todd Freeman, David Rainey. Steppenwolf Theater, Chicago. 2 Nov. 2003.

▶ If you are concentrating on one person's work in theater, music, dance, or other collaborative arts, put that person's name first. For example, if you are focusing on David Rainey's acting:

Rainey, David, perf. <u>Topdog/Underdog.</u> By Suzan Lori-Parks. Dir. Amy Morton . . . .

▶ If, by contrast, you are focusing on Amy Morton's directing or on directing in general:

Morton, Amy, dir. <u>Topdog/Underdog.</u> By Suzan Lori-Parks. Perf. David Rainey . . . .

	In-text	(<u>Kiss</u>)
		(<u>Topdog/Underdog</u>) or (Rainey) or (Morton)

Television program	Works Cited	"Bart vs. Lisa vs. 3rd Grade." <u>The Simpsons.</u> Writ. T. Long. Dir. S. Moore. Episode: 1403 F55079. Fox. 17 Nov. 2002.
	In-text	("Bart vs. Lisa")

Film	Works Cited	<u>Godfather II.</u> Dir. Francis Ford Coppola. Perf. Al Pacino, Robert De Niro, Robert Duvall, Diane Keaton. Screenplay Francis Ford Coppola and Mario Puzo based on the novel by Mario Puzo. Paramount Pictures, 1974. DVD. Paramount Home Video, Godfather DVD Collection, 2003.

▶ Required: title, director, studio, and year released. Michael Corleone insists.

▶ Optional: actors, producers, screenwriters, editors, cinematographers, and other information. Include what you need for analysis in your paper, in order of their importance to your analysis. Their names appear between the title and the distributor.

➤ If you are concentrating on one person's work, put that person's name and role (such as performer) first, before the title:

Coppola, Francis Ford, dir. <u>Godfather II</u>. Perf. Al Pacino, Robert De Niro, Robert Duvall, Diane Keaton. Paramount Pictures, 1974. DVD. Paramount Home Video, Godfather DVD Collection, 2003.

	In-text	(<u>Godfather II</u>)
Artwork, original	Works Cited	Tintoretto, Jacopo Robusti. <u>The Birth of John the Baptist</u>. 1550s. Oil on canvas, 181 × 266 cm. Hermitage, St. Petersburg. ➤ Year, size, and medium are optional.
	In-text	(Tintoretto) or (Tintoretto, <u>Birth of John the Baptist</u>)
Artwork, reproduction	Works Cited	Tintoretto, Jacopo Robusti. <u>The Birth of John the Baptist</u>. 1550s. Hermitage, St. Petersburg. In <u>Tintoretto: Tradition and Identity</u>. By Tom Nichols. London: Reaktion Books, 1999. 47.
	In-text	(Tintoretto) or (Tintoretto, <u>Birth of John the Baptist</u>)
Artwork, online	Works Cited	Tintoretto, Jacopo Robusti. <u>The Birth of John the Baptist</u>. 1550s. Hermitage, St. Petersburg. State Hermitage Museum. 5 Jan. 2004 ‹http://www.hermitage.ru/html_En/index .html›. Tintoretto, Jacopo Robusti. <u>The Birth of John the Baptist</u> (detail). 1550s. Hermitage, St. Petersburg. CGFA-Virtual Art Museum. 5 Jan. 2004 ‹http://cgfa.floridaimaging.com/t/ p-tintore1.htm›. ➤ The same artwork accessed through the museum's site and another site. Note that the sponsors of the different Web sites are listed, as well as their URLs.

Artwork, online (*continued*)	In-text	(Tintoretto) or (Tintoretto, <u>Birth of John the Baptist</u>)
Photograph	Works Cited	Adams, Ansel. <u>Monolith, the Face of Half Dome, Yosemite National Park.</u> 1927. Art Institute, Chicago.
	In-text	(Adams) or (Adams, <u>Monolith</u>)
Figures: map, chart, graph, or table	Works Cited	"Electoral Vote Map." Map. <u>Election 2000.</u> 30 Aug. 2004 ‹http://www.usatoday.com/news/vote2000/electfront.htm›.
		▸ MLA treats maps like anonymous books.
		"Ethnic Population Transfers." Map. In Chaim D. Kaufmann, "When All Else Fails: Ethnic Population Transfers and Partitions in the Twentieth Century." *International Security* 23 (Fall 1998): 120–56.
		▸ Or
		Kaufmann, Chaim D. "When All Else Fails: Ethnic Population Transfers and Partitions in the Twentieth Century." *International Security* 23 (Fall 1998): 120–56.
	In-text	("Electoral Vote Map") ("Ethnic Population Transfers") or (Kaufman, 137, map 2)
Musical recording	Works Cited	Johnson, Robert. "Come On in My Kitchen (Take 1)." Rec. 23 Nov. 1936. <u>Robert Johnson: King of the Delta Blues Singers.</u> Expanded edition. Columbia/Legacy, CK 65746, 1998.
		Allman Brothers Band. "Come On in My Kitchen." By Robert Johnson. <u>Shades of Two Worlds.</u> Sony, 1991.
		Barber, Samuel. "Cello Sonata, for cello and piano, Op. 6." <u>Barber: Adagio for Strings, Violin Concerto, Orchestral and Chamber Works.</u> Disc 2. St. Louis Symphony. Cond. Leonard Slatkin. Cello, Alan Stepansky.

Piano, Israela Margalit. EMI Classics 74287, 2001.
- The catalog numbers are optional but helpful.
- There is no need to say that a recording is on CD. However, if it is on cassette, LP, or some other medium, that should be listed just before the publisher. For example:

Holloway, Stanley. "Get Me to the Church on Time." My Fair Lady, Original London Cast Recording. Book and lyrics, Alan Jay Lerner. Music, Frederick Loewe. Rec. 1958. Audiocassette. Broadway/Legacy 060539, 1998.
- If you are concentrating on one person's work, such as the pianist, her name can come first:

Margalit, Israela, piano. "Cello Sonata, for cello and piano, Op. 6." Barber: Adagio for Strings, Violin Concerto, Orchestral and Chamber Works. Disc 2. St. Louis Symphony. Cond. Leonard Slatkin. Cello, Alan Stepansky. EMI Classics 74287, 2001.

In-text

(Johnson) or (Johnson, "Come On in My Kitchen")
(Allman Brothers) or (Allman Brothers, "Come On in My Kitchen")
(Holloway) or (Holloway, "Get Me to the Church on Time")
(Margalit) or (Margalit, "Cello Sonata")

Sheet music   **Works Cited**

Bach, Johann Sebastian. Toccata and Fugue in D Minor. 1708. BWV 565. Arr. Ferruccio Benvenuto Busoni for solo piano. New York: G. Schirmer LB1629, 1942.
- This piece was written in 1708 and has the standard Bach classification BWV 565. The arrangement is published by G. Schirmer, with their catalog number LB1629.

In-text

(Toccata and Fugue in D Minor) or (Bach, Toccata and Fugue in D Minor)

| Liner notes | Works Cited | Reich, Steven. Liner notes. <u>Different Trains.</u> Kronos Quartet. Elektra/Nonesuch 9 79176-2, 1988. |
| | In-text | (Reich, <u>Different Trains</u>) |

| Government document, hard copy and online | Works Cited | Cong. Rec. 23 July 2003: 2468–72. United States. Cong. Senate. Committee on Armed Services. <u>Hearings on S. 758, A Bill to Promote the National Security by Providing for a National Defense Establishment.</u> 80th Cong., 1st sess., 1947. Freedman, Stephen. <u>Four-Year Impacts of Ten Programs on Employment Stability and Earnings Growth. The National Evaluation of Welfare-to-Work Strategies.</u> Washington, DC: U.S. Department of Education. 2000. ERIC Document Reproduction Service No. ED450262. United States. Department of State. <u>China— 25th Anniversary of Diplomatic Relations.</u> Press Statement. 31 Dec. 2003. 5 Jan. 2004 ‹http://www.state.gov/r/pa/prs/ps/2003/27632.htm›. |
| | In-text | (U.S. Cong., Senate, Committee on Armed Services)
 ▸ If you are only referencing one item from that committee, then in-text citations don't need to include the hearing number or report.
 (U.S. Cong., Senate, Committee on Armed Services, <u>Hearings on S. 758,</u> 1947)
 ▸ If you refer to several items from the committee, indicate which one you are citing. You can shorten that after the first use: (<u>Hearings on S. 758</u>).
 (Freedman) or (Freedman, <u>Four-Year Impacts</u>)
 (U.S. Department of State) |

| Database | Works Cited | <u>Internet Movie Database</u> (IMDb). 2004. Internet Movie Database. 6 Jan. 2004 ‹http://www.imdb.com/›. |

Corpus Scriptorum Latinorum database of Latin
literature. 2003. Forum Romanum. 5 Jan.
2004 ‹http://www.forumromanum.org/
literature/index.html›.

► For a specific item within this database:
Caesar, Gaius Julius. Commentarii de bello
civili. Ed. A. G. Peskett. Loeb Classical
Library. London: W. Heinemann, 1914.
Corpus Scriptorum Latinorum database of
Latin literature. 2003. Forum Romanum.
5 Jan. 2004 ‹http://www.thelatinlibrary
.com/caes.html›.

	In-text	(IMDb) (Corpus Scriptorum Latinorum) (Gaius Julius Caesar) or (Gaius Julius Caesar, Commentarii de bello civili)
Software	Works Cited	Dreamweaver MX 2004. San Francisco: Macromedia, 2003.
	In-text	(Dreamweaver MX 2004)
Web site, entire	Works Cited	Digital History. Ed. Steven Mintz. 2003. U of Houston et al. 6 Jan. 2004. ‹http://www .digitalhistory.uh.edu/ index.cfm?›. Internet Public Library (IPL). 2004. School of Information, University of Michigan. 7 Jan. 2004 ‹http://www.ipl.org/›.
	In-text	(Internet Public Library) or (IPL)
Web page	Works Cited	Lipson, Charles. "Advice on Getting a Great Recommendation" Web page. 2003. 6 Jan. 2004 ‹http://www.charleslipson.com/ courses/Getting-a-good-recommendation .htm›.

► If the URL takes up more than one line, break
after a single or double slash and *before* a
period, a comma, a hyphen, an underline, or a
number sign.

► MLA currently suggests listing the date when
you accessed a particular Web file. *The Chicago*

Web page *(continued)*		*Manual of Style* now recommends against it, unless there is a reason.
	In-text	(Lipson) or (Lipson, "Advice") ▶ Web pages and other online documents may not have pages. You may, however, be able to cite to a specific section (Lipson, sec. 7) or paragraph (Lipson, pars. 3–5).
Weblog, entries and comments	Works Cited	Jerz, Dennis. "How to Cite a Weblog and Weblog Comments in MLA Style." Weblog entry. 11 Dec. 2003. Kairosnews: A Weblog for Discussing Rhetoric, Technology, and Pedagogy. 2 Jan. 2004 ‹http://kairosnews .org/node/ view/3542›. Kiwi (Janice Walker). "Citing Weblogs." Weblog comment. 3 Dec. 2003. Kairosnews: A Weblog for Discussing Rhetoric, Technology, and Pedagogy. 3 Jan. 2004 ‹http:// kairosnews.org/node/view/3542›. Cowen, Tyler. "Trial by Jury." Weblog entry. 24 Dec. 2003 Volokh Conspiracy. 6 Jan. 2004 ‹http://volokh.com/›. Chafetz, Josh. Untitled Weblog entry. 27 Dec. 2003, 12:06 p.m. OxBlog. 29 Dec. 2003 ‹http://oxblog.blogspot.com/›. ▶ Chafetz's posting had no title and is one of several he posted to this group blog on the same day. Listing the time identifies it.
	In-text	(Jerz) or (Jerz, "How to Cite a Weblog")

MLA uses abbreviations frequently. Here are the most common:

MLA: COMMON ABBREVIATIONS IN WORKS CITED

and others	et al.	especially	esp.	paragraph	par.
appendix	app.	figure	fig.	part	pt.
book	bk.	note	n	pseudonym	pseud.
chapter	ch. or chap.	notes	nn	translator	trans.
compare	cf.	number	no.	verse	v.
document	doc.	opus	op.	verses	vv.
edition	ed.	page	p.	versus	vs.
editor	ed.	pages	pp.	volume	vol.

Note: All abbreviations are lowercase, usually followed by a period. Most form their plurals by adding "s." The exceptions are note (n → nn), opus (op. → opp.), page (p. → pp.), and translator (same abbreviation).

In citing poetry, do not use abbreviations for "line" or "lines" since a lowercase "l" is easily confused with the number one. Use either the full word, or, if the meaning is clear, simply the number.

FAQS ABOUT MLA CITATIONS

How do I handle the citation when one author quotes another?
That happens frequently, as in Donald Kagan's book *The Peloponnesian War*, which often quotes Thucydides. Using MLA style, you might write:

> Kagan approvingly quotes Thucydides, who says that Athens acquired this vital site "because of the hatred they already felt toward the Spartans" (qtd. in Kagan 14).

In your Works Cited, you include Kagan but *not* Thucydides.

Some MLA citations, such as newspaper articles, use the names of months. Which ones should I abbreviate and which ones should I spell out?
Use three-letter abbreviations for all but the short names: May, June, and July.

APA CITATIONS

APA citations are widely used in psychology, education, engineering, business, and the social sciences. Like MLA citations, they are in-text. They use notes only for analysis and commentary, not to cite references. Unlike

MLA, however, APA emphasizes the year of publication, which comes immediately after the author's name. That's probably because as scholarship cumulates in the sciences and empirical social sciences (where APA is used), it is important to know whether the research was conducted recently and whether it came before or after other research. At least that's the rationale.

Detailed information on the APA system is available in

- *Publication Manual of the American Psychological Association.* 5th ed. (Washington, DC: American Psychological Association, 2001).

Like *The Chicago Manual of Style* and MLA style books, the APA manual should be available in your library's reference section. For more details on engineering papers, you can also consult an online guide from the American Society of Civil Engineers, available at http://www.pubs.asce .org/authors/index.html#ref.

To get started, let's look at APA references for a journal article, a chapter in an edited book, and a book as they appear at the end of a paper. APA calls this a "Reference List." (MLA calls it "Works Cited," and Chicago calls it a "Bibliography.")

> Lipson, C. (1991). Why are some international agreements informal? *International Organization, 45,* 495–538.
> Lipson, C. (1994). Is the future of collective security like the past? In G. Downs (Ed.), *Collective security beyond the cold war* (pp. 105–131). Ann Arbor: University of Michigan Press.
> Lipson, C. (2003). *Reliable partners: How democracies have made a separate peace.* Princeton, NJ: Princeton University Press.

This list for the distinguished author C. Lipson follows another APA rule. All entries for a single author are arranged by year of publication, beginning with the earliest. If there were two entries for a particular year, say 2004, they would be alphabetized by title and the first would be labeled (2004a), the second (2004b). Also note the APA's rules for capitalizing book and article titles. They are treated like sentences, with only the first words capitalized. If there's a colon in the title, the first word after the colon is also capitalized. Proper nouns are capitalized, of course, just as they are in sentences.

In these reference lists, single-author entries precede those with coauthors. So Pinker, S. (as a sole author) would proceed Pinker, S., & Jones, B.

In the APA system, multiple authors are joined by an ampersand "&" rather than the word "and." It is not clear why. Just accept it as a rule, like how many minutes are in a soccer game.

The authors' first names are always reduced to initials. Pagination is not included for in-text references, except for direct quotes (where the pages are preceded by "p." or "pp."). That makes it different from the other systems, as does its frequent use of commas and parentheses.

When works are cited in the text, the citation includes the author's name, for example (Wilson, 2004d), unless the author's name has already been mentioned in that sentence. If the sentence includes the author's name, the citation omits it. For instance: Nye (2004) presents considerable data to back up his claims.

The examples in this section focus on the social sciences, education, engineering, and business, where APA citations are most widely used, just as the MLA examples focus on the humanities, where that style is common.

To make it easy to find the APA citations you need, I've listed them here alphabetically, along with the pages where they are described.

APA: REFERENCE LIST AND IN-TEXT CITATIONS

Book, one author — Reference list

Mandelbaum, M. (2002). *The ideas that conquered the world: Peace, democracy, and free markets in the twenty-first century.* New York: Public Affairs.

Lundy, C. (2003). *Social work and social justice: A structural approach to practice.* Peterborough, ON: Broadview Press.

➤ Canadian provinces are abbreviated with two letters.

In-text

(Mandelbaum, 2002)
(Lundy, 2003)

Books, several by same author — Reference list

Elster, J. (1989a). *The cement of society: A study of social order.* Cambridge: Cambridge University Press.

Elster, J. (1989b). *Nuts and bolts for the social sciences.* Cambridge: Cambridge University Press.

Elster, J. (1989c). *Solomonic judgements: Studies in the limitations of rationality.* Cambridge: Cambridge University Press; Paris: Editions de la Maison des sciences de l'homme.

Elster, J., & Moene, K. O. (Eds.). (1989). *Alternatives to capitalism.* Cambridge: Cambridge University Press.

➤ Note that the author's name is repeated. APA does not use dashes for repetition.

➤ When the same author or coauthors have several publications in the same year, list them alphabetically (by the first significant word in the title). Label them as "a," "b," and "c." The

last item by Elster is *not* labeled "d" because its authorship is different.
- ► Coauthored books like Elster & Moene follow a writer's single-author ones, in the alphabetical order of the second author's name.

	In-text	(Elster, 1989a, 1989b, 1989c; Elster & Moene, 1989)
Book, multiple authors	Reference list	Reiter, D., & Stam, A. C. (2002). *Democracies at war.* Princeton, NJ: Princeton University Press. ► Name the first six authors, then add "et al."
	In-text	(Reiter & Stam, 2002) ► For two to five authors, name all authors in the first citation. Beginning with the second reference, name only the first author, then add "et al." ► For six or more authors, name only the first author, then add "et al." for all citations. ► Use "&" within parenthetical references but not in the text itself.
Book, multiple editions	Reference list	Strunk, W., Jr., & White, E. B. (2000). *The elements of style* (4th ed.). New York: Longman. ► If it says "revised edition" rather than 4th edition, use (Rev. ed.) in the same spot.
	In-text	(Strunk & White, 2000) ► To refer to a specific page for a quotation: (Strunk & White, 2000, p. 12)
Book, multiple editions, no author	Reference list	*National Partnership for Immunization reference guide* (2nd ed.). (2003). Alexandria, VA: National Partnership for Immunization. *Publication manual of the American Psychological Association* (5th ed.). (2001). Washington, DC: American Psychological Association.

Book, multiple editions, no author (*continued*)		► For multiple editions without authors, the form is *Title* (18th ed.). (year). City, STATE: Publisher.
	In-text	(National Partnership for Immunization [NPI], 2003) ► Subsequent references are (NPI, 2003) (American Psychological Association [APA], 2001) ► Subsequent references are (APA, 2001)
Book, edited	Reference list	Shweder, R. A., Minow, M., & Markus, H. (Eds.). (2002). *Engaging cultural differences: The multicultural challenge in liberal democracies.* New York: Russell Sage Foundation Press. Katznelson, I., & Shefter, M. (Eds.). (2002). *Shaped by war and trade: International influences on American political development.* Princeton, NJ: Princeton University Press.
	In-text	(Shweder, Minow, & Markus, 2002) (Katznelson & Shefter, 2002)
Book, online	Reference list	Reed, J. (1922). *Ten days that shook the world.* Project Gutenberg. Etext 3076. Retrieved January 12, 2004, from ftp://ibiblio.org/pub/docs/books/gutenberg/etext02/10daz10.txt ► APA does *not* put a period after the URL, making it different from most other reference styles.
	In-text	(Reed, 1922)
Multivolume work	Reference list	Pflanze, O. (1963–1990). *Bismarck and the development of Germany* (Vols. 1–3). Princeton, NJ: Princeton University Press.
	In-text	(Pflanze, 1963–1990)

Single volume in multivolume work	Reference list	Pflanze, O. (1990). *The period of fortification, 1880–1898: Vol. 3. Bismarck and the development of Germany.* Princeton, NJ: Princeton University Press.
	In-text	(Pflanze, 1990)
Reprint of earlier edition	Reference list	Smith, A. (1976). *An inquiry into the nature and causes of the wealth of nations.* E. Cannan (Ed.). Chicago: University of Chicago Press. (Original work published 1776)
	In-text	(Smith, 1776/1976)
Translated volume	Reference list	Weber, M. (1958). *The Protestant ethic and the spirit of capitalism.* T. Parsons (Trans.). New York: Charles Scribner's Sons. (Original work published 1904–1905)
	In-text	(Weber, 1904–1905/1958)
Chapter in edited book	Reference list	Keohane, R. (1983). The demand for international regimes. In S. Krasner (Ed.), *International regimes* (pp. 56–67). Ithaca, NY: Cornell University Press.
	In-text	(Keohane, 1983)
Journal article	Reference list	Lipson, C. (1991). Why are some international agreements informal? *International organization, 45,* 495–538. ▸ Notice that article titles are not in quotes. ▸ The journal's volume number is italicized, but the issue number and pages are not. The word "volume" (or "vol.") is omitted. ▸ There's no need to name a specific issue if the journal pages are numbered continuously throughout the year. However, if each issue begins with page 1, then the issue's number or month is necessary to find the article: 45(2), 15–30.
	In-text	(Lipson, 1991)

Journal article, multiple authors	Reference list	Koremenos, B., Lipson, C., & Snidal, D. (2001). The rational design of international institutions. *International Organization, 55,* 761–799.
		Hansen, S. S., Munk-Jorgensen, P., Guldbaek, B., Solgard, T., Lauszus, K. S., Albrechtsen, N., et al. (2000). Psychoactive substance use diagnoses among psychiatric in-patients. *Acta Psychiatrica Scandinavica, 102,* 432–438.
		▶ Name up to six authors, then add "et al."
	In-text	(Koremenos, Lipson, & Snidal, 2001) for first reference
		(Koremenos et al., 2001) for second reference and after.

Journal article, online	Reference list	Conway, P. (2003). Truth and reconciliation: The road not taken in Namibia. *Online Journal of Peace and Conflict Resolution, 5*(1). Retrieved December 26, 2003, from http://www.trinstitute.org/ojpcr/5_1conway.htm
		Mitchell, T. (2002). McJihad: Islam in the U.S. global order. *Social Text, 20*(4), 1–18. Retrieved December 28, 2003, from JSTOR database: http://muse.jhu.edu/journals/social_text/v020/20.4mitchell.html
		▶ Your can omit the URL when citing well-known databases, such as JSTOR or PsycARTI-CLES.
	In-text	(Conway, 2003)
		(Mitchell, 2002)

Newspaper or magazine article, no author	Reference list	The United States and the Americas: One history in two halves. (2003, December 13). *Economist,* 36.
		Strong aftershocks continue in California. (2003, December 26). *New York Times* [national ed.], p. A23.
		▶ Newspaper page numbers include p. or pp.

	In-text	("United States and the Americas," 2003) ("Strong aftershocks," 2003)
Newspaper or magazine article, with author	Reference list	Bruni, F. (2003, December 26). Pope pleads for end to terrorism and war. *New York Times* [national ed.], p. A21.
	In-text	(Bruni, 2003) or, if necessary, (Bruni, 2003, December 26)
Newspaper or magazine article, online	Reference list	Vick, K. (2003, December 27). Quake in Iran kills at least 5,000: Temblor devastates ancient city; officials appeal for assistance. *Washington Post* [online], p. A01. Retrieved January 2, 2004, from http://www.washingtonpost.com/wp-dyn/articles/A31539-2003Dec26.html Jehl, D. (2004, January 1). U.S. hunts terror clues in case of 2 brothers. *New York Times* [online], p. A10. Retrieved February 6, 2004, from ProQuest Newspapers database.
	In-text	(Vick, 2003) or (Vick 2003, December 27)
Review of book	Reference list	Orr, H. A. (2003, August 14). What's not in your genes. [Review of the book *Nature via nurture: Genes, experience, and what makes us human*]. *New York Review of Books, 50,* 38–40.
Unpublished paper, poster session, dissertation, or thesis	Reference list	Tsygankov, A. (2004, February). *Russia's identity and foreign policy choices.* Paper presented at the Program on International Politics, Economics, and Security, University of Chicago. ▶ Only the month and year are needed for papers. Cheng, D. T., Smith, C. N., Thomas, T. L., Richards, J. A., Knight, D. C., Rao, S. M., et al. (2003, June). *Differential reinforcement of stimulus dimensions during human*

Unpublished paper, poster session, dissertation, or thesis (*continued*)		*Pavlovian fear conditioning.* Poster session presented at the 9th Annual Meeting of the Organization for Human Brain Mapping, New York, NY. Reid, P. (1998). *Beginning therapists and difficult clients: An exploratory study.* Unpublished master's thesis, University of Massachusetts, Amherst. Gomez, C. (2003). *Identifying early indicators for autism in self-regulatory difficulties.* Unpublished doctoral dissertation. Auburn University, AL.
	In-text	(Tsygankov, 2004) (Cheng et al., 2003) (Reid, 1998) (Gomez, 2003)
Microfilm, microfiche	Reference list	U.S. House of Representatives. Records. Southern Claims Commission. (1871–1880). *First report (1871).* Washington, DC: National Archives Microfilm Publication, P2257, Frames 0145–0165. Conservative Party (UK). (1919). *Annual report of the executive committee to central council, March 11–November 18, 1919.* Archives of the British Conservative Party, Microfiche card 143. Woodbridge, CT: Gale/Primary Source Microfilm, 1998. (Original material located in Conservative Party Archive, Bodleian Library, Oxford, UK). ► You do not need to include the location of the original material, but you are welcome to.
	In-text	(U.S. House, 1871–1880) (Conservative Party, 1919)
Preprint	Reference list	Williams, A., Leen, T. K., Roberts, P. D. (2003). Random walks for spike-timing dependent plasticity. Preprint. arXiv: q-bio.NC/0312038. Retrieved December 26, 2003, from http://xxx.lanl.gov/PS_cache/q-bio/pdf/0312/0312038.pdf

▸   arXiv is a collection facility for scientific
preprints. The "q-bio" number is its identification number there. ID numbers and URLs are
valuable to readers who wish to follow your
citation to the database itself.

	In-text	(Williams, Leen, & Roberts, 2003)

Encyclopedia, hard copy and online	Reference list	Balkans: History. (1987). In *Encyclopaedia Britannica* (15th ed., Vol. 14, pp. 570–588). Chicago: Encyclopaedia Britannica. Balkans. *Encyclopaedia Britannica* [online]. Retrieved December 28, 2003, from http://search.eb.com/eb/article?eu=119645 Graham, G. (2002). Behaviorism. In *Stanford encyclopedia of philosophy* [online]. Retrieved January 5, 2004, from http://plato.stanford.edu/entries/behaviorism/
	In-text	("Balkans: History," 1987) ("Balkans," 2003) (Graham, 2002)

Reference book, hard copy and online	Reference list	Pendergast, S., & Pendergast, T. (Eds.). (2003). *Reference guide to world literature* (3rd ed., 2 vols.). Detroit: St. James Press/Thomson-Gale. Pendergast, S., & Pendergast, T. (Eds.). (2003). *Reference guide to world literature.* E-Book. (3rd ed.). Detroit: St. James Press. Colman, A. M. (2001). *A Dictionary of Psychology.* Oxford: Oxford University Press. Retrieved March 16, 2004, from http://www.oxfordreference.com/views/BOOK_SEARCH.html?book=t87 Woods, T. (2003). "The social contract (du contract social), prose by Jean-Jacques Rousseau, 1762." In Pendergast, S., & Pendergast, T. (Eds.), *Reference guide to world literature* (3rd ed., Vol. 2, pp. 1512–1513). Detroit: St. James Press/Thomson-Gale.

Reference book, hard copy and online (*continued*)		"Great Britain: Queen's speech opens Parliament." (2003, November 26). *FirstSearch*. Facts On File database. Accession no. 2003302680.
	In-text	(Pendergast & Pendergast, 2003) (Colman, 2001) (Woods, 2003) ("Great Britain: Queen's speech," 2003)

Dictionary, hard copy, online, and CD-ROM	Reference list	Gerrymander. (2003). *Merriam-Webster's collegiate dictionary* (11th ed.). Springfield, MA: Merriam-Webster. Protest, *v*. (1971). *Compact edition of the Oxford English dictionary* (Vol. 2, p. 2335). Oxford: Oxford University Press.
		➤ The word "protest" is both a noun and a verb. Here, I am citing the verb.
		Class, *n*. (2003). *Dictionary.com*. Retrieved January 4, 2004, from http://dictionary .reference.com/search?q=class Anxious. (2000). *American heritage dictionary of the English language* (4th ed.). CD-ROM. Boston: Houghton Mifflin.
	In-text	("Protest," 1971)

Government document, hard copy and online	Reference list	*A bill to promote the national security by providing for a national defense establishment: Hearings on S. 758 before the Committee on Armed Service, Senate.* 80th Cong., 1 (1947).
		➤ "80th Cong., 1" refers to page one (not to the first session). If the reference was to testimony by a specific individual, that would appear after the date: (1947) (testimony of Gen. George Marshall).
		➤ For documents printed by the Government Printing Office, give the full name rather than the initials GPO.
		U.S. Bureau of the Census. (2000). *Statistical abstracts of the U.S.* Washington, DC: U.S. Bureau of the Census.

		U.S. Department of Commerce. (2002). *A nation online: How Americans are expanding their use of the Internet*. Retrieved December 30, 2003, from http://www.ntia.doc.gov/ ntiahome/dn/anationonline2.pdf Federal Bureau of Investigation. (2001). *Investigation of Charles "Lucky" Luciano*. Part 1A. Retrieved January 2, 2004, from http://foia.fbi.gov/luciano/luciano1a.pdf
	In-text	(*Bill to Promote National Security,* 1947) (U.S. Bureau of the Census, 2000) (U.S. Dept. of Commerce, 2002) (FBI, 2001)
Speech, academic talk, or course lecture	Reference list	Szelenyi, I. (2003, August 17). Presidential address. American Sociological Association. Annual convention. Atlanta, GA. Woodward, A. (2004, April 14). Course lecture. University of Chicago. Chicago, IL.
	In-text	(Szelenyi, 2003) (Woodward, 2004)
Interview	Reference list	Wilson, E. O. (2004, February 1). Personal interview regarding biodiversity. Cambridge, MA.
	In-text	(Wilson, 2004)
Television program	Reference list	Long, T. (Writer), & Moore, S. D. (Director). (2002). Bart vs. Lisa vs. 3rd Grade [Television series episode]. In B. Oakley & J. Weinstein (Producers), *The Simpsons*. Episode: 1403 F55079. Fox.
	In-text	(*Simpsons,* 2002) or ("Bart vs. Lisa," 2002)
Film	Reference list	Huston, J. (Director/Writer). (1941). *The Maltese falcon* [Motion picture]. Perf. Humphrey Bogart, Mary Astor, Peter Lorre, Sydney Greenstreet, Elisha Cook Jr. Based on novel

Film *(continued)*		by Dashiell Hammett. Warner Studios. U.S.: Warner Home Video, DVD (2000).
		▸ Required: You must include the title, director, studio, and year released.
		▸ Optional: the actors, producers, screenwriters, editors, cinematographers, and other information. Include what you need for analysis in your paper, in order of importance to your analysis. Their names appear between the title and the distributor.
	In-text	*(Maltese falcon,* 1941) or *(Maltese falcon,* 2000)
Photograph	Reference list	Adams, Ansel. (1927). *Monolith, the face of Half Dome, Yosemite National Park* [photograph]. Art Institute, Chicago.
	In-text	(Adams, 1927)
Figures: map, chart, graph, or table	Credit or explanation for figure or table	▸ Citation for a map, chart, graph, or table normally appears as a credit below the item rather than as an in-text citation.
		Note: "Electoral vote map [2000]." *Election 2000.* Retrieved August 30, 2004, from http://www.usatoday.com/news/vote2000/electfront.htm.
		Note: From Daryl G. Press (2001), The myth of air power in the Persian Gulf War and the future of warfare, *International Security* 26 (Fall): 17, fig. 2.
		▸ Give a descriptive title to your maps, charts, graphs, and tables. With this description, the reader should understand the item without having to refer to the text.
		Note: All figures are rounded to nearest percentile.
		▸ This is a general note explaining information in a table.
		*$*p < .05$ $**p < .01$. Both are two-tailed tests.
		▸ This is a probability note for a table of statistics.
	Reference list	"Electoral vote map [2000]." *Election 2000.* Retrieved August 30, 2004, from http://www

		.usatoday.com/news/vote2000/electfront .htm. Press, Daryl G. Press (2001). The myth of air power in the Persian Gulf War and the future of warfare. *International Security* 26 (Fall): 5–44.
	In-text	("Electoral vote map [2000]," 2004) (Press, 2001)

Software	Reference list	Dreamweaver MX 2004 [Computer software]. (2003). San Francisco: Macromedia. SPSS regression models (12.0 for Windows) [Computer software]. (2003). Chicago: SPSS.
	In-text	(Dreamweaver MX 2004, 2003) (SPSS Regression Models, 2003)

Database	Reference list	Bedford, VA, city of. (2004). *Property tax database*. Retrieved March 15, 2004, from http://www.ci.bedford.va.us/proplax/ lookup.shtml *Intellectual Property Treaties, InterAm Database*. (2004). Tucson, AZ: National Law Center for Inter-American Free Trade. Retrieved March 15, 2004, from http://www .natlaw.com/database.htm
	In-text	(Bedford, 2004) (*Intellectual Property Treaties*, 2004)

Diagnostic test	Reference list	Tellegen, A., Ben-Porath, Y. S., McNulty, J. L., Arbisi, P. A., Graham, J. R., & Kaemmer, B. (2001). *MMPI-2 restructured clinical (RC) scales*. Minneapolis: University of Minnesota Press and Pearson Assessments. Butcher, J. N., Graham, J. R., Ben-Porath, Y. S., Tellegen, A., Dahlstrom, W. G., & Kaemmer, B. (2001). *Minnesota multiphasic personality inventory-2 (MMPI-2): Manual for administration, scoring, and interpretation* (Rev. ed.). Minneapolis: University of Minnesota Press.

Diagnostic test (*continued*)		▸ Manual for administering the test. Tellegen, A., Ben-Porath, Y. S., McNulty, J. L., Arbisi, P. A. & Graham, J. R. (2003). *The MMPI-2 restructured clinical (RC) scales: Development, validation, and interpretation.* Minneapolis: University of Minnesota Press and Pearson Assessments. ▸ Interpretive manual for the test. *Microtest Q assessment system software for MMPI-2.* (2003). Version 5.07. Minneapolis: Pearson Assessments. ▸ Scoring software for the test.
	In-text	(*MMPI-2 RC Scales,* 2001) (*MMPI-2 RC Scales,* 2003) (*Microtest Q,* 2003)
Diagnostic manual	Reference list	American Psychiatric Association. (2000). *Diagnostic and statistical manual of mental disorders* (4th ed. text revision [*DSM-IV-TR*]). Washington, DC: American Psychiatric Association Press.
	In-text	(American Psychiatric Association, *Diagnostic and statistical manual of mental disorders,* 2000) for the first use only. (*DSM-IV-TR*) for second use and later. Title is italicized.
Web site, entire	Reference list	*Digital History* Web site. (2004). S. Mintz (Ed.). Retrieved January 10, 2004, from http://www.digitalhistory.uh.edu/index.cfm? *Internet Public Library* (IPL) (2003, November 17). Retrieved January 5, 2004, from http://www.ipl.org/ Yale University, History Department home page. (2003). Retrieved January 6, 2004, from http://www.yale.edu/history/ ▸ If a Web site or Web page does not show a date when it was copyrighted or updated, then list (n.d.) where the year normally appears.

	In-text	(Digital History, 2004) (Internet Public Library, 2003) or (IPL, 2003) (Yale History Department home page, 2003)
Web page	Reference list	Lipson, C. (2004). *Advice on getting a great recommendation*. Retrieved February 1, 2004, from http://www.charleslipson.com/courses/Getting-a-good-recommendation.htm
	In-text	(Lipson, 2004)
Weblog, entries and comments	Reference list	Drezner, D. (2004, February 1). Entry post. Retrieved February 2, 2004, from http://www.danieldrezner.com/blog/
	In-text	(Drezner, 2004)

APA does not permit very many abbreviations in its reference lists. When it does, it sometimes wants them capitalized and sometimes not. Who knows why?

APA: COMMON ABBREVIATIONS IN REFERENCE LISTS

chapter	chap.	number	No.	supplement	Suppl.
editor	Ed.	page	p.	translated by	Trans.
edition	ed.	pages	pp.	volume	Vol.
second edition	2nd ed.	part	Pt.	volumes	Vols.
revised edition	Rev. ed.				

APPENDIX 3
ADVICE FOR NEW FACULTY ADVISERS

For younger faculty, advising their first thesis students, it may help to hear from colleagues who've done it before. What tips and suggestions do they have?

To find out, I asked my own colleagues, especially younger ones who have been advising for four or five years. They know the ropes but still remember what they learned the hard way. Their constructive suggestions are, in many ways, the flip side of what I've already told students. (A quick summary of that advice is in chapters 15 and 16.)

Here are their ideas for advising BA theses:

- Don't micromanage.

   Pose questions, suggest readings, offer alternative arguments, but always remember that the student writes the thesis.
- Calibrate your scales; this is a BA thesis, not an MA thesis or a PhD dissertation.

   Most students want to learn more about the subject and conduct independent research, but they are not trying to become professionals in your field. They should not be expected to push back the frontiers of knowledge. Set realistic expectations.
- The most important stage of advising is helping each student find a good question.

   Although it is the student's responsibility to find the right question, your guidance is always helpful and often essential. The question should be manageable so your advisee can study it in depth and complete the project. On the other hand, it shouldn't be so narrow that it interests only specialists and bores the student. The best solution is to find a circumscribed topic that bears on larger issues. At some point, your advisee can explore the connection.
- For students having real difficulty finding a question, it may help to think about topics that advance their career goals.

As one professor explained, "Think of a thesis that helps you tell an employer, 'I did this, which is another reason why you should hire me.' Or, to a grad school, 'I did this, which is another reason I am interested in your graduate program.' [Topics like these] help students create options for themselves in the future."

- Thesis timetables are important; missing key deadlines is a warning sign.

Early in the thesis process, ask each student to write his own schedule for the project. The ones in this book, summarized in chapter 15, should be a useful guide. You'll also have your own ideas about what should be accomplished by November or February, so you can give students feedback on their schedules. Keep an eye out for deadlines missed.

- Tell students what arrangements you prefer for meetings, papers, and deadlines. Do it early, and be specific.

How often do you want to meet? How long do meetings usually last? Should students make appointments or just drop in during office hours? What if a student has to work or take a class during your office hours? Is it the student's responsibility to bring an agenda or question to each meeting? (Short answer: Yes.)

What kind of writing do you expect? For example, do you expect to receive brief papers every few weeks? Do you want papers in hard copy, as e-mail attachments, or both?

What about deadlines? Are you strict about them? Is your department? If students want to receive comments on their work, how much lead time should they give you before a deadline?

Be clear from the outset about such housekeeping arrangements. Students will appreciate it.

- If students make unreasonable demands, explain the limits of what you are willing to do.

Inevitably, a few students have unreasonable expectations and make excessive demands on their adviser. But they may not even know their demands are excessive unless you say so and explain what you will do and won't.

One student might want you to assign his thesis topic rather than finding his own. Or he might expect you to assign his readings or tell him exactly how to research his topic. You need to explain, early on, that those are his responsibilities and that they are an essential part of the learning process. Your responsibility is to advise him.

Another student might ask you to read five long drafts of a completed paper. A third, who is well behind schedule, wants you to read a rough draft five days before the final version is due. They need to understand how many drafts you will read and what kind of advance notice (if any) you need. The student who has fallen behind should also be warned about the problem as soon as you discover it (even though it is ultimately the student's responsibility, not yours, to know the schedule and keep up with it).

If your expectations are reasonable and if you explain them in advance, your students will be on the same page with you.

- Learn about other student resources, especially campus centers for writing, learning skills, and mental health.

    Writing centers can offer one-on-one help to students who need it. Learning centers can help with a wide range of study issues, even for students who are doing well. Student mental health services are available on every campus and are confidential. One downside of that confidentiality: if you are really worried about a student and recommend counseling, you cannot find out if the student followed up on that recommendation unless the student chooses to tell you directly.

- Encourage students to take thesis workshops—they are often quite valuable—but recognize one potential problem: students sometimes receive advice that conflicts with yours. The solution: ask your students to tell you if this problem arises.

    Workshop leaders are *supposed* to give advice to students. So are second readers. Their suggestions are bound to depart from yours occasionally. Sometimes, the conflict comes from writing tutors who make research suggestions, even though it goes beyond their mission.

    There are really two issues here: discovering the problem and resolving it. You might notice the conflict in the work itself. Then again, you might not, or you might not notice it soon enough. There is a straightforward solution. Ask students to tell you directly when they receive advice that differs from yours so you can help them sort it out. In the end, though, you are the main thesis adviser. You may need to explain that.

- If you are going to be unavailable for more than a week, give your advisees a heads-up.

  You may be going abroad for research, sprinting to finish a paper of your own, or expecting a baby. If you are going to be unavailable, let your advisees know (a little in advance, if possible) and say when you'll be back at work.

- Keep an eye out for students who go AWOL.

  Some students quietly decide not to go forward with the thesis, but never bother to inform you. Others keep working, but do so privately. They might disappear for weeks, usually during the middle stages of the thesis.

  For students who are still working on the thesis, going AWOL is a bad idea—but students don't always realize it. You have to decide if you want to nudge them, perhaps with an e-mail asking for a meeting.

- If you are a second reader, be helpful but play second fiddle.

ACKNOWLEDGMENTS

I am grateful to colleagues who offered suggestions about thesis research across their varied fields. Some read specific chapters; others offered comments or answered questions; still others pointed me to specialized books James Chandler, Elizabeth Helsinger, and Kenneth Warren suggested readings in English literature, Neil Harris in architectural history. Duncan Snidal offered insights into case studies, particularly the value of "easy cases." Daniel Drezner and Patchen Markell discussed their advising experience and offered ideas for new advisers. Valerie Funk, who taught a BA thesis colloquium at the University of Chicago, made several practical suggestions. My wife, Susan Lipson, commented on how students can work more efficiently and overcome personal problems, based on her wide reading and her years of experience as a therapist.

Since this book is designed to help thesis students and their advisers, I wanted to hear directly from them. I asked several faculty to take the draft manuscript out for a "test drive" with their honors seminars and tell me how to make it more useful. I was fortunate to receive such help from Ian Hurd (political science) and Carl Smith (English and American studies) and their students at Northwestern University, and from Gayle McKeen (political science) and Woody Register (American studies) and their students at the University of the South, Sewanee. Several other faculty used the manuscript to work with individual students. My thanks to Michael Mandelbaum at the Johns Hopkins School of Advanced International Studies and Sean Kay at Ohio Wesleyan University.

They not only gave me constructive comments themselves; several passed along ideas from their students. Two of Sean's students, Dan Hlavin and Ali Chaudhry, wrote me directly with helpful comments.

In addition, I received detailed comments and valuable suggestions from several anonymous readers.

To these faculty and students, my deepest thanks. Their generous advice improved every chapter of this book.

The editors and staff at the University of Chicago Press have been exceptionally supportive. Linda Halvorson is an extraordinary editor. I turned to her for wise advice, beginning with the earliest drafts. Her enthusiasm for this project always lifted my spirits and encouraged my work. Linda's colleagues at the Press, Mary Laur and Christopher Rhodes, assisted me at every stage. So did Erin DeWitt, whose skills as a copy editor improved line after line of the manuscript. It required real restraint not to put them all on my speed dial.

Most of all, I want to thank the undergraduates at the University of Chicago with whom I have worked on BA theses over the years. Poring over their papers, listening to their ideas, and talking with them about their research have been rewarding teaching experiences—and something more. Working with these students has been a genuine learning experience for me, one that continues with each new class. It is a rare privilege to teach gifted students who are eager to learn and ready to work. It inspired me to write this book.

INDEX